BOOMER
RAILROAD
MEMOIRS

LINDA NIEMANN

CLEIS
PRESS

Library of Congress Cataloging-in-Publication Data

Niemann, Linda.
    Boomer : railroad memoirs / Linda Niemann.
        p.   cm.
    Originally published : Berkeley : University of California Press, 1990.
    ISBN 0-939416-55-7 (trade paper) : $12.95
    1. Niemann, Linda.   2. Women railroad employees—United States—
Biography.   I. Title.
    [HD6073.R22U66   1992]
    331.4′81385′092—dc20
    [B]   91-39879
                                                                                                    CIP

Boomer

Published in the United States by Cleis Press Inc., P.O. Box 8933, Pittsburgh, Pennsylvania 15221, and P.O. Box 14684, San Francisco, California 94114.

Produced by arrangement with the University of California Press.

Permission has been granted for the use of a quote from *Bound for Glory* by Woody Guthrie, copyright © 1943 by E.P. Dutton, renewed, 1971 by Marjorie M. Guthrie. Reprinted by permission of the publisher E.P. Dutton, a division of Penguin Books USA Inc.

Printed in the United States.
Cover design: Ellen Toomey
Front cover photograph: Michael Pierazzi
Back cover photograph: Lauren Crux
Logo art: Juana Alicia

First Edition.
10 9 8 7 6 5 4 3 2 1
ISBN: 0-939416-55-7

FOR ANGUS

CONTENTS

ACKNOWLEDGMENTS

I WOULD LIKE to thank my sister, Dorothy Mohr, who used her court-reporting skills to help me edit this book. I would also like to thank the following friends who read and commented on the manuscript: Angus Fletcher, Carter Wilson, Sheila Hough, and Betty Gardiner.

My experiences as related in this book are fact. The main characters are literary creations, fictional in certain respects and colored in others by the people I knew and worked with. The railroad is itself.

1

BREAKING IN

THE FREIGHTYARD lay to the east of the town, surrounded by apple orchards and artichoke fields that swept in painterly rows down to the dunes and riptides waiting in the bay. It was cool for July, with that wet smell of salty fog and rotting produce in the packing sheds of the cold storage plants. I drove my fifty-six Chevy with its four bald tires into the parking lot behind the depot. There were rows and rows of pickups, RVs, Chevy Suburbans, and the beat-up "luxury car" heaps that the brakemen used as away-from-home cars. It was solid American steel.

The parking lot was in the center of tracks in the shape of a *Y*, used for turning engines. The engines seemed huge, covered with black grime, five or six hooked together roaring and screeching to stops. I could hear the sounds of crashes from the switching yard and could see solitary boxcars floating down the tracks.

I entered a door and found myself in a long room filled with lockers. At the end of the room was a table, a beat-up couch, and several overstuffed chairs black with diesel grime and the stuffing poking through. An older man with a sooty baseball cap wedged over his tilted face was snoring away on one of the chairs, oblivious to the racket from a computer printer spewing out yards of paper onto the floor. A big man in overalls came out of the men's washroom.

"Trainmaster's office is in there. Don't worry about the herder, he's had his shots."

"OK," I thought, "fine."

Trainmaster Mohan looked at me across a beat-up walnut desk stacked with computer printouts weighted down by a brass-plated railroad spike. A coffee cup sat there with a quarter inch of what looked like diesel fuel in it. I guessed that it was cold and that he would probably drink it anyway. There were bunches of cheerful older women in the office dressed in jeans and cowboy boots and without a lot of makeup. It felt more like a softball game than an office. It felt just fine.

Mohan had a robust handshake and a very red nose.

"So you want to go railroading, do you?"

"Yes," I said, not having any idea what "going railroading" meant. The way he said it had something of the flavor of going whaling. I was going to work in Watsonville, wasn't I? I handed him a business book I had written and explained the company I did it for had gone under. Mohan took it and hefted it thoughtfully. I was glad it was a heavy book.

"Well, we got all kinds of people out here railroadin', and you'll find most of 'em are good people. I guess we got room for a writer."

For a moment, I was in a room fronting the Sahara. The Legionnaire Captain shoves a paper across his pitted desk.

"Make your mark. You are now lost to the world you knew."

"Now, you're going to hear bad language out here," Mohan went on. "It's always been that way, always will be. And railroading gets in your blood. That's the only way to describe it."

He leaned forward then and looked straight into my eyes.

"And now I got to ask you another thing. Do you drink?"

"Well, yes, I drink—I mean, I'm a social drinker."

Mohan smiled. "Well, we're all social drinkers. But remember that drinking and railroading don't mix."

On that note the interview ended.

On my way back to Santa Cruz I stopped at a liquor store for two club cocktails for the road. It was a habit of mine, and I didn't think anything about it. Being a drug user, I thought of drinking as basically legal. My whole scale of judgment was based on what happened to you if you got caught. Drinking and driving was pretty bad, but not as bad as if you got caught with dope in the ashtray or lids of pot in the trunk. I had no intention of ever drinking on the job. To my mind, the railroad was an opportunity to dry out a little.

I had been hanging around for a few years with a very party-time crowd, and my life was on a downward slide. I had gotten a Ph.D. and a divorce simultaneously. The fancy academic job never materialized, and I hung around Santa Cruz getting to know my neighbors. Soon I was playing flute in a street band, eating donated sandwiches, and spending every night in clubs dancing the night away. My living room was full of strippers, poets, musicians, and drug dealers. Gradually there was less music and more drugs, and in a few years I was living in the mountains in a shack, my lover had moved out, my dogs had heartworm, my Chevy was a wreck, and though I thought of myself as a musician, the money, such as it was, came from dealing, and none of my friends worked.

When I saw the ad in the Sunday paper—BRAKEMEN WANTED—I thought of it as a chance to clean up my act and get away. In a strategy of extreme imitation, I felt that by doing work this dangerous, I would have to make a decision to live, to protect myself. I would have to choose to stay alive every day, to hang on to the sides of those freightcars for dear life. The railroad transformed the metaphor of my life. Nine thousand tons moving at sixty miles an hour into the fearful night. I now would ride that image, trying to stay alive within it. I know that later when I sat behind the moving train in the darkness of the caboose, window open and the unknown fragrances of the landing filling the space, the blackness of the night was my friend. It felt good to be powerless and carried along by the destiny of that motion. I felt happy and at peace. I was where I belonged.

The railroad didn't believe in lengthy formal training. They offered a two-week class that covered the book of rules, a three-hundred-page document with a dual purpose—to keep trains from running into one another and to prevent any situation in which the company might get sued. Rules of the road that you had to learn were mixed in with rules that you had to ignore in order to get the work done. But you had to know that you were ignoring a rule so that in the winter, when company officials had time to sneak around testing, you could work by the book.

The rulebook was also in a continuous state of revision. Revisions appeared in the timetable that you carried with you at all times. Further revisions appeared in regular timetable bulletins that were posted at work. Soon your rulebook resembled a scrapbook, with paragraphs crossed out, pages pasted in, and notes on changes that were then crossed out and changed weeks later. It drove you crazy. You always had to be on the lookout for a company official hiding in the bushes while you did your work. This individual would pop out and ask you questions about the latest rule revisions. A notation of failure would then appear in your personal file. These notations were referred to as "Brownies," named after the official who devised the railroad demerit system. As trainmen were fond of pointing out, however, there was no merit system to go with it.

Out of seventeen student brakemen three of us were women. This was a large percentage, comparatively. The first women had been hired two years before, and they were around to give us advice. The point was to get through the class, ignore the sexist remarks and the scare tactics, and get over the probationary period known as the "derail." Then you were in the union and a railroader for life. Getting over the derail took sixty days, and if either the crews you worked with or the company officers had a complaint, you were out. At the end of two weeks of classroom instruction, you bought a railroad watch, they gave you switch keys and a two-dollar lantern, and you marked up as an extra board brakeman. It was going to be sink or swim in this business. We drew numbers to determine our seniority dates—the most important factor in our careers. One or two numbers could mean that you worked or didn't.

On the last day of class, they took us down to the freightyard to grapple with the equipment. We practiced getting on and off moving cars, climbing the ladders and cranking down the handbrakes, lacing up the airhoses and cutting in the air, changing the eighty-five-pound knuckles that joined the cars together, and hand and lantern signals. These signals were the way members of the crew talked to each other, and they were an art form. An old head could practically order an anchovy pizza from a half mile away. You would see lights, arcs and circles, stabs of light. It would repeat. You would stand there confused. Finally you would walk down the track and find the foreman in a deep state of disgust.

"I told you to hang three cars, let two go to the runaround, one to the main, go through the crossovers, and line behind. Now can't you read a signal, dummy?"

The day after our practice session, I got into my car and tried to roll the window down. My arms didn't work. This was my first moment of doubt about being able to do the job. It was hard to get the upper-body strength required to hang on and ride for long distances on the side of cars. Terror at falling beneath the wheels was a big motivator, however. Terror and ridicule. There was a lot of both during the probationary period and the student trips. On student trips we tagged along with a regular crew and tried to learn something. To me, what we were doing made no sense whatsoever. Just getting used to the equipment had me so disoriented that I had no idea where we had gone or how the crew did anything. One of the crew suggested to me that I go to a toy store and look at the model trains, to see how switches work. They say, though, that whatever you start out doing railroading, it gets imprinted, and that's what you are most comfortable doing from then on. I couldn't have picked a better place to break in than Watsonville Junction. It was old-time, local-freight, full-crew switching. Kicking cars and passing signs. The basic stuff that you have to learn at first or you never get no matter how long you're out here.

The small switching yard at Watsonville classified all the perishable freight from the Salinas Valley and Hollister/Gilroy—the "salad bowl" of America. A break in the coastal range at Salinas allowed the fog to pour into the valley, cooling it, and allowing cool weather crops like artichokes, brussels sprouts, and lettuce to grow. Strawberry fields and apple orchards skirted the low hillsides. There were cool fresh days in midsummer. The packing houses and canneries were running around the clock, with rows of mostly women working the graveyard assembly lines. Clusters of yellow schoolbuses bordered the fields, and farmworkers moved slowly through the orderly rows, bundled up against the fog and pesticides.

This map of canneries, packing houses, cold storage sheds, and assembly warehouses made up the maze of tracks in Salinas known as "the districts." In railroading, knowledge of the track system is most of the job. You have to know how many cars can fit, the slope, where the road crossings are, where runaround tracks are that you can use in switching. The Salinas districts were named for cities of the freight's destination: New York, Portland, Boston, Chicago. After a few days, the crew expected me to know how to get there from here. I had no idea. Just the idea that there were only two directions to go on a switch engine (forward and backward) hadn't sunk in yet.

"OK, pinpuller; line us up for Boston, off the Portland Main."

I looked out at this web of tracks; I knew the red switch targets were mainline and that bad things would happen if you threw one of them when you weren't supposed to. The book of rules had me paralyzed. There were six things you were supposed to look for in order to throw a mainline switch. What were they?

"Are you going to throw that damn switch or are you going to have a nervous breakdown?"

"Are you sure that we can throw it?"

"Oh Lord, student brakies. They should be paying us extra for this."

Watsonville switching crews worked fast, like a soccer team playing with boxcars. They moved in position like a team, climbing aboard and peeling off moving cars to keep in sight of one another and the engineer. On Saturday night they worked twice as fast in order to go home early. It was called "running for a quit." On other nights they worked fast so that they could "go on spot" in a little switchman's shanty tucked in beside the packing warehouses. There was a switchlock on the door and a long table inside where some serious cardplaying went on.

Since I was still learning the most basic moves, it was impossible to keep up with the pace. But how do you manage to learn? My strategy was to follow a crew member around like a baby duck, getting in the way. He then would yell at me and tell me what to do. So I'd learn something. I also wore this silly hat—a baseball cap with silver wings on it. The hat meant several things to me: one, I figured they would see the hat and not run over me, and also I wanted to bring something of my old identity into this new situation, which was threatening to dissolve my sense of who I was. The hat became the cutting edge of nonconformity in the freight-yard. It separated those who could take a joke from those who couldn't and clearly marked those people who had an attitude about women being on the job.

"I wouldn't wear that hat if I were you. I mean you don't know shit about railroading and you're wearing that hat."

I guess I wanted the hat to take the flack, and not all the other things about me that weren't going to fit in here. I wore the hat.

Summer was the busy season, and we all worked steadily as brakemen, switching out the perishable freight in Salinas, Monterey, and Hollister. The locker room would always be full of boxes overflowing with broccoli, green onions, lettuce, apples, cauliflower. It smelled wonderful and you felt included in the bounty of this part of the world. It gave me a sense of how this work fit in with the essentials of life. We moved stuff people used to build their houses, get from place to place, and to put on their table. I felt a part of it all, whatever "it all" was—something I had never felt before. I also knew I earned my pay, because at the end of the day I felt like I had been hit by a truck.

When the sugar beets stopped running in the fall most of us new brakemen were cut back to working in the freightyard as switchmen. There were three shifts a day, and when things were busy you could work a shift, be off eight hours, and come back at time and a half to work another eight hours, and so on until you had to lay off to get some rest. Around the middle of October it started to rain all the time, and the worst job in the Watsonville freightyard—the midnight lead job, went up for bid. The three women rookies, me, Maureen, and Gretchen, won it. This was big news on the railroad hotline; everyone was watching to see just how badly we messed up. It was considered extremely arrogant for a new person to bid in a foreman's job, as Gretchen did.

The midnight lead job did all the work that the other shifts had avoided all day; it was under pressure to make up the morning trains which had to be set by a certain time. We went to work at midnight, in the pouring rain, and switched out a four-page list. This could take two or three hours. Then we got to come inside for ten minutes on a coffee break. Then another two lists, followed by twenty minutes to eat dinner. Dinner usually happened around 4:30 A.M. There we were in the switchmen's locker room sprawled around a long table, not even noticing the springs in the grimy couch or the stuffing leaking out of the chairs. Wet from sweating in raingear and from water running down our arms as we held onto side ladders, feeling like deep sea divers as we tried to walk in boots encased in rubber overshoes caked with mud, gloves sopping wet, completely exhausted, we fell asleep with our mouths open—just like the old heads sawing wood on their dinner break.

We all lived in Santa Cruz and would meet at a local espresso house to fortify ourselves for the night. It was an odd feeling to be getting ready to go to work when everybody else was ending their evenings, relaxed, dressed up, and, I began to see, privileged. They were going to put up their umbrellas, go home, and sleep. We were going to put rubber clothes on and play soccer with boxcars, and on top of that, we were going to have to figure out how to do it with no old heads on the crew. Gretchen didn't seem worried; it apparently was a lot less scary than her last job, which was being a topless dancer at the Bandbox in Castroville—a tough Mexican workers' bar. Maureen was less sure. Before the railroad, she had never even owned a pair of jeans. Her first move in the yard had been to fall off a side ladder from about nine feet up, but she picked herself up and got right back on.

Tonight we were going to get some coaching from Wide Load, a switchman delegated to making sure we didn't kill ourselves the first night. We sat around the table in the shanty looking at the computer lists of the track. It told us what was in each track and where each car was supposed to go. It was our job to get them there.

"Just think of the cars as being different colors," Wide Load counseled. "All the pink ones are for the Santa Cruz local on track five. All the blue ones are for the Peddler at 4 A.M. You want to set that first. Right now they're all mixed up in the yard. You have to separate them out and put them in a clear track. OK. Got it?"

We nodded.

"OK. There's three things you do in a yard. You pull, shove, and kick. The cars have to be bled off when you kick, so they can roll. That's the field man's job, or woman's job. Anyway, you have to walk the track and pull the bleed rod on the cars so the air drains out."

We knew how to do that.

"OK, then we'll figure out how you're going to switch, how many cars to let go to what sluff tracks, and where to make your cuts."

We bent over the lists, marking them, planning our moves. It was like a football huddle.

"Hey, how do we keep these lists from getting wet?"

"Fold 'em and put 'em in your plastic timetable covers. You girls all set now? Remember, don't get in no hurry out there. Them boxcars have no conscience at all. They'll roll right over you. So keep in the clear of those tracks. All the time. OK?"

We went outside in the rain and climbed aboard our engine, which was idling on the lead.

"Two track," Gretchen said to our engineer, and he kicked off the jam and we started rocking down the lead. A small yard like Watsonville had two main lead tracks which were diagonals. The switching tracks branched off them. A diagram of it would look like a mesa with twelve lines drawn across it. There were switches where each track met the lead. The yard was full of cars and it was going to be hard to find space to switch stuff out.

The hard part of the job was in remembering where you put things. Thinking of cars as different colors really did help. You might, for example, put two cars that would eventually go to four track in six track, because you needed them first out in four track. You had to remember this when you switched out six track. Not easy when you made similar adjustments every time you did something else. It was hard to keep the final picture in your mind when there were so many intermediate moves involving these huge objects which you couldn't visually keep track of. They were just too big, they all looked the same, and the yard was full of them. After about three hours of moving cars around the yard, I had no idea where we were on our list or what our list meant anymore. Maureen was making mistakes too, and Gretchen was getting her fur up, since as foreman she was technically responsible for everything. It's lonely at the top.

We knocked off for lunch around 4 A.M., and I crawled into the back seat of my Chevy in the parking lot. It was such a wet and wild night, it had driven some of the hobos who lived in the yard into our shanty bathrooms to sleep—their sock-and-rag-wrapped feet protruding beneath the stalls. Only Nature Boy stayed out in this weather, sleeping on a bench under the tower, rain running in his ears and sleeping the sleep of the natural fool. He startled me earlier by pressing his wild moon face against the window of the car. The presence of women here truly mystified him—he would follow Maureen around like a little duck, until she yelled at him to leave her alone. But she would also give him change and relent, so he kept it up, but from a distance. Tonight his face at the window, the heavy curtain of rain, and the sound of the engines roaring around the Wye which circled the parking lot—it wasn't enough to keep me from exhausted sleep, but I drifted into a bizarre dream.

I sleep in the eye of the hurricane, in the Wye of engines and boxcars clanging slack, circling and jerking stop like wagons circling under attack. I sleep within the circle, resting, a tired fighter. The lunatic's happy face is pressed against the glass looking in upon my sleep like the moon—the moon's freightyard fool. We call him Nature Boy. A Spanish dancer twirls within the circle of lurching reefers, clanging gondolas. She wears a black dress that shows her leg, a red ruffled slip, and black silk stockings. She is the storm's voice.

"Who are you?" I ask. I recognize Maureen.

"I am the bullringer. This is my herd tonight."

She whirls, the shepherdess.

Gretchen appears, warning of attack. She wears an army sergeant's suit, medals cover her breasts.

"It's time to go back. They're coming again."

The car is shaking. The rain is in my face. I hear the engine moving down the lead. We have another list to switch. I join my dream.

The rain had let up for the last half of our shift, but the fog was worse. The yardmaster's tower was going to be no help in relaying signals, since the whole yard was socked in beneath it like a white wooly blanket. Fusees burned for ten minutes—white and red phosphorescent hot. The fire would sometimes drip down your gloves and burn them, and you had to be careful to make big signs and hold the fusee into the wind while riding on the side of the cars.

I traded off with Maureen and worked pins for the second half of the shift. The pinpuller cut off the cars in motion that we were kicking to each track. I watched Gretchen for a kicksign, and then when the engineer gunned the engine and the slack ran in on the cars, I yanked up the cutlever, hoping that the pin would stay up and I wouldn't have to run alongside holding it up. If the pin didn't drop, the car would go floating down the lead toward Maureen in the field. With bad pins, you could also ride the side ladder and hook the cutlever with your foot. But this is where you got hurt, running and getting on and off cars in the dark. And you didn't want to fall in between the cars, whatever happened. Being new at it, Gretchen was unsure just how hard to kick the cars so that they would clear the lead but not crash so hard into other cars in the track that they would knock the brakes off. Sometimes I would be running down the lead trying to hold the cutlever up while Gretchen calculated the distance to be traveled.

"Godammit, give a stopsign. I can't hold this fucker up."

It was a little like running alongside a house. A house that was rocking from side to side. A house that could mangle you. I was outraged that there were potholes and debris beside the tracks. What if you tripped over them in the dark, trying to get these pins? Why didn't somebody clean them up?

What with the fog and all, the normally crucial business of passing signs became even more important. It was hard to see the engine, which was the usual way of knowing that the engineer could see you. The standard rule was to pass whatever sign you saw exactly as you saw it. You weren't supposed to interpret, just reproduce. The stakes were life and limb. At first, it was a lot of pressure. You thought, "What if I see it wrong, that light moving a half mile down the crowded track. What if I crush Maureen?" Tonight, with the fog and the yard tracks blocked with cars it was one of those times you had to constantly move in position to pass signs.

Our move was to shove into a track with a cut of cars and couple into it. This was called doubling a track. Since it was a short joint, Gretchen rode the point and I was at the curve to pass signs. Our engineer, of course, didn't know what the move was; he just watched the lights and obeyed them. He got a "go ahead" so he started shoving hard. I could see that Gretchen had about six carlengths to a joint with the other cars, but still no slowdown sign. The rule about passing signs was firmly in my mind, and I just followed them to the letter since I didn't have the judgment to examine them. So I didn't give a slowdown either.

Two cars from the joint Gretchen finally gave a sign—two cars, two stabs of light, and I hear the brakes squealing on the engine but the cars aren't slowing down. I thought, "Wow, they're going to hit," and then they did. I saw a flash of red and something large went sailing past my face. It was half of an eighty-five pound knuckle, the stress translated back to the curve where I was standing and just sheared the coupler in half. I was too surprised to be scared. It all happened too fast.

Gretchen was stalking up the lead in a snit.

"Damn that engineer. He didn't take my sign."

Such is the arrogance of the beginner. The engineer, however, was surprisingly patient. I guess you get that way working midnight goats every night of the week.

"Look," he said, when I had climbed on the engine to explain. "It takes ten carlengths to get stopped going that fast with no air when you have ahold of this many cars. Trains don't stop like cars. They just start to stop when all the slack runs out. Double the distance if you're not sure when passing me signs. You knocked this water cooler all the way across the cab. Good thing I been braced all night."

We weren't unique in our mistakes. All beginners were this way, dangerous as hell for about two years. There was no rushing it. You had to get the habits of the work into your nerve endings so that you could do the job in your sleep. If you had to think about everything you were doing, you would miss something. And misses could be deadly.

"Far out," I thought. "Gretchen almost killed me and she doesn't even realize it." The thought started to sink in about how careful I was going to have to be.

I got off the engine and just kind of stood there looking down two track. Maureen was supposed to be there somewhere bleeding the cars and knocking off brakes. All I could see was a particulate blackness. The hobos had lit a trash can fire under the tower and were clustered around it like witches warming their hands. Soft drips melted off switch stands and padded into pools of oily water like little lakes evenly spaced down the lead. The yard lights were fuzzy yellow balls hung in the fog. I couldn't see a thing. For a moment it all seemed hopeless.

"Kind of reminds you of the *Heart of Darkness* doesn't it."

I looked up at the engineer, who clearly had his own story. It was a kind of intersection, now with the addition of literary space. A notation that this place was a book I was reading and writing, and at this moment I had found another reading over my shoulder on the same page. A kind of surreal shiver. A red light made tiny circles in the fog.

When morning and the day shift made their appearance, the all-girl crew usually headed for Pete's to drink breakfast. Pete's was a switchman's bar. This is a place near the yard which opens up around 6 A.M. for the workers coming off the graveyard shift. The walls are lined with "gimmie caps" bearing local industrial logos— those are the prize caps, probably traded for drinks. Then there are the standard trademark caps and flea-market printed caps with the little insulting sayings, like "No fat chicks," and "Take this job and shove it." The bar sponsors a softball team and has a basically country and western jukebox. It's called the Pub, the Caboose, the Whistle Stop, the End of Track, the Shanty, or Pete's. There are always rails inside drinking. Graveyard shift workers tell themselves it's perfectly natural to be drinking at six in the morning. For them, it's five in the afternoon—Miller time. At noon, it's only midnight.

This logic seemed perfectly natural to me. In fact, it seemed wonderful. Since the whole yard was now in the bar, we would start discussing the moves of the night before, play by play. Switched them out all over again. Soon the yardmaster would come in and things would really get lively. Switchmen insulted yardmasters and were insulted back. Railroading and its finer points were discussed.

"You jackass, you couldn't switch shit. Why those girls over there did a better job than your crew."

"I'll see you on the ground, buddy. You ain't even a pimple on a switchman's ass. I'd like to see a night where you don't change your mind five times a list. Oh by the way, get two bad orders off two track—after we switched it once already. Must be nice, sittin' way up there in the big picture, and all."

We would get our turn in the barrel, but this was where you got to learn things. Out on the lead, people never talked to you—you were working, and there wasn't time. In the switchman's bar, you got the inside dope—if you could stay conscious enough to hear it.

For a month, this was our routine. Our lives were beginning to adjust to the seemingly impossible. I was living on my toes, trying to react, to pick up information, to get rested, to stay alive, to get along with the old head rails. And then, in the space of a week, we were bumped off our job, and then shortly found ourselves without work on the extra board. How did this happen? I thought. Just last week they wouldn't let us lay off. What happened?

"That's railroading," a switchman told me in Pete's, where I was commiserating with the other bewildered members of my class.

"Feast or famine. Better get used to it."

"Well, when are we going back to work?"

"Oh, probably around April. You might pick up days, like at Christmas, but it's slim pickins here in wintertime. Do you know what a boomer is?"

"No."

"Well, a boomer follows the work, and if you're a rail, then I think you is one."

Our trainmaster gave us roughly the same advice. This was to pack up and follow the work the first year, so that we would learn the skills of the job. Just working a few months a year wouldn't do it, and it would be like hiring out all over again every time you got called back to work. I, for one, did not want to go through that all the time, and besides, I was locked into the struggle of learning the job. I wasn't about to quit now. Also there was the little matter of money. I was broke. Fixing my car so I could get to work, paying the vet bills for my dogs, and buying the damn railroad pocketwatch had set me way in the hole. I was in the classic position to become a boomer. And I did.

2
UNDER THE FREEWAYS

A S ONE OF the old heads explained it to me, a boomer is a railroad term for a brakeman who travels around following the rush periods of work in different parts of the country. In Watsonville, for example, there were two runs of sugar beets, one in the fall and one in the spring. You were always busy then, even in bad years. Other places had similar rhythms. In the old days, boomers were boomers out of choice; they were typically hard drinkers who would work until they had a stake to go on a run; then they would disappear. Boomers now, however, were different in a crucial respect. The old boomers were traditional rivals with the homeguard, but they went behind them in seniority. They would turn up at times of feast, and they weren't displacing anyone. In fact, the boomers brought a legendary expertise with them since they only worked in rush conditions and had been everywhere and done everything. They were good help. But now the boomer had a ranking in a systemwide seniority system and might displace a homeboy with less seniority. If hard times were on the way, boomers would show up bumped from somewhere else and keep the chain reaction of displacement happening all over the country. They were traveling in response to an earthquake whose aftershock would be felt throughout the system.

I had been laid off in Watsonville, so I decided to move south to the huge terminal in L.A. where the winter layoff hadn't yet hit. There was a company phone book with systemwide numbers for crew dispatchers. I just called around until I found a place where I could hold the brakeman's extra board. There was no guarantee how long I could hold it, but I wasn't thinking more than a step ahead at a time. I knew that my understanding of this work was based on daily repetition. It was like a detailed puzzle I was in the middle of—since I didn't know what move to make next, I asked whoever was around for advice. There wasn't any choice, really. I had already started to crawl out of what felt like quicksand—the druggie mountain life, and now this slender thread that I had somehow held onto was yanked. In much the same spirit of numb acceptance that I grabbed onto the unfamiliar iron shapes of the work itself, I now blindly moved with this new directive—to go on the road and survive my first winter as a boomer.

I quickly found somebody to live in my cabin, said goodbye to my dogs, and packed up my Chevy. I also had to say goodbye to my lover, a woman I had been involved with, off-and-on, for five years. Our love affair was on the same rocks as the rest of my life, but I just didn't want to believe it. Perhaps leaving her was a way I could keep her in my mind the way I wanted her to be. I thought of Naomi as my creation, anyway, someone whose sexuality I had discovered and brought out. I had a messianic feeling toward her, a feeling of secret possession. I thought of our love life as mystical, holy. But we couldn't get along day by day, couldn't make all the magic weekends last.

As I was leaving town, a friend gave me a book to take with me on the road—*Bound for Glory* by Woody Guthrie. The story of his days as a Texas refugee, a prunepicker, as I would later come to understand the term. I tucked the book into my brakeman's grip and headed south down the Salinas Valley, stopping in at the yard office to pick up my transfer papers. It was like the army; you needed paper to go from one terminal to another. Past twenty-four hours you were AWOL.

After the long hours on highway 101, turning off the freeway into Taylor yard left me with that kind of mental displacement you get when a rhythm is broken and the destination is suddenly there too soon. I had lived in L.A. most of my life, but I was entering a vast topography I hadn't known existed. It was around midnight, and the huge floodlights in the yard were making strange shadow sculptures of the long tracks filled with cars and engines. I drove for a mile next to receiving tracks before I entered the yard proper, and it was a bewildering patchwork of clustered buildings, more small yards within yards, running tracks, roundhouses, towers, repair shops, elevated walkways, and the muffled sounds of collision coupled with an eerie wailing like a metallic drawn-out scream. All this frightened me. I needed to find the crew dispatcher's office. I parked behind a building, and walked into a room with four men in green hardhats sitting around a table drinking coffee. They all stared at me. Then they fell all over themselves giving me advice. The trouble was, none of them knew where the crew dispatcher's office was.

"Oh yes, you must be looking for the yard office, up at the top end. Turn around and go past the roundhouse, all the way to A-yard, you know, where all the engines are."

The yard office sounded right. At Watsonville, everything was in the yard office, but the whole Watsonville yard would take up about one-tenth of what I was seeing here, and I had the feeling that there was lots more I wasn't seeing. Nothing had prepared me for the difference in scale. This was Watsonville and the Salinas districts raised to the tenth power.

After more than one wild goose chase, I finally located the crew office. It had its own separate building, and the night shift was a rude bunch of people. They didn't seem to care about my feelings or want to give me any information at all.

"OK Niemann, you're sixty-four times out."

"Well, what does that mean?" It sounded like a lot of times out. We only had seven people on the whole Watsonville board.

"It means you better get your rest."

Getting your rest is an odd idea for nonrailroad people. It seems obvious; something one, of course, does. But it's the kingpin of the railroad style. I wish I had a dime for every time some old head has told me "Kid, get your rest." At first I had no idea what they were talking about. It meant, to me, "Don't stay up all night partying and then try to go work," or "Don't get so drunk you can't sober up in time for work." I didn't understand that they were talking about an entire shift in priority for my whole life—everything in my life.

Rest has to come first. Because if you don't put it first, you may not get it. And if you don't get it, you may end up run over by a boxcar, dead on a highway trying to drive home, or strung out in unbelievable ways simply trying to live what you think is a normal life and work too. Getting your rest means going to sleep right after you get home, whether it's eight in the morning, four in the afternoon, or midnight. Because you don't know when the phone will ring again. It could be in six hours, and you might have to go back and work twelve hours, and if you haven't made some attempt to "get your rest"—in this case that four hours between getting home and getting awakened again—hey, you're shit out of luck, buddy. And don't try telling the crew dispatcher you're tired. Tired doesn't cut it. They don't care if you're tired. They want meat on that train, and you picked up the phone. I have picked up the phone and burst into tears at not being able to lay off. "Getting your rest" is one of those phrases that you kind of grow into understanding, as it sculpts your body and your life.

The next day was Thanksgiving, and I was spending it with my mother. I was going to stay with her while I worked in L.A., and it had been a long time since we had spent any time together. She didn't understand what I was doing with the railroad or, in fact, anything at all about railroads, period. As we were sitting down to Thanksgiving dinner, the phone rang.

"Gypsy, it's for you. The Southern Pacific calling."

"Oh God," I thought, "how do I explain this?"

"L. G. Niemann? You're augmented to El Centro on a seven-day stand. Are you going to drive or do you need transportation?"

"Augmented? What's that? Where's El Centro? Don't I get to come home?"

"The youngest brakeman on the board gets augmented—loaned out, and they can keep you seven days. I don't know where the hell El Centro is. You got an hour and a half to be at the depot."

I looked at my mother standing in the kitchen. She clearly wasn't taking any of this in. It was as if the police were picking me up. I had the feeling this was the first of many such bewildered looks—

from lovers, from friends, from people I had to deal with who led ordered, ordinary lives.

"You have to go right now?"

"It's the way the railroad works. It's my job; I'll be back home in seven days. I'll call you from El Centro." I didn't have to pack anything—I wasn't unpacked yet. And the grip a brakeman keeps packed with the essentials of the trade plus clothes and snacks for two days was in the trunk of my Chevy. The only problem was money. I had about fifty dollars in my pocket—hardly enough for a week eating out, and no paycheck for a week after that.

"Mom, could you loan me a hundred for a week. I get paid in two weeks."

This clearly was a giant step beyond even her most pessimistic feelings. Here I was arriving in the middle of the night with an impossible story about the railroad, rushing off rudely in the middle of dinner, and then asking for an enormous sum in cash—probably never to be heard from again. This behavior, clearly, was not to be encouraged.

"No, I don't think I can, dear. You know you can stay here this week; you don't have to buy anything."

"No, Mom, I have to go to El Centro. I just took the call."

Oh, well. I would just go with it, and the body would have to follow some way or other. Leaving my mother framed in the doorway of her Spanish-style Pasadena home, I hit the freeway on my way to the Glendale freightyard.

El Centro turned out to be a nowhere spot near the Mexican border. There were a few mine jobs and a few haulers, and their tiny extra board was always running short. The closest terminal was West Colton, a huge ultramodern classification yard at the gateway separating the Mojave desert from the L.A. basin. West Colton's extra board was also short, and therefore they augmented me from L.A. and then shipped me out to cover their outside point. The money was going to be good. We got paid a basic day or 100 miles— any mileage over that was extra pay. The distance from L.A. to El Centro was 250 miles—two and a half days' pay, and we got paid that just for going there (a "deadhead") and also for coming back. Plus the seven-day stand. This was supposed to make up for the missed turkey. At the time I thought it did, but now I'm not so sure. As the company bus dumped me at the Greyhound station in Riverside, I looked around at all my fellow travelers. Families with suitcases, going somewhere better; kids in their twenties having adventures; single men going from work to work; winos just sitting in the station; poor people visiting relatives back home. This wasn't the instant travel of the time-is-money class. This was travel that composed the fabric of your life.

It got dark on the bus, and I lost my sense of direction. We were heading southeast, towards the desert and Imperial Valley. We changed buses at some point, and I walked a quick two blocks to a liquor store for a travel pint of yellow tequila. I was going to have to get to sleep fast when I arrived so that I could "get my rest" before the job went on duty eight hours later. Getting my rest was a fairly malleable concept. It went with drinking, as did the whole patchwork of the extra board life. Upon my arrival at El Centro, an adobe bus station on an adobe main street, the company agent was waiting for me. He was a compact man, with a desert leather face, wearing a straw cowboy hat and fancy boots. The boots meant he drove a car and didn't have to do track work. He did a double, then a triple take on me.

As we drove down the tracks toward the company dorms—grim modules perched beside the mainline, I could tell he was preparing himself for an announcement.

"Well, I guess you must be one of them female brakeman. (Pause.) We had another one of them come down here one time. Seems she thought it was too dirty."

"Uh huh." I let the silence rest a minute. It probably was too dirty, I thought. So what? There clearly was more.

"You know the freightyard here's a pretty dangerous place. A lot of illegals here. A female clerk here said she wasn't going to go down there by herself at night and check the cars. Well, I say if they can't handle the job, then let 'em stay home."

He gave me a searching look.

"Me, I carry this with me," indicating a forty-five automatic resting on the driver's seat beside him.

"OK," I thought, "fine."

The idea of illegals didn't scare me. They weren't half as scary

as just trying to walk in a freightyard, or trying to do the funda-
mental moves of the job without getting severed. Illegals were just
people, like the Watsonville bo's. Most of them I'd seen seemed to
be about fourteen years old and hungry. They'd be stuck in the
middle of nowhere on a siding, hiding under the cars from the sun
and the *Migra*, afraid and unable to ask for a drink of water. It
seemed unlikely they would call attention to themselves by attacking
anyone. They needed to be invisible to us brakemen. Not that the
agent was only trying to scare me. He genuinely felt he needed that
forty-five.

The modules were grim housing in the tradition of the railway
lodges of the nineteenth century. They were built motel-style, with
paper-thin walls and one common room with a TV, always playing
a boxing match. The rooms contained a sprung bed, a small desk,
a lamp, an oil-stained carpet, and a Gideon's Bible. If you searched
the plumbing or checked for loose panels in the bathroom ceiling,
you might find a trainman's stash—a pint for the end of a run. As
it was, I had mine, and I settled in to read *Bound for Glory*, the story
of Woody's hobo ride out to California from Oklahoma in the
thirties.

For most of my life, books had been everything to me. I remember walking into bookstores and the public library and staring at all
the rows of books. I had to know what was in those books. And so
I read for ten years, and now I didn't feel that way anymore. I was
a Doctor of Philosophy and I knew what was in the books. But I
felt that same way about the world, and the boxcars in the freightyard reminded me of those books—reefers with their strange covers, the Soo Lines, the Frisco, the L&N, Illinois Central. They were
thirty-ton books on iron guillotine wheels; they had origins and
destinations; they had histories along the way. Their colors and
logos fascinated me. And they were messengers also. The hobos
would write their signs on cars with chalk, would create logos of
their own, messages of their presence. Working yards all over the
country, these logos would remind me that it was a circle I was in,
after all, and not just endless vectors with no return. What goes
around comes around, from Houston to Klamath Falls, and what
you did on the first day links up with what you did yesterday, and

the hobo with the sombrero under the palm tree comes back again heading west.

Getting bullet-proof and sentimental from the tequila, I thought about Woody's train, the real one full of hard times and freezing nights and brakemen doing the special agent's job—and the other train, the one the book was named for.

This train don't carry no gamblers,
Liars, thieves, and big-shot ramblers
This train don't carry no rustlers,
Whores, pimps, or side-street hustlers,
This train don't carry no smoker
Lyin' tongues or two-bit jokers,
This train is bound for glory,
This train

It seemed like all my friends, and Woody's too, wouldn't be riding this train. Or did the train itself turn all its riders into what Woody wanted them—and himself—to be? Was I looking for this train too?

Minutes later, the whole building was shaking and banging.
"Niemann, on duty five o'clock."
Used to literally shaking brakemen out of bed, he was in the room before I could figure out how to adequately respond.
"Oh my God, it's a girl. Sorry about that. Call the depot for a ride when you get up. You don't want to walk in this part of town."
Meeting my crew at the depot was the first of thousands of similar entrances. Everybody who was talking suddenly shuts up, and everybody starts shifting their positions—walking over to the window, shuffling around on their chairs, changing the conversation to accommodate the boulder that has just appeared in their familiar river. The cause of the problem has just arrived, the reason for the late start, the extra L.A. brakeman, which is bad enough, and a girl brakeman, which is lots worse. The foreman, a thin, mean-looking old guy, gives me a disgusted weasel look and heads for his caboose. The field man is going to have to handle this one. He turns out to be OK, the kind of guy who wouldn't be bothered by my winged hat.

"Just ignore the old fart. But stay out of his way."

My first move of the night was to run the engine through a rigid crossover switch. It was kind of a trap. The other two switches on either side were variable, meaning they would flop over with the weight of the engine wheels. Rigid switches had to be thrown, or they would crunch over and need to be sent back by a track maintainer. Cadillac, the fieldman, was grinning.

"Seems like all them L.A. brakemen run through that switch."

This is what breaking in was all about. It's totally dark, the track layout is unfamiliar, you are groggy from not much sleep, and the old heads won't talk to you and explain the moves. Old heads just didn't communicate with words, and they didn't believe anyone could learn anything by having it explained. You were supposed to watch what they did, copy them, and be ready for whatever hand or lantern signal would come your way. The only time they communicated in language was to chew you out. But they did allow you to make mistakes, which was in fact how you learned to do anything. We were dealing with objects, after all, and not words, and objects have to be understood physically, with your whole body in relation to them, and not just conceptually.

Cadillac was checking me out. In his opinion, L.A. brakemen were "mainline brakemen who couldn't switch their way out of a wet paper bag." Well, we weren't mainline brakemen in Watsonville. Suddenly I was grateful for those confusing student trips in Salinas, learning to string yourself out along a line of cars so that the point man is always in sight of the swing man who is always in sight of the pin man who has to keep in sight of the engineer. The teamwork of peeling on and off moving cars to stay in position and pass signs, relaying stabs and curves of light. Those nights in the rain switching out list after list.

"OK, now, we got to make up our train. Can you read a switch list?" He didn't seem to feel it was at all likely.

"Sure," I said, pulling out my pen and marking off cuts of cars. "Where you going to make the first cut?"

"Well, what do you know. Line twenty, but we'll pull the whole track up first. I'll pump the switch and give the kicksigns. You be at the cut."

Cadillac and I got a good rhythm going switching out our train.

He seemed to feel I was some kind of prodigy for being able to keep track of how many cars to let go on each cut. I just marked them on the list and tried to remember where we were. I also was grandstanding a bit—riding cars to be at the cut and hooking bad pins with my feet. I was showing enthusiasm. Putting out more energy than I had to. Thinking with my feet. It made the old heads feel good about themselves.

From that point on, though, I was cut in with Cadillac, and he protected me from harassment by the locals. The railroad is really a closely knit family. The early nepotism and the crazy way of life supported this. In the early days, the company built houses for rails, and they all lived in the same part of town. They understood each other's problems with ordinary social life, and they stuck together. It's the same way now. Railroaders travel a lot and need places to stay temporarily. They drop in on one another's families and make their spare rooms or floorspace available to each other. Stories get circulated quickly. Cabooses and engines are moving signposts, covered with graffiti pertaining to finks and trainmasters. First impressions count, and anything you do tends to follow you around. Cadillac's comment on me was that I'd do "to ride the river with." Later in Texas, reading Frank Dobie, I understood what he meant.

Cadillac had a way of looking at you and then keeping on looking. I had the feeling I was being read like a newspaper. And Cadillac didn't believe everything he read. One night when we came to work, an old guy was hanging around the trainmen's room, talking to the conductor. He was clearly a wino, but everybody seemed to know him. Later that night Cadillac told me about him. A former conductor, now just hanging around the old spots. Never got out of town and no place else to go.

"You know, I used to drink pretty good myself. But I had to quit."

He looked at me with that rock steady gaze.

"That stuff just about wupped my butt."

My other friend in El Centro was an L.A. brakeman named Juan. He was a fellow sufferer, augmented like myself. He was my first introduction to the fellowship of the road. We had something in common because he was Hispanic, and they, along with the blacks, had taken the flack that the women were now in line for. Juan lived in a black-and-white schoolbus he parked behind the yard office in L.A. The lot was like a trailer park with boomers from everywhere saving on rent and taking showers in the roundhouse. The crew-caller would just go outside and pound on their doors to give them calls. When Juan found out that I was eating at Taco Bell because I was broke, he lent me twenty dollars to eat on that week. Gifts from strangers when your own family can't see through their rose-colored glasses. Gifts that aren't coming to you. The world, while dishing out hard knocks, occasionally passed out roses. I gave him *Bound for Glory*, and we went over the border to drink tequila from those little bottles, followed by pieces of fresh lime, while we walked the dirty streets and talked about our struggles hiring on.

Just what struggles Juan had to deal with came home to me as I was coming off the hauler job one afternoon. I asked the agent if anyone had left a message for me at the station. He looked at me with contempt.

"Some Mexican guy was here, asking about you."

"A brakeman, you mean. A brakeman was asking about me."

He turned to the other good old boy propped behind a computer.

"Just looked like some old Mexican to me."

Juan and I rode back to L.A. together. The new twist of fate was that I was now cut off the brakeman's extra board and forced into the yard to work as a switchman. Juan had the seniority to work in Colton. So all I saw of him after that was the black-and-white bus sitting in the parking lot. I was glad to have something friendly to associate with Taylor yard, and that bus was it. Period.

L.A. switchmen weren't thrilled to have me working there. I was the only woman on the ground in the whole yard, and I got to hear about the few other women that had been run off. The implication was that they were finks, sissies, and cowards. "OK," I thought, "fine." Since these were the standard charges against us, I didn't pay any attention to them. The men were reluctant to trust us; they weren't used to being working partners with women. We were therefore spies, likely to turn them in to management. We had to have some protection other than ourselves didn't we? So naturally we would rely on company officials. Or we would expect the men to do our work for us. And while they would resent it, this is how they wanted us to act. Since you can't tell anybody anything, the only thing to do was to shine it on and do the work.

The work itself was very different from small yard switching, and I could understand Cadillac's impatience with L.A. brakemen. The L.A. yard was vast, consisting of four yards: the receiving yard and hump, the bowl, the tracks for making up trains, and the separate shops yard, which held container freight. There were hundreds of tracks. Switch crews rarely got to do any complete moves. They did half of something—like doubling one whole track to another. Then another crew would put the caboose on. There was very little switching out. That was done on the humpyard by a separate job that did nothing else but pull pins on hundred-car cuts being slowly shoved over the hill by a switch engine. The yardmaster's voice would come over a P.A. in the switchman's shanty announcing some move or other, and the crew would leave their card game or nap to go do one move, then back to the shanty, then back on the lead, in short choppy meaningless bursts all night long. The yardmasters were generally abusive and sarcastic, and the switchmen retaliated by moving slowly. They did not have what you would call esprit de corps.

My main concern was still pure survival. I didn't have the basic moves of the craft to where they were second nature. I had to think about them. I also didn't know the tracks and where dangerous situations were likely to occur. In a huge yard, many jobs are working at the same time. You may know where your crew is, but the other five crews may surprise you. The rule book has a phrase for it—to expect movement on any track at any time. Also, yards are not lit up like Main Street. You need your lantern. And boxcars, particularly flatcars, are silent. They roll silently, floating down those bowl tracks making only an occasional creak as they roll from side to side. That creak will wake you out of a sound sleep. An instant nightmare.

I had a nightmare like that the first few weeks working Taylor yard. It was one of the few times I got caught by the crewcaller when I was loaded. This is bound to happen to an extra man sometime. In this case it was past the regular calling time and I thought I was safe, so I smoked a joint and got into playing my guitar. With that narrowing of perception that happens with pot I was really able to get into the music and to feel on top of it and together. Then the phone rang, and being inexperienced, I picked it up. It couldn't be the railroad. It was past calling time, nearly midnight. Wrong. Somebody had failed to show up for their job. I was it. Because I had felt so competent playing music, I figured I wasn't really very stoned. Wrong again. When I hit that freeway, headed for a place I'd never been before, the disorienting panic that comes when there is too much sensory input kicked in. I had to talk to myself in the car. "OK, calm down. Turn on the radio. Think one thing at a time. You're here now; you're going there. One thing at a time."

I'd look out the window, and none of it made any sense. Where was I? Why was it midnight? Finding the shops yard involved several tricky maneuvers with cloverleaf offramps and left turns through industrial gates and container freightyards, asking directions of nightwatchmen in lonely little booths, and a long drive down the row of giant insect cranes used to load and unload piggyback rail-packs. This was starting to feel like a trip to the moon. I walked into the shanty and met the crew. Luckily they were ready to go to work, so I didn't have to sit there and talk. That would have been hard. I found myself in the field, trying to concentrate on what was happening. It was difficult to think about several things at once. Pot narrows your peripheral sensitivity—a deadly side effect in a freightyard. You might look around and notice how interesting the hook-shaped moon looks suspended over Chinatown, and the next thing you know death has brushed your cheek with her soft sable wrap. Without knowing it, I stepped out of the way. Some other crew had been shoving a long line of piggyback flatcars—silent floaters, on the track next to me. Only I wasn't standing in the clear and I had my back to them. My body decided to move. After it did, and the river of creaking steel went riffling past me inches away, I had a moment out of time. I knew I hadn't done that. And I didn't know how to interpret it, either. I decided that I wasn't going to smoke pot much anymore. I would just drink. It was safer.

The winter went on, and it rained, and rained, and rained. Coffins were floating down the freeways. I worked mostly midnights on the hump. Wearing a yellow slicker and being out all night in the rain pulling pin after pin on endless cuts of cars as they were shoved up to the crest of the classification hill, I began to feel that there was no night or day, that shelter was the body itself, that it was the home I lived in. For companionship, I went to bars. Mostly gay bars, since I felt safer there. It was instant companionship. A few martinis, and whoever was sitting to my right or left became a confidential friend. I created myself in conversation. And after an hour or two, I could slip out the back door and leave my sculpture intact, and I could revel in it on my way home. As I careened my way home.

The L.A. freightyard, winter of the flood, L.A. river over the top, up to my knees, swimming down the rails. Midnights I discover I don't need to sleep, don't need shelter from the rain, can sleep like a cat on the floor of the engine, the diesel throb a comfort. In the yard, camaraderie, talk of the old days, steaks barbecued in the bullpen, beer in the coolers, free beer from warehouses. On the Santa Fe hauler all-night job, the drunken conductor swings aboard with vodka and O.J. and sets up a bar in the second unit. We slip back there all night, do lines of coke, Slick the engineer and Fang, his fireman dog. Nights, I lie on benches in the switchmen's shanty, eavesdropping on men talking as if I wasn't there, a woman, among them. They really do talk about their dicks.

"And then we had the short-arm inspection, in the army, you know what I mean, boys."

I am among the few who know the land now, its shape, the L.A. railmap. Unknown roads through the city, following invisible rivers, our hump yard screaming over Mt. Washington, the shops container yard at Chinatown's feet. Sunrise creates skylines I had never seen. On New Year's Eve I found a haven as a herder for the engineer's locker room, a pajamas-and-slippers job. The Dolores crew came in at three, after a delay at Watts, the windows of their caboose shot out.

"Better lie on the floor and lock the doors. You don't walk your train no matter what. Brakeman cut up with a church key, while the railroad agents watched. Chickenshit assholes."

Winter went on, long midnight shifts, then fewer shifts, then no shifts at all. Roma, Watsonville brakewoman and boomer extraordinaire, calls me from Houston. The railroad women are there, the party is there, the streets are paved with gold. Overtime, hurting for men, free roundtrip tickets, the Texas open checkbook policy, a free hotel. I look under "Weather" in the paper. Houston, eighty-four degrees in February. I pack a small grip and I'm on the big bird headed for the tropics, worst hangover of my life from tequila for all the night before. My suitcase lost in Dallas and a Blue Norther arriving with me, I give the cabman a twenty for a ride to the boomer hotel.

3

BOOMER IN A BOOM TOWN

THE CENTER CITY HOTEL was located on the corner of Mug and Murder in downtown Houston. It was the kind of location where, if you went out the front door to hail a cab, drivers would pull over and ask you what you cost. As a matter of fact, if you sat in the lobby even in overalls and work boots, men thought you were hustling. Houston was at the end of the oil boom, and thousands were still moving there every day. Street maps were instantly out of date. Freeway exits went to ski jump endings. People were living in foyers of storefronts—every storefront. The kind of people who wear underpants over their pants. It was a wino fad. Everybody carried guns. White office workers used the network of underground tunnels to get around downtown. At 5 P.M. they got out of town, followed by the police force. By 7 P.M. the downtown belonged to the street folks and to nocturnal workers like us.

Boomers from all over the Southern Pacific system were at the hotel. They were mostly new-hires who had worked a few months and had then been cut off. Utah, Texas, Oregon, California—word had gotten out. Roma, Teresa, and Maureen were already here. There was another woman from El Paso, and myself. Five women boomers with sixty male boomers staying in a free hotel, with free taxi vouchers, and enough work available to make everybody feel rich.

"Be careful around here," Maureen advised. "Yesterday I saw this couple having a fight on the street, and this guy just rips this baby out of the woman's hands and throws it down on the sidewalk. I think everybody's crazy around here. You can stand on your balcony and watch people getting killed."

It was true. The homicide had almost a carnival atmosphere. The effects were that you couldn't go anywhere alone at night. We all stocked supplies in our rooms and went in pairs to McDonald's two blocks away. I had been in urban slums before, but this action was different. There were no rules, no right way to act. The street people were improvising too—they also were boomers, but they weren't getting in on the action. It was, of course, a tense racial situation. Blacks who managed to get jobs in the service industries took the chance to strike back against white racism by outdumbing 'em. This meant that they became incredibly incompetent when it was your turn in line. It was an effective strategy. But it approached the surreal with respect to taxi service, which was the only way we had to get around. Cabs would come or not come. You might or might not get to your destination. Maureen and Roma were taken to a "rock house," instead of back to their hotel, while their cabbie did a dope deal. I had a cab driver stop in traffic, get out, and go inside a building to pay his phone bill, leaving me and the cab sitting in the middle lane of heavy traffic. I got out, found another cab, and continued on to work. When you consider that we only got about five hours sleep between shifts around the clock, this cab roulette was nerve-wracking. Some disgruntled California boomer even got a cab driver to drive him to California. He just got in a cab and said "California," and the driver took him there. On a company voucher. Even the Texans couldn't believe that one. Finally we discovered Taxi Unlimited, a cab-within-a-cab company. Those taxis actually arrived. It had come to seem like a major blessing.

In the midst of all this confusion, a renaissance was happening. The Chamber of Commerce put on events in center-city parks every weekend. Musicians from all over the South came to Houston to perform and hit it big. Arts and crafts of surprising quality sold on the streets. Texans could really laugh at themselves—their work was self-reflexive, whimsical, and fantastic. If someone liked what you were wearing, they offered you money for it on the spot. Lots of money. Working people had hundred-dollar bills, and they weren't drug dealers. And they were spending them.

The first day on the job, I found myself working with an all-extra crew. Hardly anyone worked regular jobs here, since the money was on the extra board working eight hours on and eight off, around the clock. The people on the crew were boomers who had arrived in Houston hours before I had. The hoghead was from Oregon; the other two trainmen from El Paso. Our assignment was to take a drag to the port. None of us knew where the port was. It was a surprise to me that there even was a port. I thought you needed an ocean to have a port. Englewood yard was even larger than L.A., but with tracks in much worse condition and none of them numbered. All of the other switchmen in the shanty were extra, and none of them knew where anything was either. It took us about an hour to locate our engine and the track where our train was made up. The yardmaster was a boomer from California who had been hit in the jaw by a puzzle switch the week before. He just wanted us off his chessboard.

"Just get on your train, and do the best you can. You'll probably die on the law before you get there anyway."

Hours later we were creeping out of town. We had ten hours to get these cars to the port, a distance of about twenty miles. In the meantime, what Texans call a "Blue Norther" had entered the picture. This was a vicious windstorm with an icy bite that had "nothing but barbed wire and tumbleweeds to stop it" as it blew out of the north. The temperature was not eighty-four degrees any-more; it was ten below. Just getting out of the cab to go line a switch left you feeling cut by the cold like a hard-boiled egg intersected by a wire egg slicer. We took turns doing anything outside. The engine rocked from side to side on the rotting ties and swampy ground. All the track in Houston and in the yard itself was in terrible shape. There were daily derailments, and nobody thought anything about it. The tracks would just spread under the weight of the engine, and boom, you were on the ground. There were often no spikes holding the track to the ties, or the ties had just rotted away. This was at a time when ten-million-dollar trains were rolling out of

Houston every hour, carrying petrochemicals north and west. Southern Pacific was playing catch-up, throwing money, track crews, and extra help at the problem. We were all working overtime and, it seemed, not getting much of anywhere. It was a scene of mass confusion. We put in our twelve hours wandering on creaky track toward the port and then tied our train down on a siding to await the company carryall that would bring in the dogcatching relief crew. We were now dead on the law. Time to make plans to get warm and eat dinner.

One of the boomers had a car, and we all piled in and headed for a gumbo house. Logan, one of the El Paso brakemen, passed around a pint of bourbon, and the fiery warmth hit me right in the knees and built a campfire in my empty insides. I began to feel that we were all old friends and that Houston was an exotic and mysterious location. Logan was having similar comradely impulses.

"You know, you Californians talk like Yankees, but you act more like you were from the South."

"I didn't even think of Texas as being South. I mean, I thought it was Western, but I guess this is as far South as I've ever been."

"Well, there's Texas, and then there's West Texas. These old boys down here don't even think we're Texans in El Paso. Me, I say put the *J* back in Tejas, if you know what I mean."

I didn't really, but I felt like I did. We were drinking Old Weller 120 proof. You get telepathic pretty quickly on that stuff. Then a song came on the radio that went right through my bourbon bravado. It was Lacy Dalton singing "Tennessee Waltz." She was from the Santa Cruz mountains and used to sing in my local bar. I felt how lonely and homesick I really was here. And how scared. But I also felt grateful that something from my old world could find me, that I couldn't just lose myself completely like my suitcase in Dallas.

The hurricane ambience of Houston brought to the surface all my old struggles to fit in, to feel located in an identity. I had never found a niche where I didn't violate some of the membership rules. I was an intellectual, and I looked like an all-American bimbo. I was bisexual, but lesbians thought I looked straight, and straights thought I looked gay. I was middle class, but I was living a working-class life. I was extremely ambitious, but in a curiously spiritual sense. Money was not it for me, nor status, nor happiness. I didn't know what was it, but I always wanted to see more of the picture, as if there would be an illumination just around the bend. This belief kept me moving through life. Hiring on the railroad, though, I felt the brass knuckles wrapped around the heavy hand of conformity. I needed an identity out here, and I needed it fast.

In Houston, I was instantly asked to choose up sides—racially, sexually, and regionally, I had not been outside California in ten years, and the small community in which I lived was a throwback to the sixties. It was a home for misfits and outlaws, all the folks who wouldn't be riding Woody's train. While living up in the mountains, all my possessions from the mainstream culture—like blenders, TV sets, and pantyhose—had fallen off my train a long time ago. I did not even own a dress. I hadn't worn one in years. I realized quickly in Houston, from the empty-cash-register looks from people on the street, that I didn't even know what I looked like. I looked at the people around me. Women wore skirts, high heels, and hairdos requiring rollers. And lots of makeup. And little bags that matched their shoes. I had awakened on the set of *Invasion of the Body Snatchers*, and I was a pod.

With a truly serendipitous twist, I lost my California driver's license. I could no longer prove who I was. All I had with me was two suitcases filled with workboots and overalls. Eyes on the street looked through me. Street person? No. Woman? No. Man? No. Boy? Must be.

"Sorry, sonny. You have to be eighteen to buy liquor."

This was getting to me where it hurt. Thirty-four and couldn't buy booze. Women didn't wear flat shoes. Women wore makeup. I must not be one. Was I one? I began to worry about it. I felt erased, like the hole in the donut. I went to Woolworths and bought girl drag—pantyhose and makeup and razors and pink blouses and shoes with little heels. I thought, "I feel like a drag queen. What's going on here?" A Walt Disney hippo ballerina armed for a day at the office. Work in the real world. But I needed to exist in the mirrors of other people's eyes. I needed to survive here; it was yet another decision to hold onto the side of the car. Railroad work had made me aware of my dependence on other people. I needed the other members of my crew to keep me alive. I needed to exist for them. In between the cars, my body inches from the wheels, I was powerless and vulnerable. A signal passed or not passed, and I was history. That fact settled in and lay resting in my consciousness, quietly altering all my relationships to the world.

One of the sources of my vanishing sense of identity was the attitude of the men on the job. A real woman wouldn't be doing this kind of job; therefore, if you were a real woman you couldn't do the work, and vice versa. Since we all were learning the work, we could do the job to the extent that the old heads allowed us to. It was a tricky give-and-take situation. All of the women had to deal with this problem—to be thought competent or to be thought feminine. How to get a balance? My tendency was to erase what would trigger a standard sexual response and to blend in as "one of the guys." I figured I could reclaim my sense of sexuality later, when I could survive out here. Other women made other choices.

Frankie Lee wore one of those Texas Dolly Parton hairstyles. She was a boomer from El Paso with seven, count 'em, kids to support, and was in Houston because that's where the money was. Frankie's ex had run out on her when she was in the hospital with number five, and he now lived nearby in Cut-and-Shoot. She was trying to figure out how to collect on back child support, and he was in deep shit if she ever figured it out. The guy's life appeared to be hanging by a thread.

"If he's giving you problems, why don't you just take a contract out on him, Frankie?"

Frankie looked thoughtful. "No, the kids need the money. But I thought about it plenty."

She was about five feet tall plus another foot of hair, and no matter what, Frankie looked good. She would come back from an eight-hour shift with six hours to rest and spend two of them setting her hair. This happened around-the-clock, leaving Frankie with not much time to eat. She sent all her money home, anyway, and ate peanut butter sandwiches to keep going. When they threw us out of the hotel, Frankie moved into her van and took showers at the roundhouse. This kind of existence would kick a Marine's ass, but Frankie managed to project an image of helplessness all the time she was doing her superwoman changes in phone booths. She had the men convinced she couldn't do anything really. They liked that, and they liked Frankie, but they also talked about her behind her back.

"She don't do her work. She's afraid to get dirty. Why, I had to kick a brake off for her last night on the hump."

Switchmen's wives would call Frankie up and tell her she ought to be home with her kids instead of out working with their husbands. What were Frankie and the kids supposed to eat when they were all sitting home together?

The truth was nobody cared. There was a certain hardness and rudeness that ruled here. The company took almost a terrorist attitude toward its workers. Crew dispatchers yelled at us on the phone. Coworkers called us California queers and prunepickers. In response to this, I came to learn something about myself. I found the end of my personal fuse. I started fighting back. Texans harassed you until they got a response. They had a ways to go with me. On the hump job, the pinpuller walked along the crest of the hill, pulling pins on the cars. It was a hard job physically. Unlike other yards where you read cut numbers on a board or from a list, in Houston the foreman yelled out the cuts from a little tower overhead. The elevation gave them a godlike feeling of superiority. They yelled out other things besides the cut numbers, usually a running commentary on the pinpuller's attitude, appearance, and competency. After your third shift back-to-back, this shit got annoying.

Texans were the same way on the radio. Yak yak yak. With all the jobs working in Englewood yard and all of them using radios to switch, it was downright dangerous. Switchmen giving car signs had to compete with good-old-boy CB talk. When it became clear that a woman switchman was making a move, then everybody in the yard got talk-itis.

"SP4540 back 'em up two cars to a joint."

"Sounds like somebody's wearin' tight underpants, hee hee hee."

"One of them California help, s'all."

"One car, 4540."

"Hey foreman, get on down there and see what's going on."

"Easy 4540."

"Gawdamn. Yehaw." (Sounds of snuffling, kissing.)

"Will you gawdamn yahoos git off the gawdamn radio. I can't hear my headman."

"Headgirl, don't yew mean? Hee hee hee."

"Back a carlength, 4540. The joint didn't make."

I was down in the bowl wrestling with a drawbar on a piggyback car. Pig drawbars are a bitch to move over since they are longer than normal ones, but I had a method. I planted both feet on the inside of the rail, my ass against the drawbar, and shoved back with my legs. The sucker moved right over. The standard way to do things was based on male body mechanics, but women had to figure out their own best way to deal with the oversized equipment and their own center of gravity. Men just couldn't figure out how women could move things. They couldn't make that leap that women are strong but move their bodies differently. I was engaged with the drawbar when my foreman showed up to the rescue. He motioned me out of the way and started to give signs to the engineer. This turned out to be my limit.

"I'd just as soon do my own job, if you don't mind."

"Well, honey, I'm just getting things moving for ya."

"Well, if you want to do my job, then I'll go sit on the engine all night, and you can pull pins and be the foreman."

I really had surprised him. But it was a good surprise.

"Well, I'm sorry. I guess that tells me you really do give a damn about your work."

Railroaders wanted to find out where you were at. They had to know if they could trust you, and they weren't about to take it on faith. They pushed until they found out, and then they were nice to you. With my Pasadena background, it was hard for me to be impolite. I kept waiting for other people to come to their senses and stop being rude. In Texas, however, hell would obviously freeze over first, and I had to learn to stick up for myself. Nobody else would.

In celebration of my newly discovered porcupine identity, I decided to buy a genuine Texas cowboy hat. I had a sympathy for the fact that hats meant something here. They were what got picked on first in bar-macho posturing.

"Gawd, I never saw a hat that looked quite that sat-on before. I think I might be ashamed to wear a hat like that into a public establishment. Now tell me, did your wife sit on that hat?"

The American Hat Company was on Old Market Square in downtown Houston. I was prepared to have to pay a lot for a hat, but I wasn't prepared for the number of decisions required to buy a hat. I walked into a large carpeted room with hat-sized shelves circling it in layers. These shelves contained "blanks"—unshaped hats with varying crown heights, brim widths, colors, and quality. The blanks looked like the hats the Indians wore in old Western movies. The colors started with white, cream, silverbelly, grey, tan, brown, dark brown, black, blue, and ended up with the wilder cowgirl shades of yellow, lavender, royal blue, and red. The ceiling of the two-story room was decorated with finished blanks, with brim and crown styles labeled. There were names like Alpine, Old West, PRCA, Bullrider, Gun Club, and Goatroper. A tall glass case stood in the corner, containing examples of the possible textures, starting with XXX beaver and running to fuzzy mink. Slick-looking sales-people in tight jeans and exotic skin boots held blanks over steam jets, lovingly forming creases to order. Men in business suits and lizard boots stood around while their immaculate silverbelly minks were steamed into perfection. Celebrity photographs of the Oilers in such headgear decorated the walls. I clearly was out of my league.

My second attempt went better. I knew what to expect. I got as far as the models hanging on hatracks, but I was still too intimidated to ask for my size or to even admit that I was there to buy a hat.

The third time I entered the store with presence. The urban cowperson approached, boots creaking.

"I want a black, triple beaver, size seven, with a three-inch crown, Alpine crease, and a four-inch Bullrider brim. Please."

"Yessmam." The blank came down; the jets did their work. Twenty minutes later I emerged, feeling reborn. The part of the process I hadn't considered was the hatband, and I had put myself into the hands of the hatmaster there. As a result, I left the store with something that looked like it had better not get rained on. Tail-feathers extended down my neck, over the Bullrider brim. I felt outrageous.

I later bought another hat in Houston at one of the crafts fairs that filled the city center nearly every weekend. This hat was a parody of itself, a straw shaped like it had been stepped on by a horse and then shellacked. It was pure art, on the line between insult and self-irony. A Texan could wear it, but maybe not a Californian. It was in the class of my baseball cap with wings. It was a right-to-life-o-meter.

I noticed that I was drinking a lot in Houston, but I thought of it as joining the mainstream and blending in. I was, after all, staying away from drugs. So drinking was being good. I didn't connect it with the strange feelings I was having about who I was, that I didn't seem to belong inside myself. I felt that I was being seen incorrectly by other people and that I had to be secretive. But, in fact, I didn't know what it was I was hiding. The fact that I thought I had to hide meant I was letting other people define my "secret" self, too. None of the identities fit except one—the one that was drinking. But that one I mystified too.

It was OK to drink at seven in the morning because I was coming off the night shift, and I had to get my rest (pass out) fast so that I could go back to work. Since I was working, I was functional. The hangovers were the price you paid for the quick knockout which I needed or I would feel worse. Right? I would get out of the cab, change boots and walk two blocks, stepping over the bodies, to a cockroach saloon that was open at the crack of dawn. I didn't think much of the clientele at that hour. They were obviously alcoholics. They clearly weren't nightshift workers like me. Occasionally I would run into other boomers there, and I was glad to see them. After three or four bourbons, the aches stopped and the loneliness went away, and it felt like a welcoming evening was approaching, an evening that held possibility. More bourbons, and the bar became picturesque, the country music moving, and a kind of heroic self-image appeared. It was easy to talk to strangers; they became my intimate friends. We shared something. I started waking up in other rooms in the boomer hotel. I told myself I would have to be more careful. I made up a little saying for the bartender.

"When I start calling them tiled wurkeys, cut me off."

I found a braking partner in one of the boomers from El Paso. We were right next to each other in seniority, so we worked a lot of the same jobs. Braking partners stick together, share housing, go booming together. We weren't lovers, but everybody thought we were. Lovers would have been risky for me. Logan called black people "jungle bunnies" and gay people "faggots." I wasn't going to share my inner life with him. But I needed backup in the yard, and so did he. We also were drinking partners. We went to happy hours, ate mountains of oysters, and drank. We went to honky tonks, danced our asses off, and drank. We went to street fairs, threw our money around, and drank. At the yearly union dance, we stood around the stage and watched a beer-drinking contest. I had an uncomfortable feeling as the woman who won kept pouring the amber liquid down her throat. She looked ill. Her face was green. And she kept on drinking.

Boomers out on the town, we take free cabs to country western bars, and ride the mechanical bull. Roma and I jump on its back together. A stranger joins us, and somebody plugs it in. At the first buck our crotches are slammed into the saddle horn and on the second buck we are all airborne. A flying cowboy boot catches me in the thigh. I am told that I executed a martial arts roll and landed on my feet. This makes me feel invincible. That's not the way I feel the next morning, covered with black and blue bruises. Why didn't I feel any of this the night before?

After two months of free rent and double shifts and crew callers screaming when you wanted to lay off, the boom tapered off and the warm welcome got cold all of a sudden. The company had been housing around seventy boomers at the hotel. We came off a shift one night and were told to get out by tomorrow or start paying rent. The party was over.

I went to see the trainmaster, who was on the phone with somebody in the hospital who had just been gassed. He had been working at a place called Strang. He hung up the phone and fixed me with a warden-like stare.

"You're forced to Strang," he said.

It sounded awful, like a disease or the heart of darkness. The horror.

"Where's Strang?"

The other switchmen were encouraging.

"Strang? You watch out or they'll send you back to California in a pine box."

The cab ride out to Strang was surreal. I was called for the midnight shift, a bowl job in the small switching yard. About ten miles outside of Houston the smell began—the sweetish odor of petrochemicals and swampy pools of evaporating liquids collecting in depressions beside the road. It got noticeably warmer, and the light began to change. Soon it was daylight from the incandescence of towers and steaming caldrons looking like they were built from erector sets and decorated with prison floodlights. Gas burnoffs flared into the humid atmosphere. The number of plants increased; they clustered together until we were in the land of the petrochemical, the industry tracks skirting the highway and filled with round, black, deadly tank cars.

The Strang yard was where all these chemical cars were switched out and trains known as "bombs" made up. Since the railroad was shorthanded, crews working Strang were mostly new-hires and boomers, some of them with as little as a month's railroad experience. They handled cars loaded with flammable gas, deadly chemicals, nerve gas, sulphuric acid, anhydrous ammonia, propane, and God knows what else. Since the chemical plants were working overtime also, the cars weren't always carefully loaded, and leaks were common. Can you picture it? Someone down in Strang bowl, learning how to couple up a track and making the kind of mistakes Gretchen, Maureen, and I made on the all-girl crew? Hit a joint hard with a leaky tank car full of corrosive, say, with the hatch not fastened down, and the results would not be pleasant. I heard about some hideous accidents. There was the standard description of what happens when you get coupled up; this was told to all new brakemen to scare them into being careful. The unfortunate victim gets coupled up, and only the pressure of the couplers keeps him alive. He will die the moment the cars are separated and his blood pressure drops. His wife rushes to the freightyard to say goodbye, and then they give a backup sign. They pull the pin on the guy's life. The Strang version of this story included the victim's being eaten up by acid while coupled up. I remembered the guy in the hospital on the phone. Oh, that was common, I was told. Seventy-five percent of the regular crews here had been gassed last year. It was a good way to get a suit against the company, make some big money. How could you get gassed? It could happen from leaking cars when you were down in the bowl coupling up a track, or it could happen when the petrochemical plants decided to vent some gas in the middle of the night. This was illegal, but they did it anyway. The first time I was on a switch engine working one of the plants, I wanted to turn around and go home. The plant had an employee whose job it was to follow our engine around on a bicycle, carrying gas masks. He was supposed to run to our aid if we all suddenly dropped to the ground.

I reported for work the first night at Strang at the switchman's shanty, where we played one of those "walk into a room nobody says anything" scenes. I finally deduced from the grunts and heads thrown back, chins pointing down the hump, that my job went to work in the bowl. This meant we were going to spend the night coupling up the tracks that had been classified by the hump job and hoping that the cowboys on the hill didn't send any cars into our tracks by mistake or didn't hump any dangerous cars that would explode or gas us. It hadn't been too long ago, after all, that the Texans had managed to blow up Englewood yard by humping a flammable gas car. It sailed like a deadly balloon right onto the drawbar of another car, was pierced, and began leaking LPG. A switch engine passed by on the lead, and KAZOW the whole yard blew up. The Texans were really pissed off that they didn't get to hump LPG cars anymore and slipped a few by on the sly to prove they weren't scared of officials or demolitions.

There were two or three cabooses that belonged to the bowl job on a spur next to the parking lot. In the old days, each local had its own caboose, and the crew could fix it up like home. The bowl job's caboose was a gesture left over from this tradition. It was a cupola caboose, wooden and old-style, and every square inch of its interior was papered with hard-core porn. We were talking split beaver here. Hairy-mouthed vaginas lined the roof like spiders waiting to gulp up whatever dumb fly had abandoned all hope and entered here. Melon-sized breasts poked out like torpedoes from the walls. Like a Byzantine chapel, its cruciform shape, drab and earthly on the outside, gave no hint at what would be revealed within. Passing through its portals, one understood that the interior was really the gateway to the universe of stars, following the processing of Saints and Martyrs who have gone before. The vagina, gateway to life, certainly, and now re-enterable, following the procession of big bazooms, disclosed the jewel-like interior of the body of life itself. But to what universe were we heading here? No ethereal place or feeling, but a closing in, a breathlessness, I would have thought, an anti-erotic concentration. The pictures were too dark, too—well, hairy. Women tend to paint themselves as vulva flowers, perhaps in a desire to turn themselves inside out, to give birth to themselves. The vulva becomes flowers and swirling water; it is brought to light. The caboose regarded snatch as a dark and bushy place where the sun definitely did not shine. No wonder men had trouble with the concept of foreplay. I bet they didn't spend much time in this caboose either.

Not to say that stepping into this caboose was not a slap in the face. But its placement here, in the deadliest switching yard in the Southern Pacific system, raised it into the realm of the artistically surreal. It felt like a tall tale, like another dimension had been added or subtracted from an ordinary perception. Suddenly you are within a joke, and things have just gone a little too far out there, and the mind suspends judgment. I just thought, "OK, fine. Hairy vaginas and sulphuric acid tank cars and cowboy macho switchmen and so what next."

Next was the everyday occurrence of derailments due to the poor condition of the track. Houston was just plain old swampy, and the ties were rotted away. You went on the ground so often that nobody even reported it unless you couldn't rerail the engine with old boards or you tore up track. One day I was hanging on the point of a hopper car and the car just jumped the track and went bouncing out into a cottonfield. It took at least two good hops before the air blew and we came to rest in the dirt.

"Gawdamn, girl, how'd you do that?"

I just smiled, and we both sat down to wait out the rest of our twelve-hour day while the track crew came and put humpty back together again. You always had to expect the unexpected working Houston, and it was good survival training—if you passed the course. You couldn't count on whoever had been there last—that included switch crews or industry crews. The rule was "Don't assume anything. Check it out." One night I turned my back on a cut of cars because I assumed they had handbrakes on them. It was an industry track, and I was doing the simple move of coupling the engine to the track. The joint didn't make at first, so I backed the engine up to have some space to straighten out the coupler. I stopped in front of the engine and started wrestling the coupler over, and I turned my back on the cars. Suddenly the hair on the back of my neck went up and I stepped out of the way as the two knuckles coupled up. The cars had been left with no air and no brakes, and the missed first joint had set them rolling. I always checked for brakes after that.

This was what the first year was all about, a struggle to make safe habits instinctual. Things like never standing foul of any track at any time, always knowing where everyone on your crew was, always keeping one foot outside the rail so you could step out, always keeping one hand on a grabiron in case of slack action, never setting your lantern in the toepath when you went in between the cars. Your light represented you, and if the engineer saw the light, he would figure it was safe to move.

Logan also found himself at Strang dodging poison gas, and we had t-shirts printed up that said "I survived Strang." One night I read in the paper that Lacy J. Dalton was playing at Gilley's, and Logan and I went to see her. This was her first road tour, and she was glad to see a groupie from home. Logan was very impressed that I knew a country star, and we went backstage and ate pizza with her and the band. She looked at me with those wise eyes of hers and wrote something on her pizza box and handed it to me.

"Home is where the art is. Love Jill."

Clutching my pizza box, I watched her ride off into the humid night with some flashy dude on a Harley. Logan and I hitched a ride with the harmonica player back to Houston. We had to get up in a few hours and dodge poison gas. I wondered where my art was, what it was, or could a brakeman's craft make a home?

After a month, we were allowed back to Englewood yard, and we went gladly. It was the old Western dilemma of whether it's better to be scalped or snake bit. I started catching a lot of hauler jobs going from Houston to Strang and jobs working the little switching yards around the city. Often the train would be held at a red signal for hours, and you would have to get out and walk the train. Now it was other people you had to worry about, and not chemicals. A brakeman from Oakland got off to walk his train one night and found himself looking at a shotgun and some dude telling him to cut the road crossing right now. Houstonians didn't have a lot of patience, and they were armed to the teeth. They didn't intend to sit in their pickups and wait for some train to get moving.

It turned out they weren't the only ones with guns. The train crew had them, too. Kids in the ghetto neighborhoods we ran through would pack the switch points on power switches with rocks, hoping for some excitement. They would also run out and turn the angle cocks on cars whenever the train stopped—which meant that the brakes stayed set up on half your train and the brakeman had to get out and check each angle cock, and by the time you had done that, more were turned. Rocks came sailing in open windows—and bullets, too. The cowboy engineer would pull out a three-fifty-seven magnum and fire back into the night. God, I thought, beam me up. Get me out of here.

God answered in the form of the oil bust and the mellifluous voice of the crew dispatcher.

"Niemann, you are cut off as of 12:01."

"You woke me up at three in the morning to tell me I'm cut off?"

"That's correct. You're cut off."

I left Houston in late May when the killer heat wave was just gathering to strike. It already felt like someone was standing on my chest. I had nearly a year's experience as a rail and a carpetbag stuffed with money. I was used to drinking bourbon and jumping ten feet when I heard a loud noise. I also felt partially deaf from the screaming retarders on the hump and standing next to steel wheels being dragged with brakes on. I wondered if I could still play flute by ear or hear soft subtle things. I was very homesick. I wanted my friends, and lover, and dogs to have been waiting. I was right about the dogs.

When I got back to Watsonville, I found to my surprise that I could hold the brakeman's board. Being tied to the agricultural cycle, summer was its boom time. I soon found myself knee-deep in strawberries, passing signs in the fog, just like always. God, what a relief. Sweet, harmless boxcars, reefers humming, filled with fruit, lettuce, and things that didn't blow up. The switchmen's shanty was filled with boxes of produce crews had brought off their runs. Apples, green onions, lettuce, broccoli, cantaloupe, bright red chiles. It was hard to believe this place had seemed so intimidating a year before. Now it seemed like the Garden of Eden.

4
BRAKETTES INVADE TUCSON

OVER THE WINTER, the railroad women gather, have potlucks, tell stories. In the Bay Area, women from all the railroad crafts organize around safety, working conditions, and job discrimination. We imagine that there will be other women who follow us in these jobs, and we want to set up some structures to help them. This is, however, the moment of our greatest numbers. Roma, Maureen, Teresa, and I had gone to Houston. Gretchen had staked out Carlin, Nevada. Rose had been working San Luis Obispo. We share our stories and talk about next season—what we'll do, where we'll go. We share rumors of where the work is happening. These rumors are a tangible part of a boomer's life; they are like a seasonal flu or the smell of a certain food from a childhood table. You fell the blood pounding in your ears. In March, the low-seniority boomers are packing their cars. Roma, Maureen, and Rose leave for Tucson, and I pack up to follow them. We decide there is strength in numbers. I know now that I may not be home again soon, and so I give in to the life, find tenants for my cabin, and homes for my dogs. Trainmaster Mohan's prediction has come true. Railroading is in my blood, and it's spring along the desert highways.

Naomi had bought a house in San Francisco and was growing ever more remote. She would tell me I didn't really know her, and

I suppose it was true. I only knew how she was with me. My belief was that I allowed a part of her to live that didn't exist anywhere else. We had photography in common and from the beginning would photograph each other as if we could create a floating place where our love affair could live. A place that didn't exist in the world anywhere, but came to life in the developing tray, in the darkness in each of our private minds as we, separately, printed these pictures and sent them to each other. These were our secrets with half-lives as long as uranium ore.

In the redwoods' cathedral light my naked body is banded by the shadows. I am looking into her eyes; my arms rest against my thighs, hands in a curved hook of desire.

She lies facing me on the beach at Seaside. She wears a denim cowboy shirt that barely contains her breasts. The sand is dusting her thick brown hair. I know the way she should smell—salty, her body permeating her clothes. My image, photographing her, is reflected in her glasses, in the joy of her smile.

I take her to the Owens Valley to see the bristlecone pines, oldest living things, hunched in dolomitic soil on their high and ancient hills. Sentinels of the desert. She is leaving me again, going abroad to another desert country. The pictures show a woman twisted like the trees, a survivor, with a part asleep and a part that's green, alive and opening to me. Her photograph of me shows blond hair blending with the burl, smile creases like the wood grain, and a hawk's eyes.

I pack these photographs to take with me on the road, carrying my past with me in a bundle. Then I call a woman brakeman I know who is gay and has less seniority than me, a great choice for a braking partner. I knew she had been laid off all winter. We sit on Telegraph Avenue in Berkeley, sipping wine.

"Come booming—the streets are paved with gold. We can caravan down there, and Roma has a place for us to stay. What have you got to lose?"

Donna sat there thinking about it. She had two cats to lose, and a nice apartment in Marin, and probably a lover or two. But she was a rail. She wanted to be working.

We leave the following week, leapfrogging each other's cars through L.A. and into the desert siroccos blowing out of Mexico.

I'm still driving the Chevy and the hood latch is loose and getting a real workout in this wind tunnel. I keep expecting the windshield to suddenly go black. We stop for the night in Gila Bend, along with Death Valley, the hottest place in the United States. Donna stands looking down the tracks, two steel bands headed off to infinity to meet. Her mind is looking out of her window onto the wet and foggy headlands; she should be seeing San Francisco Bay.

"Where are the trees?"

"You're looking at them. Think of them as bonsai trees. That's the bad news. The good news is that from here on out, the drinks are free. This is cowboy country. Women only buy the first one."

The temperature hit 100 that week and never looked back. We found our outlaw band camped on the floor of Psycho Ward's place. Psycho and his roommates were California boomers who had moved to Tucson and settled in. The place was knee-deep in beer cans, the shades were drawn, and the blue light of the perpetual TV illuminated the cave. If the three laws of the desert were hibernation, nocturnal predation, and protective adaptation, they were being practiced here. It was daytime, and everyone was sleeping like bears. One of the guys had broken his leg and was in a hip cast. On the kitchen table were photographs of their latest picnic, one of them depicting a switchman named Rabbit fucking a cantaloupe.

The women decided that our time camping on this floor was definitely limited. Two days later we moved into our own place. It was a kind of railroad sorority house, or stewardess crash pad. With all of us working different shifts, the hairdryers were always buzzing and the phone always ringing. We threw a big housewarming bash to get acquainted with the locals and to outmaneuver the sour grapes contingent that was campaigning against all boomers. Printed signs saying "Boomer Go Home" and "Reinstate Home Rule" appeared on lockers, engines, and cabooses. Tires were slashed and boomers' wives got obscene phone calls when their husbands were out of town. Roma was the first one of us to arrive, and while she was having a beer in the local switchman's bar, a Tucson switchman threatened to break her legs. He picked on the wrong boomer.

"Break my legs? Who's going to break my legs?"

Every head in the bar turned, and Joe homeboy was now on the spot. Was he or wasn't he going to break this woman's legs? Roma was just getting warmed up.

"Now, why do you want to break my legs? You haven't even met me. When you hired out on the railroad, didn't they explain to you that you were going to get bumped? Haven't you ever bumped anybody? Or are you one of those people who can dish it out but can't take it? I bet you think women should stay home and have babies. You think that way, don't you? I think you're a Nazi, but I'm going to talk to you anyway and see if I can straighten you out."

We, of course, were in Tucson because Oregon boomers had bumped us out of Watsonville, but we didn't hold it against them. Californians are philosophical about foreign invaders; we are used to it. The Southwest wasn't. There had only been two invasions in the last three hundred years—the Spanish, and the North Americans. These groups were still busy duking it out and weren't prepared to accept any new contenders for their patch of sagebrush. In Arizona, outsiders were supposed to start their own town, like Ely or Miracle Valley where black people were supposed to live, or South Tucson where Hispanic people were supposed to live. Gay people weren't supposed to live anywhere. Texans had called us Californians "prunepickers" out of their disdain for deserters in the thirties; Arizonans called us "granola"—flakes, fruits, and nuts, out of a cultural paranoia. We were supposed to be sophisticated, loose, educated, in the fast lane. They were afraid we were going to be snobs, and make them feel small-town. And so our plan was to head the grumblers off at the pass.

We decided on a softball game, followed by a keg and lots of food. Space wasn't a problem since we didn't have any furniture— perfect for a dance floor. Curiosity guaranteed a large turnout. I got elected to pitch, an activity that was to have serious ramifications for the next two weeks of my life, but which seemed perfectly possible at the time. The game broke the ice. Here was the terror of the lower end job, Chainsaw Murphy, coaching me on my next pitch. Chainsaw was famous for flying into a rage and continuing the argument while switching, speeding up the job, recklessly kicking cars, like words, on top of his fieldman, who understood that he'd better be out of the way. A man impossible to avoid tangling with, and here he was, coaching like a dad at an afternoon softball game.

"OK, Gypsy, easy out, easy out, the batter's blind."

A Tucson afternoon just pours through you, changing the content of your cells every hour, as you drink gallons to just stay even with what's sweating out. But it feels good to the body to work like this, and the light-headedness feels good too, and you feel as though staying alive just means something all on its own. As shadows appeared, and the raw energy floating in the air turned into something shared and laughed about, we all drifted back to the hacienda for drinks and salsa and tacos and showers. Some people went home to change, others arrived for the wilder time of night. Soon there were clumps of men and women in circles on the patio, the sonority of party voices filled the rooms, and someone put on dancing music. Hands reached over heads for ice and mixers, and cameras appeared.

"Let's get you girls all together."

Walking through the rooms, there was rail talk and the kind of edge-of-challenge talk you found in switchmen's bars, but a friendlier dialogue was beginning. This was, in fact, our house, and the rules of hospitality made themselves felt. The threatening edge was gone. I had my guitar with me, a vintage fifties Gibson sunburst LS-125, a blues guitar with a beautiful shape. I set her up in the back bedroom, with an amp and a chair. I didn't really expect anyone to play, since it's taking a risk to open up and play music. You show something of yourself or you can't play. But sure enough, some of the rails drifted back there, and soon there was a roomful. This would have been rare in California, where the vicarious curse of high tech has made people shy about homemade music. I played a standard twelve-bar, and a Tucson switchman fished out a harmonica, and we were there, wherever there is. Musicland, I guess. Donna had quietly entered the room. There was a different feeling in here than in the rest of the party. We were all here together, breathing together, the very air felt heavier—shared. It had a certain color, like a blanket. Donna stood up, and you could feel that curtain move aside. There was a space for her to take a well-worn guitar case from under the bed and slowly unsnap its latches.

"All right, lady," one of the switchmen said. "Give us a song."

"She would have a Martin," I thought. I was expecting a bell-like folksinger's voice. Pretty, gentle.

She began to play, and suddenly there was no war anywhere in the world. Clouds were moving across a clear sky. You had the long view of things, the ones the birds have. Like seeing the coastal town where I lived from a small boat offshore, there was the river, its dark green cut in the hills, the white steeple of the church, the white foam canvas of a painter's shoreline. I wasn't alone anymore. No one that I knew had died. Everything was forgiven. I was crying. It felt like being in love.

There was a warm silence in the room after her song. She played a few more and then handed the music over to the homeboys to sing their country western songs, their blues. I stepped out on the patio, to catch up with my mind.

Donna came out through the sliding glass doors, holding a can of Tecate and a handful of quartered limes. She leaned back against the adobe fireplace and fluffed out her curly long red hair. The hot night wind dried the sweat off her neck and raised goosebumps on her bare brown arms.

"Hey, it's quiet out here. I can almost hear the surf break."

"That was beautiful, Donna. The music. You can reach inside people."

"It's the only thing that I can really do. I've had people tell me I should get an agent, record." She took a long drag on the Tecate. Her eyes looked into mine.

"Oh, God," I thought, "we're going to go underwater. We might be there a long, long time."

"This is a kind of set up," I said. "You and me being here inside an adventure."

"Oh really," she said. "I wonder what's going to happen."

Both knowing what was going to happen, we lay back in the arms of the evening and hoarded our private anticipations. What would begin now would be a long stringing out of desire, until one of us gave in and broke the tension, became the first one to touch. Women love long flirtations, want to be electrified by the act of choosing to desire. The scenario of being swept away is preceded by a long journey across the sea and the complication of a desert island. The moment is fortuitous. Actually, it is agreed upon. One of you simply cannot wait another minute. But women need to get to that acrophobic edge and suffer there for a while. Men don't seem to understand this about sex. They rush into it, and sex is over before the woman has even noticed that they are there. It's like the sun waking up a sleepy earth. It just doesn't turn the lights on. It sneaks up on the earth, lights a subtle fire somewhere else, makes the earth turn over in her sleep and face him. He throws a few drops of red into the inky waters of the sky, and lightens the palette with orchestral resonance. He also makes it colder. The earth realizes she wants to warm up. Unknowingly she starts to desire the sun. She creates the sun in her mind, and then there he is, her creation, child and lover, returning from the dream of her sleep. Who would resist such a lover?

The sun in Tucson rose with a brass band and accomplished its miracle in seconds. The town was a sundial surrounded by mountains. Working the freightyard, you became highly conscious of the movement of the light as different canyons and ranges received their intensities of color, light, and shadow. The temperatures on the ground were fierce—105 on the street, and 115 on the track. The black slag roadbed reflected the heat, and the iron sides of the reefers blew overheated air like monster breath as you walked the tracks. You couldn't drink enough to pee. It just sweated out as fast as you put it in.

The day after the party was a payback. My head hurt, my eyeballs hurt, my tongue felt like a dead rat, and I couldn't move my right leg without a sharp pain zapping me from my kneecap to my thigh. This was going to be fun later when I had to show up for the midnight yard job. This was hard lesson number two, right after "Don't show up for work loaded." If you work a physical job, you can't take chances with your body. Adventure sports and weekend athlete stuff are out. You could kill yourself.

The Tucson yard was built on a steep grade. It was used to make up trains for the mine jobs and for blocking pickups from the through freight on its way to Houston and L.A. It was a difficult, busy yard. Because of the grade, each cut at both the top and bottom ends of the yard had to be secured with fifteen hand brakes. That's a lot of handbrakes. Every time you wanted to move cars, you untied and tied brakes. Think of it as working on the top end of a huge ski jump. Any mistakes, and you had potentially lethal runaways that could kill switchmen working the bottom end of the ski jump. That's why you never kicked cars at the top end. Separating cars was done by testing a brake, tying the brake, stopping the engine to bunch the cars, and pulling the pin. The swing switchman then released the handbrake and rode the car down to a joint. Once the joint was made, the handbrake was retied until there were fifteen brakes on the cut. Then you could let cars roll on their own against that heel. When you pulled cars out of a track, you replaced all the brakes you knocked off. You made sure you never left cars in a track with insufficient brakes on them. Not with Tight Fit as your foreman, anyway.

Tight Fit got his name from letting a car get away once at the top end. By the time it hit the derail three miles later at the junction of the yard and the mainline, it had given the yardmaster and three yard crews grey hair and something to talk about for years at the switchmen's bar. Tight Fit was born. Like most everybody else in the yard, Tight Fit drank a lot. The switchman's bar, the Pub, was across the street from the top end shanty, and it was home-away-from-home for lots of rails. When Tight Fit couldn't get his boots tied before work, you knew that he had probably forgot to catch some sleep in the Pub parking lot. In that case his field man ran the job, and Tight Fit rode the engine when an official was around and dealt pinochle when they weren't.

Because my injury had been sustained while drunk and playing softball, it qualified me for sympathy. Rails took care of their injured in the line of duty.

"Now you sit right there and deal. That's your job tonight. You can let your partner here cover for you. There's a six-pack in the back of my pickup if you need to get straight."

The Tucson switchmen had invested their union dues in a hand-crafted walnut tabletop so that the top end pinochle games could proceed with class. They were as serious about pinochle as they were about handbrakes. If you didn't play, you worked. We all learned to play.

The night passed with Tight Fit and Donna disappearing between hands to couple up tracks and double over rails. I watched

Donna riding the brake on three heavy gravel hoppers we were letting drift down two rail.

"Get two brakes on that cut right now," Tight Fit yelled from the switch.

She cranked down one, and you could see the cars were picking up speed. She got the second brake tied and they slowed down some, but it took three brakes to get them rolling at a safe speed. They were just so heavy. I watched her work and I was glad she really put her heart in it. I think I was harder on the women rails than I was on the men. I wanted us to be the best, and I could tell by the way she worked that Donna felt that way too. She would never take the easy way out. Donna wanted to understand things first; then she wanted to be left alone to do it. Getting things explained was going to be her hard part since old heads rarely talk to you. Tight Fit was actually a good foreman to work for because he cared passionately about doing the work right. His own way of communicating this was to swear and yell and carry on, but beneath the form the content was good solid information.

About one o'clock a white Bronco pulled up outside the top end shanty, and the yardmaster and another man got out. Pretty soon Tight Fit came up the lead and went inside. Ten minutes later he came out with a paper in his hand and headed for his pickup. Inside, the other top end crew and the yardmaster were filling each other in.

"Godamn that's cold. Wife serves a man divorce papers on the job."

"Well, maybe she couldn't find his truck behind the Pub. You know he don't go home much. Just sleeps in the parking lot in his truck, wakes up, and goes to work. Sometimes she doesn't see him for days."

"Still, it's cold to serve a man at work."

Tight Fit spent some time in his truck, then sat down in the dirt on the lead. Being left alone again while the crew made a move, I hobbled on over and sat down next to him.

"Well, that's twenty years down the shitter."

We both sat inspecting the rail closely.

"Well, I guess I'll survive, move a trailer out to my dad's place."

I could picture the trailer and the piece of desert it rested on.

This was an old story around the railroad; men buying fancy vacation RVs and Broncos to drive to work and then moving into them when things went wrong one more time at home. I knew about things going wrong at home. My current solution was not to have a home. I could see Tight Fit was headed that way too.

By the time 6 A.M. rolled around I could tell we were in for a heavy morning at the Pub. They opened up whenever the switchmen got off the graveyard shift, and by eight everyone was pretty well lit. One double-edged consequence of our getting accepted in Tucson was getting through all the free drinks at the Pub. I would sit down at the bar and soon there would be eight shot glasses turned upside down in front of me. This meant eight people had bought me a drink. How nice. The only problem was I didn't drink beer, I drank tequila. I looked over to where Donna sat surrounded by switchmen and noticed she also had those shot glasses in front of her. And she wasn't drinking just beer either; she was drinking shots of Stoly vodka with beer chasers. I remember liking this. Soon Maureen and Roma came in off an all-night road trip and the drunken sun rose on another day. I moved over to Donna's table to listen to Diamond Jim trying to scare her about snakes.

"I'll tell you about the snakes out here, lady. One night on the Hayden job I come off a boxcar and stepped right on a rattler. I had the fucker wrapped around my leg, man."

"Shit, what'd you do?"

"After I pissed my pants, I start banging my leg against the side of the car. Really kicked hell out of my leg, man. I was hollering and kicking till he dropped off. I retired those boots. They have fang marks in 'em. I keep 'em on the mantle. So look before you go stepping off them engines. I kid you not."

"Maybe I'll stay switching," Donna said. "I wouldn't mind if something like that never happened to me."

Everybody tried to think of a scarier snake story, but none came to mind. Diamond Jim had clearly won that round. There was a pause in the round of stories, and Maureen got off her bar stool and in slow motion went over backwards. When Donna and I got to her we could see that her eyes were crossed. It was time to go home.

"I'm fine. I can drive, no problem."

"No driving, OK? We can get your car later."

We put Maureen on the seat between us, and in the blast furnace heat of ten o'clock started down the street toward the Brakette hacienda. We put Maureen to bed, and I noticed that we weren't doing too well either. Donna was stumbling holding her up and I was having trouble negotiating the doorways. There seemed to be a lot of them in the house.

"You can stay in my room if you want. But you know that, don't you?"

"I'm fucked up, Donna. I'm fucked up."

"No, just hold me. Just stay with me, that's all."

We lay down together on the mat on the floor and held each other into sleep. Her hair was like a cloud filling my nose and breath and I fell down the long blackout tunnel into dreamland. Outside the sun was moving its white intensity across its playground, earth, but we were safely tucked away in a sleep beyond sleep. This was the only safety I knew, and I had found a partner who knew it, too.

Tucson, the sundial, was an interesting town. It was split between the white conservatives and the Hispanics, and the borderlines were rough. There were street gangs, violence, theft, traffic jams, and overdevelopment, but also a strong music and art scene. Local bands had loyal followings; there were gay bars, jazz clubs, discos, and acoustic music. Every other kid on the street had a guitar. In July the flash floods turned certain streets into rivers and traffic became impossible. Hikers were swept away by flash floods in the narrow canyons, and houses newly built on the floodplain disappeared. Winter realtors will sell more of them next year to still more snowbirds. Here were the very young and the very old. Tucson rested on a plain, sucking the water from beneath itself and air conditioning too many paper-walled apartments. Its time for crisis was approaching, but it still held the memory of a railhead cow town. We live at the core of that old identity of the freightyard— the single most defining place, the hub, the starting point of its shape.

When you work braking out of a terminal, you catch runs that go in a 250-mile radius. From Tucson you went to Yuma, Phoenix, Nogales, Douglas, the mines, or Lordsburg. On the long runs, you spent the night at the railroad modules or some seedy railroad hotel. Crews waited in rotating order for trains coming the opposite direction. You could get stuck in these holes-in-the-wall for days. In July the women brakemen found themselves able to hold the road, and we started working these braking jobs. The antiboomer agitation was stronger on the road because that's where the money was. I was glad there were so many of us, because one woman alone will always get picked on by a group of men, whereas two women won't. The lone woman switchman in Tucson before our arrival was called "No Balls Smith," for example. One striking irony of the antiboomer campaign was the accident suffered by the homeboy who threatened to break Roma's legs. He broke his legs falling off a water tower in Lordsburg while trying to nail up a "Boomer Go Home" sign.

In late July I caught a run on the Stormy, which was the run from Tucson to Lordsburg, so-called because in summer the thunder and lightning storms put on free lightshows against the amphitheater of red and black rock. At times it was hard to tell if the head end of your train was in a dust storm or if it was on the ground. They looked about the same from the caboose—huge clouds of dust boiling up the length of the train. I knew Donna was already in Lordsburg, but I didn't know if I would get to see her there. It all depended on the westbounds. We were headed down the grade near Benson when the dispatcher put us in the hole for a hotshot. It was still intermediate light, the fragrant hour before Mr. Sun made it up over the canyon walls. The greasewood was coated with moisture and the earth smelled like five different things, like a Chinese name for some ordinary noodle.

I was riding the headend, and as we stopped in the clear on the siding, a snake dislodged itself from a bush and draped itself across the track in front of us. The rail is four feet eight-and-a-half inches wide, and that snake was draped. And fat. He had come from the place where I would have to stand to roll the westbound by. I thought, "OK, fine. It's gone now. Chances are slim there would be two snakes in the same place. Just hop right on over there. No problem." I climbed off the engine and crossed over the mainline into the desert. I would wait now for the pulse of the westbound's headlight on some part of the landscape, or smoke drifting and disappearing. You often saw the approach of a train in parts. Unless you knew the territory perfectly, it was hard to know how far away it was. Its appearance was always a surprise. Out of the complete silence, waiting alone in the desert listening for a sound, suddenly the monster was there. Ten blackened units belching noise, rocking the track, creating a hurricane. It got your heartbeat up.

Waiting now, I hunkered down and looked around me. A large orange fly buzzed by—black, actually, with shiny orange wings. I watch it land behind a mesquite bush. Minutes later it reappeared dragging a tarantula. It painfully hauled the tarantula at least ten feet and then let the spider go. The orange fly then did a little drunken dance and flew away. The spider twitched sluggishly. "Far out," I thought. "Life and death in the desert. I'm not sleeping on the ground out here—no way." Then a large ant covered with yellow fur appeared out of nowhere and attacked the spider. It was followed by a horde of regular size ants, which started to drag the spider off. The spider was waking up, however, and started shaking off the ants. "My God," I thought, "Who's going to win?" Just then I heard the noise and felt the wind tunnel of the westbound at my back. I turned to see the Memphis Blue train highball past, containers rocking and rolling as the cars hit the joints on the rail. Sure enough, Donna was on the porch of the caboose highballing me back and hanging on for dear life. I knew what she couldn't say. Suddenly my trip was going to be two days longer, home receding with the red light in the pinkening horizon.

We had moved in together into a snowbird condo at the base of the Santa Catalinas. It was an air-conditioned cave with a view of ocotillo and desert trails lined with white rocks. We had a barbecue, a coffee mill, and a bottle of Russian vodka in the freezer at all times. Our life was a unique mixture of independence and companionship. We never got too much of each other; the unpredictability of trains created intense physical longing. But since braking was a life we shared, the one left behind never felt martyred by the job. Your turn to leave a soft warm bed and the arms of your lover would come. You did it and respected the demands of the life and each other's responsibility to it. To get away, we fled to the mountains and to gay bars. The women didn't hang out in bars much, but some wealthy lesbian had donated a house for a private club, and beyond the ordinary gravel driveway and wrought iron gate, women were shooting pool and swimming naked in the backyard. Inches away from the redneck main drag. Donna and I spent a lot of time there, particularly when one of us was on a run. It was good to have an alternative to the pub. It was a gentler place than the men's discos, which were cruisy and somewhat antifemale.

One night after a particularly hard week, Donna and I went out to a men's bar to get drunk and decompress. We had just come off the Phoenix run and had to literally carry the conductor the whole time since he was comatose from the moment he showed up for work. We had never been in the Phoenix yard before, and our passed-out conductor neglected to warn us to work in pairs and watch out for muggers. I was walking the tracks for a double-over and the police were running past me chasing suspects. On the way home we proceeded by guesswork on where setouts went and took a lot of flack for it on the radio.

"Ya'll going to tie up the mainline all day switching? That California style or something? Are you girls having problems again?"

After two days of this bullshit, we felt like kicking ass or at least like getting looped and talking about kicking ass. Hence our demeanor at the disco. We were not ladylike, admittedly, but the ice cube that came sailing in our direction and missed Donna's face by inches seemed distinctly out of line. It had come from the bartender who was also more plastered than he should have been and ruder than he should have been. With my short Irish trigger, I was out of my seat and in his face in minutes.

"Did you throw that goddamn piece of ice? That's not cool, man, that's not cool at all. I didn't fucking appreciate that, man."

"Oh, it's no problem. I didn't see you sitting there."

"You almost hit my girlfriend, asshole."

"You're the asshole. You're not wanted here. Why don't you dykes go find your own place?"

"Why don't you try to make me, dickhead. Penis breath. Fartface." I was getting warmed up.

Suddenly the guy went flying across the patio and ended up in a heap. Donna had been getting really uncomfortable with him so close to my face and decided to get him out of striking distance.

Donna was not a big person. Both the bartender and I were taken aback. We blustered some more and exchanged opinions about who ought to leave, but Donna and I soon headed for the door, fur up, but leaving gracefully.

In the car it started to sink in. I had been in a bar fight. Me. From Pasadena. And in a gay bar. Like, there wasn't any protection for us here. And I had started it, not even thinking about what might happen to Donna, that she might get involved. I was so used to being on a solo trip, to making decisions for yourself alone that I never considered that I was making a decision for her too. Because it never occurred to me that she would back me up like that. No one ever had.

"Donna, I'm sorry I did that. I don't even know why I did that."

"Well, we are a little drunk. I guess these things happen. I thought he threw the ice at me, too."

"Yeah, but there's something I don't understand about it. It's like I was watching myself act, and it all was inevitable and scary."

"We've been working time-and-a-half too much. Let's lay off and head for the mountains."

We followed the Salt River and wound up higher and higher into Apache country in the White Mountains. In midsummer a cool fog clung to the skunk cabbage and it rained the cold rain of the Northwest. The Indians prohibited swimming on their reservation. It wasn't something they thought people did. For some reason, this bothered me. I started wondering about loopholes. If you fell out of your boat, could you then swim? Would splashing in a stream be considered swimming? It was really too cold to swim, anyway. It was too cold to do much except lie in our sleeping bags and drink brandy. Maybe the cold was inside as well, as I had something hard to bring up with Donna. My California lover was going to come visit me.

I don't really know why I said yes to this. It seems stupid now. And I knew at the time that it was stupid, but it also seemed inevitable. Naomi and I had a long history. We were never able to make a commitment and never able to let it go. Why I held onto it was complex. I felt that I needed her, that she was an anchor for me in my drifting life. She presented an image of strength and, most importantly, of someone who had alcohol under control. We were drinking partners, but Naomi never allowed others to have an image of her as a drinker. She cloaked it with all the disguises. And as my drinking got more and more uncontrolled, I needed someone who could drive. Drive in life. Next to my stash, I needed my old lady.

You might ask why couldn't Donna be that for me? Why couldn't I choose her? In the first place, I couldn't choose anything. I had lost that ability along the way. Things happened to me. I couldn't choose not to drink. I couldn't choose not to repeat human mistakes over and over again either. I was living in an endless cycle of hope and disappointment. In every area of my life. Hope that things would change, disappointment that they didn't; hope that a drink would fix things, disappointment at another hangover; hope that things would change. There was simply no integrity in my life or I was chasing it like a runaway boxcar, projecting it as something out there I had to get a brake on.

I was also frightened by the freedom that Donna and I had together. She was too much like me, and our shared life felt like a boat drifting toward a dangerous rapid. Anything could happen here; she was someone who would say yes. Who would be the brakeman to this runaway train? I wanted her, but I wanted brackets around her. I wanted to be safe also.

We were both caught up in a romance of the desert. We felt the absence of ordinary boundaries, the conviction that there was room for anything to happen. This was at the beginning of things, at the creation of another fragile hope. The trust growing between Donna and me was such a spring flower—beautiful, delicate, and about to be changed.

We drove home in the silence of anger. Donna never said "Don't bring her." She had taken this escalator before. She knew the rules. Don't get mad, get even. Have a drink down at the pub, or the gay bar. Perhaps true love will be listening this time. Was I aware of this? Yes and no. In the same way that I hadn't considered my actions in the bar, I now didn't consider the effect my actions had on her now. I was incapable of acting any differently no matter how guilty I felt.

When Naomi arrived we got out of town, heading south for

Tombstone and the Mexican borderlands. I had enough cocaine for one good drunk, and we fell in with some miners celebrating a silver strike. We sat with our backs to the wall in a stagy saloon and played out our pretend world of partnership. It was a pretend marriage, really, eight years of lost weekends and Monday face-the-world-alone returns. About midnight it seemed wise to go the powder room, do a line for the road, and exit out the back way while the getting was good. The road to Bisbee rushed interminably before my headlights as toads slicked the blacktop with their crushed bodies, sacrifices to the Monsoon season and the intermittent rains. We spent the night in the Copper Queen Hotel listening to the black lung hacking of half the town echo through the deserted streets. With the coke and the tequila, I slept in pieces until a dream tackled me with all the subtlety of a charge of landrovers. I was a child again and watching my older sister and her best friend play dolls. I was their audience and couldn't interfere with the play. Two women were talking about a third who was an alcoholic. I realized they were talking about Donna. That's right, I thought, Donna is an alcoholic. Then in slow motion, one of the women turned and faced me. I watched as her face became my own and I heard my voice say, "You are the alcoholic." I woke up shaking after that one. "File that," I thought. "File it deep." And I did. I filed it deep.

The day after Naomi flew back on the big bird to her world without me, I found myself in the condo alone. Donna wasn't around. I called the crew dispatcher who told me she had been laid off for three days. This put me into a panic. I had to have my world back the way it was, had to get Donna placated. I was on to the next problem in life. This was the way things went for me—from problem to problem, each requiring maximum energy and verbal magic to straighten out. A little daily miracle had to be performed. I figured she would be at the club. That's what I would have done. I did some asking around and found out that Donna had smoked off with a woman named Rosa, and that her friends were wondering which woman would win—Rosa, or Donna's other lover. Triangles beget octagons. I decided that a trip to Frederick's of Hollywood was in order. When Donna finally returned to *nuestra casa*, she was facing a woman who was armed.

"Oh hi, Gypsy," Donna said, sliding her long legs out of her Fairlane. "How long have you been home?"

"A couple of days. Fifty-one hours and thirty minutes to be exact. You might have left me a note."

"I didn't think you'd be here, and I didn't get a chance to stop by the house."

"Look, Donna, do you really think it's a good idea to go running around with Rosa while we're living together—I mean in the same town and all? I mean, think about it. I know why you did it, and I can't blame you or anything, but . . . "

Donna was just staring at me. "How did you know about Rosa?" She clearly had another moment in mind to spring the news. This *blitzkrieg* had her off balance.

"I'm close to you, that's why. I'm going to know what you're doing. I can't help it."

"Well, I don't know what to do. Two months ago I wasn't in love with anybody, and now here I am, in love with two people." She gathered up her bags, and headed in through the front door.

I waited until she had taken a shower and then came into the bathroom behind her, wearing a soft robe. I put my arms around her waist and held her. I could feel her tense up and then give in to the rush of emotions.

"I'm sorry, Donna. I don't want to hurt you. I was missing you the whole time. I didn't know that I would be, but I was."

I took her hands and put them under the robe. I was wearing a titless push-up bra with red lace borders, a red garter belt, and black net stockings.

"I know you're not bored with me yet. Are you?"

Donna's mouth fell open, and she couldn't help the smile.

"You bitch, don't you have any scruples? Fuck you," she said, digging her nails into my ass as we headed for the bathroom carpet. "Fuck you."

In the morning we marked up, and resumed our life as braking partners and lovers. But the Ming vase had been dropped, and no amount of glue was going to reassemble it. We started to spend more time in the pub and less time in bed, and it was harder for both of us to get vulnerable. The sex became more like sex and less like love. It became a way to solve our problems, another drug in my long list of drugs. And drinking, which had carried us into the forbidden playground, now became the liberator of all the hidden resentments and fears. Part of it was the intensity of the jackhammer summer, added to the intensity of our life. It was August, and it seemed as though the heat would never end, would continue to rise and blacken the planet into some star for other worlds. I began to think of fall and winter, to imagine it here. I was starting to count the days. It didn't help that I was still drinking tequila shooters in the Pub everyday. I just couldn't pour back enough Gatorade the next day to keep my brain cells alive. I was starting to overlook things at work. Like lining back switches and other habitual moves. Even Tight Fit was starting to get protective.

"Well, herder, I just lined back the storage switch for you. Or did you figure that hotshot coming up two track was going to fit in there on top of them engines?"

One day the Spook, an old head switchman who knew his stuff, came up behind me in the Tucson yard. I was making the air behind the engine, and there he was, raising the hair on my neck like a rolling boxcar ready to couple me up. I jumped ten feet.

"Hey kid, who's chasing you?"

The Spook had an eerie quality of speaking the truth. That's why they called him the Spook.

"Slow down, or one of these days you'll kill someone. And from then on till they run you off or you retire, you will be just a number out here."

I thought about what that would be like. Not just a name like Tight Fit's, but a nonexistence in this world, a facelessness. The Spook was somebody you listened to. Somebody you wanted to learn from.

"Don't you know how to do a double runaround, kid?"

Who was chasing me? Why was I on the road, really? Was it something in my life I was running from, and the easy money booming just the excuse? To be sure, it wasn't the stories I told myself—it wasn't "railroading in the blood." It was fear everywhere. I was chasing me. And that "I" was becoming more and more a picture of Dorian Gray, and I heard the Spook through a carpet of denial, like my unremembered dream of the alcoholic, my flirtation with death the train, with oblivion—the silent rail-packs you can't hear or see in the dark—the yards of Strang. Yes, the Spook knew me.

Late in August Donna and I caught the Hayden mine job, and we rode the headend as the engine climbed the narrowing canyon walls on the Gila River. It was slow track and the late afternoon would turn into night before we reached the mine set deep up in the hills. It must have been Indian land, for the horses and livestock ran free, often ending up dead on the tracks, the decaying odor lingering for weeks. The air in the canyon was humid from the river, which was buried in dense shrubbery—alder, cottonwood, and mesquite. Herds of javilina darted through the waving bush. At night the rattlesnakes curl up beside the rail to warm themselves on the radiating slag, and we now watched them in the engine lights jerking away from the roadbed. There was one spot—the Woolly Wash, that had to be flagged on account of flash floods. I got down carefully from the headend and set out across the sand, checking the rail and checking for snakes. A childhood memory came back to me of a scary saying my sister used to taunt me with—"I'm the woolaby Woost, and you're the one I'm after. I think I'll run. I think I'll run. I think I'll skin you just for fun." The Woolly Wash Wust. "Crickets," I thought. "They're only crickets." The darkness was singing.

We got there at midnight, and Donna and I checked into our separate rooms in the miner's dorm hall. These were clearly walls with ears. The regular Hayden railroad crew was also sleeping here. Their job worked seven days a week moving cars around in the smelter. The crew ate and slept free. Since there wasn't anything to spend money on, crews could save most of their paychecks. In the morning the Hayden cook set out enough food to feed a line-backer. Steak, potatoes, beans, coffee, fried eggs, homemade bread, fresh salsa. Donna and I and our conductor sat around an enormous table and ate and ate and ate. The miners and the other brakemen were up at the mines. Our job would go to work in the afternoon when the ore cars we brought them were loaded. In the meantime, the joys of Hayden were ours.

Stepping outside was a mistake. We found ourselves in an amphitheater with way too many lights on, the noontime sun ricocheting off the exposed rock, the rotten smell of sulphur billowing out of the two gigantic smokestacks that defined the mineworks. We walked from the dorms to the dirt road that led into the company cluster called the town of Hayden. It seemed too far to struggle in that acidic air. Today was better spent in a cave until the sun got behind the tall walls of the box canyon. Colors could not exist in this light. Nor thought. We both went to Donna's room, left the lights off, and lay on the floor. We started kissing, but in a distracted way. We both had things we wanted and didn't want to talk about. I had just heard from a friend of mine, Luther the Millionaire, who was building a personal Winchester Mystery house of his own in Santa Cruz. He wanted to know if I wanted him to build a loft for me over his garage. Would I like skylights? It seemed like an offer I couldn't refuse, and it also answered the question we both had about what we would do when the boom was over in Tucson. I could avoid the problem of Naomi and Donna being in the Bay Area together by moving in with Luther. A neutral third place. Besides, Luther needed someone to help him snort his coke. He had way too much of it.

"Well, I guess it would be fun having someone to visit in Santa Cruz. I haven't been down there in a while. I'm glad you're not moving in with Naomi. But I don't know what it's going to be like when we get back. I don't know if I can handle it. I guess I'll see."

"You'll like Luther's. It's this mansion at the beach, with the hairless chihuahuas and a swimming pool. It's two blocks from the gay bar. We won't even have to drive."

"Hairless chihuahuas?"

"They're these little dogs Luther got because his wife was allergic to normal dogs, but two weeks after he got them she moved out, and there he was with these two weird puppies that are all teeth. They look like piranhas with legs."

"Are you sure you can live with Luther? I mean, it doesn't sound very relaxing. Didn't you tell me some story about friends of his that came over for dinner and ended up making a fuck movie in his bedroom and then showing it at dinner? Wasn't that the Luther you mentioned?"

"Yeah, well that's Santa Cruz. Nobody works and everybody does things like that, or at least everybody accepts you if you do things like that. It doesn't fit these surroundings does it? I mean, it seems like we're on some other planet. When Luther told me about it, I was in the rec room in Lordsburg with all these brain-dead brakemen smoking cigars and spitting on the floor. I thought, 'How can I be on the phone with someone who is telling me this?'"

Donna just rolled over on top of me and lay there, feet on top of my feet and her head resting cheek-to-cheek against mine. We were exactly the same size; it was as if a cookie cutter had made two of us, quietly breathing together, weightless, and drifting.

"We're here now," Donna said, as she knotted my hair in her fingers. "You and I are here today in this room up at the end of this canyon. I don't care about what's going to happen tomorrow. I don't want to think about it. It will just happen."

Then she put her tongue in my mouth, and my body tightened around her. The clean arrows of desire feathered through the white afternoon, and I could feel her heartbeat, blood to blood, in rhythm with my own. My skin wanted to feel the coolness of her skin, my breasts wanted to press against hers, our legs entwining like jungle vines in a sudden phototropic surge for the sun. Her fingertips brushed my nipples as if casually. And again. I pulled her under me, clothes coming off, soft short kisses, trying not to make noise, trying not to roll into things. Donna's voice just drove me wild. The gentle deepness. Her singer's voice. But intimate now. Speaking to me alone, calling my name like it was the first human sound heard in the new green world. I wanted her to say it now.

"Gypsy, Gypsy, fuck me."

I wanted the saltiness on my lips, the acrid entry of scent to the back of my brain, painting me with her as if we had bathed in the same Colorado River, like twins. Her hands on my shoulders carried with them all the female touches of childhood, older sister's tickles on baby skin, mother lifting me weightless in the water, my face between my grandmother's breasts, fragrant with sachet.

How to have her close to me? How to have her close enough? I wanted to press into her, entering the looking glass, two identical forms becoming one.

And she put her fingers into me, and I wanted all of them.

"More, do you want more?"

"Yes," and I did want more, and her hair was in my mouth, her long red hair webbing us, and it was hard not to scream, biting her so I wouldn't cry out, so we would be safe here, together, in the dark room. Listening in the flooding darkness, peppered now with pinpoints of light, I felt her heartbeat in my mouth, and waited for her orgasm to comet across our intermingled mind, unrolling a grey fog blanket of sleep behind it.

About four in the afternoon, we could begin to smell the river again, and the mine job had our cars switched out and our train made up to head down the canyon. The conductor decided to ride the headend with Donna, leaving me in the caboose. It had become beautiful late in the day. We had a mile-long train, heavy with tankers of acid, ore cars, and gondolas with great slabs of solid copper shining like pennies. As the train entered the first of four tunnels, a cool, wet smell filled the caboose. Emerging into the light, I noticed the buds on Teddy Bear Cholla, small shocking pink flowers waxy yellow inside. Strewn against the map like free money. An insistent hot breeze followed us west, carried sulphur, river, and mesquite blended into a fragrance that was acrid and rich. I opened the door to the caboose and lay on the conductor's bunk, letting the canyon in. I took the memory holograph of Donna and me in the room, lying together, and brought it into the caboose with me. Everything was in everything, in the smallest thing, the color of a rock, the waxy center of a cactus. Suddenly, the air blew for emergency brakes and we were stopped. The echo continued for a few seconds, and then there was silence.

I knew I had to walk the length of the train, to come back to reality, to watch out for snakes. I felt an unusual panic. I hadn't been expecting this. Then I remembered the drag detectors. I hadn't been watching for them, hadn't bothered to look them up in the timetable. Had we set one off? I would have seen the flashing light, seen something other than my mind and the canyon. Behind the caboose, I could see marks on the ties, like a giant's fork tracks. I can hear Tight Fit in my mind.

"If you were a good brakeman, you would be watching behind your train, instead of making up poems to javalinas."

It was starting to get dark, and I would need to be able to see the snakes. Was my lantern going to be good enough? I took some fusees with me and lit one as I started down the tracks. Great for light, but this wasn't Watsonville fog country. The hot wind turned the fusee into a sparkler, and it occurred to me just what might happen if one of those sparks caught in the dry brush. Panic again, and I ground the fusee out in the roadbed. "Hold on here," I thought. "What's going on? Go sit down for a minute."

Back in the caboose I waited until the conductor called me on the radio.

"Well, we got a busted train line somewhere. Looks like you'll have to walk the train. The headman's walking back."

As I started out again, I could smell something burning in the dry air and found the fusee had set a tie afire. Back to the caboose to fill a wastebasket with water. Back to the fusee. What was going on here? After the fire was dead out, I headed downtrack fast. Make lots of noise; scare the fucking snakes. The canyon was no longer friendly; it had turned mean.

I met Donna at the derailment about thirty cars from the head-end. One of our acid tank cars was nose down in a ditch, its trucks at a weird angle to the track, ties uprooted like matchsticks. It was like seeing bones sticking through skin. The scale was confusing. How had such large pieces ever rolled together as a car? How had they ever been a whole thing? Donna must have been upset, too, because it took two guys to knock off the brake she tied on the car we still had on the track.

"God, Gypsy. I didn't know they looked like this. What if one of these things fell on you? What if you had been riding this car?"

"I hope to shit we didn't set off a dragger. I was just spacing out."

"The conductor was wondering that too. But you would have seen it. You can't miss those."

We both just sat there on one of the upended ties. It was dark now, and the night sounds were closing in. There was nothing to do but wait for the hook. They were going to have a hell of a time getting to this spot. Good thing there wasn't a forest fire on top of it all.

"Well, it could have been worse."

"How?"

"Trust me—it could have been."

When a working season dies, it happens all of a sudden. One day you can't get your rest or do your laundry, and the next day you can't even work the yard extra board midnights. It was not the end of summer, with still no break in the weather, and Donna and I were perched in our high-rent cave considering our choices. We could head home and try to pick up work in the L.A. yard or scramble for a spot here in the outside locals which suddenly were desirable jobs. The bump within our reach was to Douglas on the Mexican border, a Phelps Dodge smelter town. The railroad would pay our rent, so we decided to pack up and move into the railroad hotel. Douglas would be our last stand.

The Gasden Hotel had seen better days, as had the cattle-queen dowagers who waited in the lobby for some unknown return. It was built on a grand scale, with open balconies providing a view of the lobby floor, the scene of the Wednesday- and Saturday-night dances. The Gasden's pillars were lofty even now, and the walnut counters at the front desk were polished by a hundred years of cattle kings, mining barons, and gambling gents checking in. There was room in the hotel to move—for waltzes, western swing and polkas, boots and western dresses twirling on the onyx floor. A grand entrance was possible down the center staircase, the grand view of the ball-room and a clear shot to anywhere in the room. Donna and I checked into a suite with corner light and an ornate iron bed. A single-blade fan was the Gasden's only admission that their hotel was not on the coast of France or somewhere other than the Sonoran desert on the Mexican border. The Douglas switcher went to work in the morning and picked up and delivered cars to the border and the smelter. It also rearranged the Douglas yard according to the whims of the crotchety agent, Walter, who had been there since the wilder days, or dressed as though he had. Walter wore a bow tie, with a stiff collar and vest, a porkpie Buster Keaton hat, and was oldman lean. He liked things clean—his small station at the end of everybody's line got only extra crews—hooligans from Tucson who came in red-eyed and rumpled every morning and messed up his yard. Walter knew what he wanted where. He handed you the list and then walked the yard tracks, clipboard in hand, checking it again.

"Oh no, sonny, that car don't go there, don't go there at'all. The

Tucson drag is gonna use that rail. Those border cars are kept on number five. You got the time now to switch the slag pit. Plenty of time before beans."

The crews made fun of him, but Walter was ubiquitous. He had nothing else to do but order his disappearing world, struggle with the new and careless, scoff. He appraised us with his old man's eyes, the first women brakies in his station; they said "We'll see." But he told us about the Saturday-night dance, and liked us better than the young men brakemen, those barbarians from the north.

Working Douglas was an exercise in grime. The refinery filled the air with black ore dust that got up your nose, into your ears, and even filtered through the pores of your boots so that white socks were black at the end of a shift. I tried to wear goggles and a cowboy bandanna, but it was 105 degrees and the goggles fogged up and the bandanna choked me. There were a lot of blackface jokes. One of our spots on the job was a spur called the highline. The engine climbed a ramp fifty feet high where the cars were loaded with fine black ore dust. All around were huge cooling pools and chimneys firing off loads of sulphur high into the air. At night, pulling toward Douglas, you could watch the little carts move to the crest of the slag pit and tip their molten contents in a fiery trail down the darkness, and the intense heat would travel to you across the quiet desert night.

In a corner of the Gasden Hotel was the saloon, the Last Gasp. It was our watering hole after work, and it was still home to the brakemen Donna and I had bumped when we came down here. Douglas was their last stand too, and they just remained in the bar drinking. Their winter had begun. Ours was to begin shortly. The atmosphere was not unfriendly; they just moved over two seats at the bar. A week later, we moved over for our replacements, and we also kept on drinking. Half of Tucson was going to wind up in this bar, waiting, like the cattle queens, for the Saturday-night dance.

It was a memorable occasion. By mutual agreement, Wednesday night was Mexican music and Saturday night was country and western. Everyone came from both sides of the border and from all the towns within drunk driving distance. There was quite a little group of boomers and Tucson brakemen here, ready to let down and get down. I wore an Indian squaredance dress, of gauze cotton, with a full skirt with ruffles, and tall red cowboy boots. Soon the lobby was awash with two-steppers sailing like yachts in a regatta. I loved the western fast polka, turning in tight circles, brushing other dancers with the slightest touch, leather boot soles skimming the polished floor. Cowboys followed the fragile rules of macho conduct while spinning the woman almost out of control on the periphery of the dancer's twirl, the men keeping tight asses, tight circles, and their hats on. Donna and I had fun, found ourselves the last to leave, the boomer table littered with cerveza, soulful conversation struggling to be heard over the last waltz. Stumbling to the elevator we carry the party and Rose, who happened to be down here on the Douglas local, to her room. The guitar appears, and my flute, and over Rose's comatose body we sing drunken melodies in the cavernous hallways of the Gasden's second floor, carry on until even this desert sirocco finds its last note and becomes a thin whisper in a sidewinder's dream.

I knew it was morning by the humped shape crawling from the bathroom and the sound of the flush. It hurt to move and wisdom said lie still for days, don't open the eyes, do not converse. There was a green light in the room, and it seemed to be rocking in slow motion, like a large sick ship.

"Gypsy, the phone. It's your mom. Something's wrong."

Donna's voice seemed to come from far away. I got the phone to my face and heard my mother's quiet voice speaking in an undertone, sounding strangely rehearsed.

"Oh, Gypsy. I have been robbed. I've had a burglar here. It's a young man."

"What? Did you call the police? When did this happen? Are you all right?"

"Don't speak so loudly, dear. He's here now. In the front room."

"What? Go out the back door right now and call me from the neighbor's. How did you get this number, anyway? You must have been calling everywhere. You have got to leave right now."

"Yes, I've got to leave right now. But he was here before, and then he came again today. I talked to him for a long time. And I'm sure he's in the front room. He comes quite often. It's gotten to be annoying. Very annoying. This taking things. I want you to come home, Gypsy."

My thought waves suddenly took a parabolic shape. Something was not adding up to four here. But one thing was clear. I couldn't tell anything from here. I needed to get to Pasadena.

"Mom, I'm coming home. It will be a few days. I'm going to call Mrs. Jorgensen and tell her to come over and stay with you."

"Well, I don't think that would be necessary, dear. I just want you to come home. I think we both could talk to him."

It took me a whirlwind few days to pack my boomer's life into my Chevy and point it west. There was no problem about a transfer; Tucson wanted the boomers gone now. Donna was going to join me in L.A. sometime later on, and we embraced in the back parking lot of the Gasden Hotel. We held each other and wished away all the things done wrong. Then we gathered our wills into the hard knot needed to go on and be alone. As I headed my Chevy west, I thought of the ocean, a calm thought in a burning land.

5
PASADENA GOTHIC

I HAD THOUGHT, when my mother began telling my old friends that I was picking crops in South America, that it was her genteel way of expressing her disapproval. As I walked in the door, following the narrow path between the rows of stacked newspapers and *Time* magazines, it became clear that it was something more. She did think I was picking crops, and nobody had thrown anything away in this house for over two years. No wonder things were missing. I found her in her darkened bedroom, searching for her keys.

"Gypsy, I'm so glad you're here. He's been here again and taken my keys."

She spoke with a helpless fury. I could see why. Every surface in the room was two feet deep in paper. Bills from 1946 were lying on top of current bills which were next to old newspaper clippings which were next to recent magazines.

"What's all this stuff doing here, Mom? What are all these old clippings doing out?"

"What clippings? You know, I need to find my glasses. He's taken them too. It's maddening."

Gradually the story began to unfold. She had no short-term memory and had begun to make up stories to account for the problem. Her wish was for me to join her in trapping these thieves who had stolen her familiar life away. I would move back home, and everything would be restored. But she wasn't about to surrender any control. I would assist in carrying out her plan. I remembered a trip we had taken, a grand tour of Europe, a visit to Mad Ludwig's Bavarian castle. I was in his bedroom now, an infinite regress of mirrors. Find the checkbook, the keys, hidden and forgotten; discovered to be hidden, confirming the presence of a thief who hides things; the new checkbook, the new keys. Which are which? The hidden glasses. Drawers full of keys, shoes full. Thirty-five years of receipts shuffled like a pack of cards, objects from four households, the world telescoping backwards into its original disorder.

I needed a drink. I stayed for two months, and I did what I could. Took truckloads of paper to the dump. Tried to reason. Escaped to the local gay bar every night, was awakened much too soon every morning with the ongoing drama.

"Gypsy, quick. He's here again. He's taken my bathrobe. And while I was in the shower. This has got to stop."

I found notes to the police and receipts for contributions—to the Latino police officers' fund, to the neighborhood watch, to anyone who came to the door.

The world of the L.A. railroad yards seemed similarly cluttered. There was a little work for me on the yard extra board, but I found myself getting disoriented at work, unable to remember Taylor yard and the huge railmap of interconnected tracks. I trained for a job as a retarder operator in one of the towers overlooking the hump. It wasn't dangerous, but it was slightly unreal. The operator sat at a board with lights indicating the power switches and threw them remotely for the cars rolling off the hump. You also had to calculate the weight of the car and apply the giant steel claws on the track, the retarders, to keep the car rolling at a moderate speed.

An error would send a heavy car crashing into the rest of the track, knocking off brakes and possibly pushing the cars out the bowl tracks on the other end. Brakemen were working in the bowl; I had been one of them. Now I was the great retarder god operating the pinball machine in the sky, watching the cars roll off the hump and scrambling to push the right flippers on the board. I could feel a knot of panic like the rat's nest of wires I was working with. Where were the connections? Everything seemed to be an act of memorization of some random order, and God help you if you got off the freeway an exit too soon, or suddenly you couldn't recognize your own notes to yourself. Mister Confusion was hiding under the bed, under the retarder tower, under the web of lights that L.A. was—the country's most shallow surface, my home.

I began to be aware of what my drinking was when after four o'clock there were two of us being crazy in the house. And when in the morning her terror was matched by my pain and rage. I had gone to the corner bar one night to drink Bombay gin and to go to a fantasy place where all this wasn't happening, where I was still footloose and young. I was spinning stories to whoever sat next to me, weaving an interesting web, and over the magical bottles holding wealth, I saw my face in the mirror behind the bar. I saw a woman out of control, not young, frightening in her pain turned on itself, and beyond anyone's reach. This was not an attractive face; this was vampire bait. And I realized I was unequal to what was happening here.

As it was, this situation would bury me. Right now, I could only do so much—balance the checkbook, throw out old keys, alert her friends. She refused to accept any compromise suggestions—a live-in nurse, a move to a retirement home. The problem was out there. It was trap the thief or nothing. I was going to have to wait until things got worse, until my mother reached a surrender. I knew I was going to have to take over completely and that it was a matter of time. I planned to come back every few months to clear out the paper and to get my sister here at Christmas to decide what to do. For now I could only keep her increasingly leaky boat floating toward the falls.

My own leaky boat I moved into a loft at Luther-the-Millionaire's mansion. Business on the railroad had hit the skids, and in the next year and a half, I would only work a few months in the summer, scrambling for days here and there. I had a lot of time on my hands and a lot of problems to run away from. I don't remember too much about the days at the mansion other than the trays of coke and my car parked on the lawn or at odd angles to the curb as the dewy Northern California morning arose with its habitual chamber quartet, an event that Luther and I missed with as much regularity as possible. Christmas came, and with it my sister and her two Parisian cats, who were in need of flea treatment and could not be left alone for a minute. We assembled in Pasadena to help out. The cats became the totem victims, my sister quickly becoming occupied in rescuing them from mistaken lockups in closets and drawers. I began to wonder about my whole family. Would I too become like that? Chasing cats through plate-glass doors on Christmas morning, shards and blood among the wrapping paper, the discovery of a lapsed insurance policy.

"Well that's what I wanted to mention. The insurance lady, Cecelia Fastener, she's the one who's responsible."

"Mother, you don't have insurance. Why did you let your old policy run out?"

"Cecelia Fastener, that's her name. We must do something about this. She was here, you know. I've told the police."

We painted a Christmas tree over the plywood tacked on the broken door, drank manhattans in cut-crystal glasses, and hosted a tea party for my mother's old friends. We brought out the hand-made lace tablecloth, the silver service, and spent an afternoon cutting the crusts off cream cheese and date sandwiches. Just like old times. They all came, whispered discreetly they were glad we were here, too polite to mention the toad in the silver sugarbowl. Two days later my sister's cat got leukemia, had to be hospitalized. We made more trips to the dump. I scored coke from a friend of a friend for the drive back to Luther's; it lasted till Salinas, my last line snorted in the gas stop restroom. I called my connection from a pay phone in case Luther was on a dry day. I was going to spend time in the bars getting over this one.

Donna was pulled into the funnel cone. I would drive up to see her in the city and sweep her with me on my mad escapes, going from her to Naomi who would give the scotch its weekend furlough when I appeared out of the night, a wild creature of the veldt who could be tamed by a saucer of Stolychnaya. Who would sleep beside her and vanish like the devil in a mirror on Monday morning.

All the while the before-dawn phonecalls continued, an infuriated wavering voice that I could not medicate away and could not comfort. No, I could not help to trap the burglar. There was no burglar. I felt brutal, insisting on the truth. I hated the truth. Both for her life and for mine.

In the midst of this downward spiral, Donna quit drinking. I had been with her the night before; we had been fighting. When I woke up Donna was drunk again, had gone out in the middle of the night to get more.

"You asshole, don't you know that this is how it is? That I had vodka in my coffee all the time? That I don't blame you for not wanting me, that I wish I was dead?"

"God," I thought, "she's really fucked up. She can't handle it." I guess I thought that I was handling it. I had to think that.

I really felt sorry for her. And guilty. And yet, when she called me a few weeks later and said she quit drinking, I felt funny about it. "God," I thought, "she needed to." But I didn't want to see Donna as much. And when I did, I was very hard on her, watching with a buzzard eye to see if she was having fun, was relaxed, was magically transformed. She wasn't, and part of me felt vindicated. "See, she's so weak she can't handle drinking, and now she's going to have to be miserable forever. Ha." As if my life was all Club Med. Perhaps it was. Donna stayed around, though, and tried to help out.

In the spring we went down south together to dig my mother out from under again and find a lawyer so I could take control. What an idea. While we were there, I noticed a huge rummage sale in progress at the civic auditorium. Donna and I ventured in. There were long tables of things heaped up and little old ladies elbowing each other at the counters. I didn't find anything good. Donna, however, found lots of good things. She was really happy about finding two men's white silk shirts. They had a wonderful hand and were monogrammed. I felt this knot of envy. I wanted one of those shirts. I asked her for one. And she said no. A part of me turned away and hid in the shadows. Polonius was about to die. I thought, "I'll never trust you again." And then I thought, "This is insane. These are two-dollar shirts." Then the sulking away returned, and I embraced it.

I left her from that time on. As we drove back north, I began blaming her for my life, for what was happening to my mother, for the overwhelming odds against my winning this battle. I thought,

"Donna has more than I do; her mother just gave her a car." And she had the shirts—she was wearing one of them. I never told Donna what was bothering me. I was ashamed to tell her. It's hard to admit it now, when I know what the shirts were. Something valuable she had found that I had not; something she could not share with me. And that was what had come between us.

Summer on the Coast gave me the chance to work a few days here and there, but the recession had railroad work cut back to almost nothing. The railroad is an economic weather vane. If they close a plant, they pull a railroad crew. Bad copper prices; we don't switch the mines. Trouble in the housing industry; the Oregon hump yards shut down. I would catch a day in the Watsonville yard in June and see a brakeman younger than me get off a through freight from San Luis. That night I would be down there marking up to the San Luis extra board. Two days later, I would be cut off there. I'd head the Chevy east to the San Joaquin Valley and mark up in Tracy. August was its busy month, but it was an undesirable place to work. Low-mileage runs and a hard-ass trainmaster and twelve-hour hauler jobs down the valley to Fresno, stopping in every grain bin and molasses plant from Manteca to Merced. It was in Tracy that I decided to try an experiment. I thought, "I'll quit drinking for a month before I have to go down South. Then I'll be able to handle the problem there." It seemed like a sensible idea. I began to notice something. Everyday at four o'clock a little voice would speak in the back of my mind. It said, "Hey, it's time for a drink." I had to answer it.

"Fuck off, we're not drinking."

Next day, same time same voice. The next day, a louder voice.

"You asshole. We haven't had a drink for three days. Count 'em. Three days. We'll get to Fresno tonight before last call, and if you walk across the yard, there'll be a switchmen's bar."

To my surprise this voice did not go away. Talk talk talk, day after day, rocking into Fresno or Roseville—hungry, tired, and alone. I found myself in bars, clutching bottles of Perrier, ignored by the bovine drinkers on either side, happy at their trough. Nobody would talk to me. I felt excruciatingly lonely. It made the other rails nervous that I wouldn't drink. They thought I was a company spotter.

I lasted a month. Then the railroad laid me off and Naomi swept into Stockton for one of her weekends. Everything seemed rushed and hectic, in high gear. In a frenzy we packed the car and pored over maps. In the absence of a definite plan, Naomi stepped into the breach. Within hours we were on the Amador wine loop, sipping and bickering from chateau to chateau. I got drunker than I'd ever been—and faster. At a joint whose specialty was a brutal tannin-and-charcoal liquid called Hangtown Red, we got into a lengthy argument over goals in life. I was picking visions of a happy life from the orchards of farmhouses we passed beside the road, old frame houses sleeping at the end of gravel driveways, dogs that wouldn't move for cars.

"Look. We would be happy living there. Planting Chardonnay, you handling the technical side. It could grow into a musical salon; Sundays, people would come."

"You know I couldn't do that. I work. You just ignore me with your impossible dreams. It's all for you. Everything is all for you."

The silver dragon momentarily holding passage with the sky began its downward plunge, recalled hand over hand by the stern kitemaster, became only mylar and wood, only a wish, a hopeful idea stepping out into the sunlight from a wine-soaked cave.

"Don't you tell me what to wish for. They're ideas, that's all. They don't hurt anybody."

Our arguments were resolved not substantially, but through driving. We drove through them like you drive through Yosemite. Like everything else in my life, they were natural phenomena, unconnected to causes or resolutions.

Naomi arrived, we fought, we made love; Naomi went home, and I headed south to Pasadena, buried under smog and summer and madness. I was going to take legal control of my mother's welfare, sell the family home, find her a refuge, and untangle her Byzantine financial affairs. As my friend Sybil the drummer said: "Gypsy, you drive a fifty-six Chevy and you play the saxophone." I'm afraid that just about covered it.

The first thing I had to do on arrival in Pasadena was to locate her keys and checkbook. I had copies made. Finding the checkbook was deceptive, as there were many checkbooks. Every time she lost one, she opened a new account. Then she found the old one and commenced writing checks on closed accounts. Then that one would disappear, and she would write on the new one. The same principle applied to keys. Lose the old ones, change the locks. Find the old keys which don't fit the doors anymore. The burglar has changed the locks. This is getting subtle. Find the new keys, the locks work. For a while. Drawers full of key tangles. I throw them all into a box, start hiding places of my own, then realize that no place is safe—it's her house, she'll find them and re-hide them. I start making discoveries: contracts signed for roof repair, termite inspection, large amounts of money, dents on the car bumper, money hidden all over the house, unpaid bills, insurance premiums. My going through things disturbs her, but I have no choice. I have to put the puzzle together. I will have to look at every piece of paper in the house and decide what to do with it. Lately it has been hard for me to decide whether to eat a Whopper or a Big Mac. Hung over, I would lie on the floor at Luther's and turn the alternatives over in my mind. Whopper with tomato. But the Mac has double size. And better french fries. The demands in Pasadena put me into a frenzy, and I act mechanically, driven by desperation to get it done. Feeling the weight of Everest, the lack of oxygen near the top.

Going through the family papers, I had a moment that stopped me in my tracks. Old yellowed papers from the 1880s. A newspaper clipping from a New York paper. Otto Flohr, my German immigrant great-grandfather in a sealskin cap. "Patent for improvements in bar couplings," beautiful mechanical drawings of the railroad knuckles and drawbars, a detailed explanation of the automatic coupler that made fingerless brakemen relics of the earlier craft. I had always heard this grandfather was an inventor, but it gave me a chill to realize the unbroken chain of events—how I was working with these very same pieces, how my doing the job at all was the result of these same safety improvements. An uncanny bridge to the past, great-grandfather's work, granddaughter's occupation. A handshake over a hundred-year gap. What would he have thought about it all?

When my sister arrives from Paris we are able to go to court. My mother's shoes do not fit her anymore, large boats she has to shuffle to stay inside. She has hidden the ones that fit. On the witness box she has her day in court and tells her story. The burglars. Cecelia Fastener. The keys. The judge gets the drift of things, moves his sympathetic gaze to me. I am it. Certified, bonded, and accountable for yearly reports. That is, the judge knows I'm accountable. My mother does not. I can tell she isn't taking this in. The refusal aspect of her delusions starts to become apparent. I am vaguely aware that I should pay attention to this. That I should learn some lesson from it. That it's something we all do, and I'm seeing the extreme problem it can grow into. The revealing extreme.

My sister sticks around for two weeks. We find a retirement home that suits; old friends of hers are there. The only question is can she maintain—get through the door, get on the care-for-life track?

"She's having a little trouble with her memory. Forgetting things. She might need extra help with her keys, the adjustment."

"Yes, yes—some of our residents are a bit forgetful. We are quite used to that."

"OK, fine," I thought. As if you could get used to an infinity loop of questions that are contradictions. As if it could be handled, genteelly, by anyone. "Oh well," I thought. "Worry about that one later. Plenty of time to worry about that one."

There was no lack of odd problems. Like finding our father in a box in the cupboard. A cardboard carton like any other, I toss it down to my sister, who reads the label and drops it with a shriek. "Carl Niemann." Dad.

"Mother. What's dad doing in the closet? That was twenty years ago. I thought you scattered these."

"Oh yes, dear. I meant to. Don't worry about that. I need to talk to you about Cecelia. I want you to help me."

My sister and I made a quick flight up the Coast, the tricky sensation of taking dad through the airport check in a suitcase. I mean, how would one explain? We dug a hole under a big tree on my place in the hills, and I said a few words from the gravedigger scene in *Hamlet*. It was all I could think of. Did any of this make any sense anyway? Wasn't it all improvisation?

I found myself calling my friend Roger Singleton almost every night. He had known me for fifteen years and was a conversational anchor in my life. A phone friend who lived in New York. An insomniac. An academic. Someone who knew me from my former life. I was transforming, as I usually did, the events into a story. I told him that I had tried to stop drinking, but that now, it seemed, I needed to drink to deal with all this.

"Well, perhaps now is not the best time to try to stop something like that."

"No, now is definitely not a good time. I mean, things are really crazy here."

"What you might just do, though, if you are interested, is to find a twelve-step program meeting in Pasadena. You know, that deals with alcohol. Just to go and see."

"Yeah, OK. I mean, I might do that. I know it would help if I could cut down. But the pressure here is really intense."

"It sounds intense. What were you saying about the Warfdales? Who are these people, and why are they visiting your mother?"

"She invited them last year sometime. She insists on having them stay with us, and we are all putting on this production of acting as if everything's fine. They have the big picture, but we are doing it anyway. It's a play within a play. And Sir Warfdale keeps chasing me around the kitchen, the minute his wife turns a corner."

"This sounds like a Restoration comedy, my dear. I hope these people are leaving soon."

"They have to leave. I have to paint the house. I might paint the lawn too."

My mother, like a lot of older Pasadena ladies, had begun to live in banks. Not keeping their eggs in one basket, they dress for company and set out to visit their money, going from bank to bank, waiting in hushed lines on plush carpet and sipping coffee or tea with sugar cookies.

"I think it's a shame what they've done to this bank. Redecoration. Such a big fuss. And look what they have achieved. It gives you a headache to stand on this carpet now."

It was true. The carpet in Pasadena Federal Savings would not have been out of place in Caesar's Palace. Garish red semicircles on a golden lawn, heavy red drapes gracing the marble pseudoclassic columns. Mother and the other little old ladies took this all very personally. The banks were their club. They were greeted by name.

"And how are you today, Mrs. Niemann?"

I was taking all this away from her, replacing her at the banks, tracing her steps in the carpet, investigating checkbooks and pass-keys and savings account books. In the mornings I escaped from the house at ten and hit the banks, dressed as best I could remember as a Pasadena woman—panty hose, designer loafers, raw silk pants, a cotton blouse, a purse. There the resemblance ended. Inside, I was a seething mass of redneck anger ready to gush. Texas language, like black gold, was waiting its moment to be.

I sat in the client's chair at the bank, waiting for my customer representative to untangle my case, unlock funds from the computer so I could play my next hand at the retirement home, the thirty thousand dollar ante. My customer representative rose from her chair, adjusted her coif and, carefully balancing on her stiletto heels, negotiated a route through the plush carpet to the computer bank, where a line of similar teenagers in similar tight skirts and high heels waited for the host and wine. They spoke in hushed whispers, as if their makeup would crack. Then one of them would remove some papers from the machine and square them into a neat pile as if she were folding a complex dinner napkin. I wanted to scream, rip the pages out of her hand, tear her shoes off, and tell her to get her goddamn butt in gear—I had shit to do today. But of course, nobody says that in a Pasadena bank.

Finally, my customer representative began to negotiate her return. It was a windy day on the marina, and the small boats tacking upwind resembled handkerchiefs whose position scarcely seemed to change at all. I suffered awaiting her return as part of a general groan, like a cough suppressed, shared by all in the lines except the little old ladies in their hats and gloves. Their serenity had the force of gravity, keeping the tone the way it was, the way Pasadena had always been.

"I'm sorry, but there seems to be a freeze on those funds. We cannot release them at this time. We need a letter of authorization from the court."

"What do you think you're looking at?"

"I have been informed that this is a general letter. We would need a specific one. Specific to this account."

"You don't need shit." The perfect crystal paperweight suddenly became superfluous. Someone was shaking the cage. "Five other banks accepted this letter, and I don't have time to fuck around with your bullshit, so you get this approved now, today, like right now. Get on the goddamn phone."

A blush appeared somewhere under the other blush.

"You are not allowed to talk like that in this bank."

"You just get me some action, OK? Let me worry about how I talk." A ripple ran through the lines of floating seaweed at the series of little windows. I needed lunch. And the mug-sized glass of cool white wine that went with it. If only this bitch would get out of my way.

Returning home from days at the Social Security office, the retirement home, the real estate office, the DMV, and other horrors, I would find my mother in a frantic rage, just barely concealed for the benefit of the Warfdales. "Thank God for propriety," I thought. It was the underdog against insanity, but just barely. I knew what she was thinking.

"How dare she leave me alone with thieves about, and go out without me to have a great time at my bank."

It was one of life's little ironies.

Things continued in this way for two months. The Warfdales left—no more confrontations around the garbage cans ("This weekend—we'll slip away to the mountains. What d'you say?"). I set mother up to fail her driving test; sat in the backseat while she terrorized the examiner, argued with her interminably over the results.

"He told me I could continue to drive."

"No, Mother, he said you flunked. You can call him up and check. Here's the number."

"I distinctly remember his saying I could continue to drive."

When moving day came, I should have been prepared for her last-ditch stand, but I wasn't. The movers were there, we had measured furniture, decided what would fit in her new apartment, or I thought we had. As the men were carrying things out to the truck, she started giving instructions to move other things. She blocked the door with her determined body, ready to lie down, if necessary, in front of the truck.

"I want you to take the chest of drawers. I order you to."

"Mother, it won't fit. Remember we measured it."

"I don't remember anything of the kind. You are becoming very officious. I don't care for that at all."

Here we were at the Battle of the Alamo. We were both going over the top, but I had the luck to remember my last card. I called one of her lady friends to come with us. I knew she would pull herself together for company. And, sure enough, it worked. The movers got the stuff in the van while Mrs. Jorgensen and Mother and I sat in the living rom—minus the couch—and looked on. I was on adrenalin for the long haul through the day—the smiles at the retirement home, the explanations, the creation of an instant reproduction of home. By five o'clock, I had pulled it off, sweated through my clothes, and banked my Chevy around the offramp leading to Termites, the women's bar on my way home.

It was still hot, a Southern California summer outside, but Termites was dark and cool, the out-of-focus colors of the TV illuminating the stools at the bar. The other woman sitting at the bar had been here all day watching some sports event. I put down two tall Bombay-and-tonics as if they were lemonade. I felt instantly better; the elephant was off my chest, and there was a pleasant warmth in my knees. It was like drawing a deep breath and sighing a deep sigh. I wished I had coke so that I could do this all night, so that the two-hour drop could be avoided and also the numbing descent into the evening—never as good as right now, but inevitable. I now was going to tell this lucky woman on my left the story of my life, the sad story of my day.

I returned to a house that was now truly a ruin, an archive of my history. The garage sale of my life was about to begin. I was into the bourbon now, gaining enough energy for my mind to finance its theatrical productions. In the middle of the fifth act, the phone rings. It's my sister, calling from Paris, about a silver tea set I had auctioned off the week before. It seemed she had changed her mind, wasn't really definite about it before, and, anyway, had not understood the sale was to be so quick. How could I proceed in this

PASADENA GOTHIC | 87

careless manner? Well, the shit really hit the fan. The hysteria of the day came pouring out, all over this last straw and necessary object—the teapot. I blamed her for the mess my life was in, I blamed her for making me watch while she and Susie Jorgensen played dolls, I blamed her for leaving me alone with all these problems. I blamed Mother for being old and frail, and her for giving me shit about things like tea sets. Didn't she understand that I was falling apart?

"You reek of self-pity, Gypsy. It's not a pretty picture."

"Fuck you, asshole. Fuck you. Asshole."

"I have heard quite enough. Goodbye."

It is hard work, the demolition of a home, the eviction of objects that have sat by certain walls for years, for my lifetime. The furniture grooves in this carpet are deep. I have traced them with small fingers, looking up at grownup feet.

I vacuum up after my past is wheeled off can by can. A raucous retreat on the quiet, tree-lined street. It is hard to know what to save, what faces I want watching me from walls in future rooms. I lived in motels, carry a quilt to make any room my home. I gave my dogs away years ago. I left my mother's house long before that.

I think by now you are getting the picture of the way things were going in my life. You are probably thinking, "Why doesn't she quit drinking—why doesn't she go to that twelve-step program meeting?" Well, I did go. It was in the basement of a church I went to Sunday school in. My parents, who were admitted atheists, sent me to Sunday school—for social reasons. To me, it was one more place I had to wear a dress. My sister tells me I used to scream things like "God doesn't care if I wear my chaps." OK, fine, so it was in the basement of a church. I parked. I went in. There were about ten women sitting around a table, and nobody paid much attention to me. I had been dry for three days, trying to straighten up on my own, and I was feeling kind of jumpy. Everybody listened while one person, then another, talked about her problems. They seemed like pretty dumb problems to me, nothing like my problems. I could write a book on problems. Finally, one of the women said that she didn't know if there could be a God if He let her poodle get run over by a truck. Then everybody got up, held hands, and prayed.

I stood there looking at the floor, as I always had in this church. Then they all said, "Keep coming back; it works" like some kind of football cheer. Then they all left.

I walked out to the parking lot and got into my car. I wondered what Roger thought was so great about this. I couldn't imagine him at one of these meetings. He was too smart. I never understood, either, why he had quit drinking. We used to drink together, and it was a lot of fun. Those people at the meeting didn't seem to be having any fun. And Donna. She wasn't any fun anymore either. Speaking of fun, I needed some now. And I went from the meeting straight to Termites, where a musician I knew was playing with her band. There was a chance I could sit in with my flute. I really needed something to make me feel better about myself down here. I needed a lift.

Sure enough, Rhonda and the Rondos were playing, and Rhonda asked me to join them on the last song of the set. I thought, well, maybe I should have a glass of white wine to warm up, but not too much or I'll lose my embouchure. Termites' shots of wine were eight-ounce tumblers, and I put down two of those while waiting for the set to wind up. I distinctly felt more relaxed, and when the moment came to join the Rondos onstage, I felt that suave glow of good timing come over me. I would float like a butterfly, sting like a bee. Sure enough, I got in the music groove all right and was ready for the power surge when Rhonda handed me a break. I took a double one, spilling harmonics over the top of the chords, diving and landing within the scale, fading to a perfect harmony note for her re-entrance into the song.

"All right," I could hear a few women in the audience say, and I was "all right" inside for the moment. I had been rescued with the help of the wine, the genius of this place, Termites, my space for home. Not some church basement with no joy. Here, surrounded by my own kind.

6

THE
MONTEREY
LOCAL

IT WAS NOW early December, and I was sleeping on the floor in an empty house. It, too, had been sold, and I was now free to go. I had somehow muddled through. There were more problems in the future with my mother, of course, but for now, she was safe. I turned my Chevy up the Coast, leaving Pasadena crisp and polished on a winter's smogless day. Happiness was L.A. in the rearview mirror, and I drew a breath of freedom as the skirted oaks of San Luis Obispo and the whaleback mountain that guards its pass to the north came into view. King City, Salinas, and a thought occurred to me to try a new way home, a road I didn't usually take, down highway 68 toward Monterey to try a Zinfandel that I remembered with a memory of raspberry and the color pink within its darker hue. I wanted to taste this year's new wine. A curiosity led me up the road and back along a brick path to a weathered barn. Yellow flowers blanketed the barren rows of vines, and a warm patch of sun lay on half of the picnic table adjoining the field. Its other half was wet like the grass and the dripping barrels that lay on their sides outside the winery door. A tall slender man in rubber boots and faded jeans was fooling around with a hose. He raised his head, and I looked into dark eyes set in an Etruscan face that changed from intense concentration into a sunny smile. "Hi," he said, as if he'd known me all his life. "Come in."

I entered the cool barn and walked past an assembly line bottling operation, a corker, boxes filled with printed labels, cartons waiting to be filled. The rest of the barn held large oak barrels resting on racks in rows and three huge stainless steel tanks with metal ladders winding up their sides. The smell was old, complex, and rich. The man I was following had gone through a door at the back of the barn. I noticed he walked gracefully, but with a slight limp. A path led under a trellised arbor to a round brick building with a polished wood floor. The tasting bar was a crescent of curly maple buffed to show the grain and it faced a row of windows that looked out on the fields. He now turned over two immaculate wine glasses, poured two inches of salmon-colored wine into one of them, held it up to the light, buried his nose in it, and reversed the contents into his mouth.

"Is it safe to drink now?"

"I'm alive, so it's safe. If I'm not the jester, instead of the taster. This is my white zin."

He watched while I swirled the wine, washed it into my mouth, and gurgled the contents before swallowing. A faint taste of apples lay in my mouth; the light from the field was dazzling, I felt carried away, lifted.

"I remember a raspberry Zinfandel last year. Did it happen again?"

His face became more personal. It was important I had remembered the wine.

"Yes, that's right. Well, it's never the same. I have a bottle of that, if you'd care to try it again. I'll let you compare them."

The new Zinfandel was fine, but falling into a pit of purple. The other wine had pink and wildness in it somewhere. You were hot and dusty and walking up a trail when a scent of sage raised goosebumps on your arms. Unexpected where it was. Our conversation drifted into politics and hard times.

"Tell me about the recession, I haven't had work in over a year. Not real work."

"Well, what do you do?"

"I'm a brakeman on the train. You hear us going through town — the Monterey local."

"You're a brakeman, are you?" He paused a moment and swirled the inch of wine up the sides of his glass, pinkly coating it and catching beads of light. "That means you probably know what a day's work is. I could give you a job here. I need good help."

He poured a straw-colored wine into my glass. "This is my white, from a Sauterne. My name is Anthony Lucero, by the way."

I held the glass up to the light. The ascending bubbles formed a prism and threw rainbow flashes back.

"OK, Anthony. You have yourself a cellar rat. Yes—the answer is yes."

Leaving Luther's at nine in the morning to go to work, the beaches at Santa Cruz would already be resting in full sun, and in the artichoke fields and apple orchards of Watsonville the dew had melted off the plants and soaked into the warming earth. Sheltered by the mountains, the vineyard road still lay in shadow, and the dirt driveway to Lucero's winery still crunched with frost as I drove up to his sleepy house. The dogs were awake and glad to see anyone, but the winery cats were curled like snails on the porch, waiting for the sun and food. After several long knocks, Lucero came to the door, looking a little worse for wear. He motioned me in and disappeared into the back rooms of his farmhouse, and I could hear the sounds of a shower and what sounded like weights being dropped on the floor.

Anthony clearly lived here alone. Things were thrown around— t-shirts, rubber boots, socks, wine glasses, magazines. Many layers of dust covered anything dropped more than a week ago, and cobwebs hung from the corners of the room. The woman in me felt a little tug. I thought, "Boy, he really needs some help around here. Needs someone to straighten things up." Then I thought, "I bet every woman who walks into this house thinks that, and it still looks that way." I sat down on his sprung couch thinking, "This place needs a guitar around." Soon a clean Anthony appeared and got me in focus.

"Good. You're wearing the right stuff. Are you ready to work outside?"

We headed for the barn and for the next three hours worked steadily crushing pomace in a crusher and pumping the free run into large stainless steel fermenters. We then dumped the remains in the field and washed everything. Then we washed more barrels.

He had a lot of barrels that had been fermenting and were now ready for their first rack, and we did that, too, pumping the clear red liquid into new barrels and dragging the remaining lees, a clay-like pink substance, out to dump in the field. Although it was January, I worked up a sweat in a t-shirt, and the steam rising off the dump heap was heavy with a sour, yeasty smell. It felt good to be working outside, like switching boxcars in a rhythm with a part-ner. It felt familiar and easy. Around one, Anthony announced "We will stop for lunch. I will prepare it for you."

I sat around the Spanish-style dinner table in Anthony Lucero's kitchen while he cooked me lunch. It clearly was something he loved to do; each herb and pan had ritual places within the general chaos. We would have pasta dressed with olive oil, fresh herbs, capers, and grated parmigiana. Crisp lettuce tossed with oil and local vinegar. Anthony sniffed the bottle lovingly and handed it to me.

"Get to know that smell. It's important."

He began sawing up a loaf of bread.

"Could I clear the table or something?"

"No. Sit. You work for me. I make the lunch."

He reached into a tub of soapy water and fished out two wine glasses, held them under the tap, shook them, and with a soft clean towel wiped them clean in seconds.

"Watch how this is done. Hold it here. Never touch the glass with your fingers. The tasting room is all show biz, and the glasses must be perfectly clean, no spots."

The final touch to lunch was the opening of a bottle of the wine of the house and the pouring of the first drink of the day. This, too, was ritualized.

"As you pour the wine, give a slight flip of the wrist at the finish so that you do not spill, but also it adds drama to the presentation. Show biz. Now, *buon appetito*."

Damn, this was good.

Time started to slow down. The warmth of the day was allowed in the wide farmhouse windows, and the disorder of objects in the room became comfortable, familial, a part of the way things were. We began to talk of little things. After the meal, we took our time clearing up. The push of the day was over, and now we did things like wash cartons of glasses and visit the barn to do smaller procedures like slurrying the bentonite clay used for fining white wine and topping off the oak casks with pitchers of new wine to keep the air from what was aging. Around three, a few tasters found their way back to the barn, and I found myself on the other side of the bar pouring flourishes of Cabernet. "Anthony is thinking all the time," I thought. "He has the sun behind him, enhancing the color of the wine, and in their eyes, giving him the power of observation."

"Would you care to taste in order, or do you have a special preference?"

"Oh, I think we'd like to try a white wine, nothing too sweet."

"Nothing we have is too sweet, sir. Although the grape is Sauterne, I think you'll find it quite dry. We have a case price on this. A very drinkable wine."

The afternoon was punctuated by sipping here and there. We carried our glasses from cask to cask, nose to the bottom for suspect smells, good smells. In the tasting room I tasted, too, and when the sun had started to dip below the redwood ridge, the course of the day seemed painless and wonderful, like a river broadening as it neared the sea.

At five o'clock, Anthony pulled out a battered checkbook and wrote me out a check for thirty dollars on wine-colored paper with a gold winery logo. That was what one overtime hour on the railroad would pay me. And somehow I didn't want those equivalences here.

"Anthony, why don't you just pay me in wine? That way we're traders. It would feel better to me."

"Choose whatever you like. I'll pay you a case a day."

I collected my pay from among the bottles in the tasting room, and Anthony helped me carry the case to my car and waved me up the road home.

"You do good work, Gypsy. Come Wednesday. We'll bottle. Take care going home."

"Pleasure working with you, Anthony. This is going to work out fine."

I headed home past the Salinas artichoke fields I had worked in as a brakeman. I felt even more at home in them now. When I got to Santa Cruz, it seemed natural to stop in at a local winery to taste the competition and get acquainted. Wine followed wine and made easy the way home. I banked the Chevy into Luther's drive, and still humming a Jerry Lee Lewis tune, threw open the trunk, revealing the riches inside.

"O spo-dee-o-dee drinking wine, drinking wine. O spo-dee-o-dee drinking wine."

"Well, you certainly sound cheered up." Luther's small voice carried from the balcony, where he sat in a dressing gown perusing *Forbes* magazine. "I'd say your troubles are over."

It certainly felt that way. Even when I returned to Pasadena at Christmas to visit my mother, the memory of the open fields stayed with me as a vision of retreat. Roger was around L.A. at some literary conference, and we arranged to meet for dinner in Little Tokyo. The night before I went out on the strip with friends, and one thing led to another and another, and it was three o'clock in the afternoon before I could get out of bed with a sick hangover so bad the idea of being in the same room with a raw fish seemed impossible. By five, I was able to drive, and Roger and I sat at the sushi bar catching up on old times. I ordered a beer, but the sight of it nauseated me. I could only drink a couple of sips. As we got into the car, Roger said something that I found oddly reassuring.

"If you were an alcoholic, you wouldn't have left half a beer sitting there on the bar."

I didn't say, "That's because I'm so hungover I can hardly walk." I just thought, "Well, good. I'm not an alcoholic." Then I proceeded to tell him all about the winery and how wonderful it was.

"He pays you in what?"

"Wine. Cases of wine. But I can trade it for other things."

"Like the phone bill? Those kinds of things?"

"Well, it's Santa Cruz. Everybody is into trades."

"Oh, OK. It would be hard to do that in New York. I guess I just don't understand how Californians live."

I thought Roger should do more research. He was smoking way too much, and he seemed nervous and worried. If he was going to kill himself with cigarettes, why didn't he just drink? It was lots more fun.

One day in January it dawned on me that I was in love. Anthony had been making little come-on noises for weeks, but I was so used to ignoring passes that they sailed right over my head as possibilities.

Men just hadn't been very real to me sexually for a while. I was used to looking at them as if they were part of the equipment, like a handbrake or a switch handle. On this day we had driven over to another winery to borrow a part for a filter. We were out behind the barn when the resident ram decided to run us off and began short charges aimed directly at my crotch. The little fucker could hit. Anthony gallantly distracted the beast and took a direct hit in the jeans while I located a ladder to hold the monster off. Something about the scene switched a light on somewhere, and as we backed down the winery road holding a ladder at arm's length, and absorbing successively weaker rammings, I looked at Anthony with new eyes. Poor guy, hit in the crotch by a sheep. There was something charming about that. Charming and disarming. The necessary thing happened; I became convinced that it was my idea and that I would have to seduce him.

I turned this idea over in my mind for a week, and, when I just could not wait one minute more, stayed late one afternoon in the tasting room. It got to be after five, then six, and I noticed the martini glass had replaced the wine glass in Anthony's right hand.

"Why don't you stay for dinner?" Anthony was just noticing that I hadn't left at my usual time.

"I'd love to. I hadn't noticed it was getting so late."

This was the first time we had been alone together in the dark, and we were both slightly embarrassed. The dark does that. We bustled around the kitchen, trying not to accidentally touch, like bumper cars on good behavior. Finally, sitting at the table, I reached over and took his hand. Slowly, quietly, our fingers made friends, started working things out while the two brains pushed the panic button.

"Oh, we shouldn't do this."

"I know."

"Let's do it. And then pretend we didn't."

"OK."

Our bodies crashed together, fingers squeezed love handles, caressed hair, lips met softly, then with bites.

"Oh God, let's get somewhere soft."

Tripping over the barbells we fell into the bed. It smelled like the essence of bed, and thank God it was built to last. We crashed around like wrestlers because, in fact, we were wrestlers and happy drunks falling through the roof into one more lobby at the end of the play. Wrestled out and licked by some wild tiger who was on a chase around the moon we lay in one another's guilty arms.

"I forgot to brush my teeth. I'm going to fuck your mind away. So sleepy."

"Mmnn. Blanket. Turn out the light."

Life was now taking a turn towards a closed utopia where recycling is the governing providence. We made the wine. Anthony paid me in wine. I took the wine to Luther's garage. Anthony drove up the coast, and we drank the wine. I drove down the coast, and we made the wine. Luther couldn't quite handle this unexpected turn of events. He had thought he was getting a lesbian roommate. Now here I was dusting counters and polishing silverware to impress some other guy.

"About the only thing you haven't done is put on a formal and sit in the living room waiting for him," Luther muttered peevishly.

"How about this music? Is it too obvious?" Dinah Washington crooned from Luther's audio rack.

"Well, I was trying to concentrate. You know I'd appreciate it if you would screw the lids back on these pickle jars before you put them back in the refrigerator."

Anthony usually arrived bearing gifts for Luther, bottles of wine and handfuls of garlic. Men understand other men.

"Luther should eat more garlic. It would help him. And he should put a little weight on. Why don't we cook him dinner?"

We took a walk down to the beach and exchanged paragraphs in the stories of our lives.

"Well, I've been in this long-term relationship with a woman, but we don't get along, and I think this time we won't get back together. She's Italian Catholic and she really wants me to marry her. And I know it wouldn't work out."

"Well, I've been in this long-term relationship with a woman, too, and we don't get along, and I think this time we won't get back together. She's Jewish and she doesn't want to get married. And I kind of do. You know it really blew my mind that I got attracted to you. I had been thinking for a lot of years now that I was just gay."

"Well, maybe you're gay sometimes and you're not sometimes."

Anthony looked at me and smiled.

"I guess this means I'm going to have to give up making fag jokes. We say they have cork breath. But I just do it automatically. I don't really mean it."

He looked down at his Adidas.

"I just started wearing these a couple of years ago, when I discovered Bruce Springsteen. He changed my life. He has such an incredibly vulnerable and sensitive voice. And the stuff he sings about—men feeling things. All except for that fascist song about wanting his girlfriend to sit on his lap when he gets electrocuted. That song is really fucked."

He stopped and grabbed my arm.

"Look," he said, pointing to a saloon marquee. "A neon martini. And they're open."

"Anthony," I said. "You are really crazy. But good crazy."

"Hey," he said. "I have an idea. Let's have a drink. A real drink."

In February, Anthony and I went on a trip. It was really his trip, and I was just going along. He wanted to make that clear. Trips were obviously a source of anxiety. He was going to pour at a posh vintners' convention—forty small wineries. The thing was in San Diego and included a party beforehand with the elite group of Laguna Beach Wine Tasters. These were the kind of folks who wandered tasting conventions with their own silver cups hanging around their necks and carrying mini tape recorders to capture their impressions for posterity.

"Bunch of pretentious hypocrites. Just plain garden variety drunks. All this wine snob shit. I see these people staggering out my driveway. They fall down in my parking lot."

I arrived the night before so we could get an early start on the trip. But I was restless and wanted to go out. And so we drove into town to a farmworkers' bar, from the outside a casual kind of place. I thought we could have a beer and shoot some pool. Anthony gave me a searching look.

"OK. But don't dance with anyone. And stay close to me."

I saw what he meant when we hit the door. The only woman in the place was the one serving beer. Everyone was yelling and packed in. About two minutes after we reached the bar, a big guy with a straw hat and a hard-on pressed up against my leg and put his arm around Anthony. He was bleeding from a cut wound on his face. We were all going to chat. At this point things were all right because some of the workers knew Anthony from the winery, but they were only just all right. Then Anthony pulled out the biggest roll of money I had ever seen and proceeded to pay for a round. He stuffed it in the back pocket of his jeans.

"Jesus Christ," I thought. "We'll never get out of here alive."

The god who watches out for fools and drunks was on duty, however, and hours later we were weaving out the door and across the road to my car.

"How much money have you got in your back pocket? You're nuts to flash that kind of money in a bar."

"Ten thousand dollars. I won it in Reno when . . . "

In the middle of this sentence, Anthony decided to lie down in the road. It was going to be hard to get him moved. I started looking out for trucks.

"Goddammit will you get out of the road?" I grabbed an arm and started to pull. "I'm going to leave you here if a truck comes."

"I want to do it in the road," Anthony sang, clutching his own shoulders and rocking back and forth.

Finally, a truck did come, and Anthony did get out of the road.

"I don't trust banks. I'm going to take the money with me."

"OK, fine. Just keep it out of sight in bars. I'm getting kind of used to having you around."

In the morning I made the coffee and packed my little bag. It was resting beside the front door when Anthony emerged from the bathroom and looked distractedly around the room.

"I'm afraid we can't leave till I find it."

"Find what?"

"The money. I hid it last night, and now I can't find it."

"You hid it. Now you can't find it. Where have I heard this before?"

The next two hours I spent searching Anthony Lucero's shoes, mattresses, the backs of drawers, the backs of books. I was an expert. I knew all the places. I didn't find the money. But I found a lot of other things. Either Anthony hid things regularly, or he was living with a pack rat who could press its weight.

"OK, what's this gun doing in your shoe?"

"Good. I'm glad you found that. I'm going to need that."

"You have cartons of fat girl fuck magazines in your closet."

"Some people enjoy these things."

"Here's a banana clip for an M-1."

"How do you know what that is?"

"I have one, too."

We stood looking at each other in the living room. I was close to tears. How could I be in love with a person who hid things? This was the one thing I really couldn't handle. The whole world was going into some kind of endless repeat. An echo chamber of horrors.

At last Anthony came up with the cash.

"I put it in my red wool socks in the dirty-sock box. Now we can go. I forgot to tell you that we can't take my truck. It's so late now that we'll never make it unless you drive."

"I thought this was going to be your trip. I mean, I can drive, but that doesn't make it absolutely your trip then."

Anthony gave me a suspicious look as he climbed into the front seat. I started the engine, and we were off down the Coast—Salinas, Gonzales, San Luis one more time. At Pismo, Anthony wanted to stop for a break. Pick up some wine, eat lunch on the beach. It was twelve o'clock. Time for the wine. We were still drinking as we got back in the car; Anthony was thrashing around in his seat, spilling things. Soon the inside of the Chevy had that sour familiar smell. "Just like home," I thought. "This guy really doesn't like leaving town." As if to confirm this thought, Anthony started getting undressed.

"Phew," he said. "There, that's better."

It was clearly a big relief to get the clothes off and into a heap on the front-seat floor. It made a weird kind of sense to me. I started to take my shorts off too, so we could be at home here in the car. It was a turn-the-car-into-a-living room kind of move, like you would do on acid. Anthony was trying to make the space safe.

The walls of the car in fact became more interior, with a kind of glow, but I was driving and my mind felt more exposed as if it was the car and anyone could now look into it. Like a cop, for instance. I started to wish I wasn't the one driving and that it wasn't three hundred more miles and an infinitely expanding time frame now glooming down the road ahead.

"Here," I said, handing him a fox fur hat I had brought with me. "Play with this; some little old ladies in the senior citizens' crafts co-op made it."

"Whee," Anthony said, making odd shapes with his mouth. "Tickles."

Touching and drinking and having fun with the fur, we did all right until we hit the L.A. maze. Then it was rush hour, gridlock, and all the other fun things about the Valley at five o'clock. Anthony started climbing the walls. I wanted things to straighten up. Playtime was over.

"Would you get your clothes on now. As a big favor to me."

He looked at me strangely. Why spoil the fun? Why on earth would I want to spoil the fun?

"Because I'm driving, dickhead, and I'm not having any fun. You are having the fun."

"Well, I need to get a drink."

"Well, they don't have drinks in the middle lane of the Hollywood freeway. Open a bottle of wine."

"I mean a real drink."

Since there was no way we were going to get to the Laguna Beach Wine Tasters' little party by seven if we stopped for a real drink, I just pushed on. Watching Anthony was like watching a cuckoo clock become unsprung, gear by gear, wheel by wheel. He began chanting, long rhythmic vowel sounds punctuated by repetition in the upper octave. He sounded like my musical calculator gone bass. I don't think I have ever been as tired as when I parked the Chevy outside a faceless condo on a faceless street in a faceless part of Orange County, our destination for the day.

"Late—we're late." Anthony's clock had just rung the hour to be.

To my surprise, he stepped out of the car, fluffed his hair, changed his shirt, and became Mr. Business, as if he had just emerged from a restful afternoon beside the pool.

"Gypsy, would you mind getting that mixed case from the trunk. And comb your hair. Showtime."

"God," I thought, "I'm going to kill this motherfucker," as I started grabbing the wine and trying to look glamorous and refreshed. "I'm going to kill him."

The door opened. The honored guests arrived. The bash was in full swing, hors d'oeuvres, expensive clothes, a hostess clanging a silver spoon against a glass.

"And now we have our guest, Mr. Anthony Lucero of Lucero's Vineyards, to speak to us tonight."

"As I always say, there are ways to describe Miss America, and there are ways to describe a wine. And I only wish people wouldn't get them all mixed up. Just as I wouldn't say Miss America has an incomplete malo-lactic fermentation (pause for effect) I also wouldn't say that this wine has a good nose. If nose, why not legs?"

Boy, did they eat this up. I even found my energy to kill evaporating. He looked so cute in his shirt and tie. He had such charm. By the end of the evening I was warm again, basking in his reflected light. All was forgiven as we got into the car to find a motel.

"Look," Anthony said. "Liquor. Open."

I looked at him in the blinking neon light. The unsprung clock was returning.

"I didn't get enough," he said.

"OK, fine. We'll stop."

In the liquor store, it was the old moneyroll in the back pocket story. Along with chanting and some more fuck magazines. Some of the customers—pretty scary looking dudes, were watching Anthony closely.

"Hey, we're leaving now, OK? Time to find a motel. Time to go nighty-night."

At the motel, the surface tension remained poised at the edge of the glass. We read the magazines; we made love. We drank the gin-and-tonics and talked about desire. As we held each other close and watched the random freeway headlights make starlight on the stucco walls, I felt like holding the world away.

"Do you feel safe now?"

"Yes. Do you?"

"Yes. Anthony, you didn't hide the money, did you?"

"No. I won't."

"Good. It's OK here. I'm here too."

"Goodnight."

In the morning, I knew it wasn't OK. Anthony was sitting at the table. He had a guilty smile.

"Oh, shit. You said you wouldn't."

"I got up in the night. It's got to be somewhere in the room. I can't find my checkbook either."

In three hours you can look just about everywhere in a motel room. No money. No checkbook. The repetition was wearing me down. I knew what the rest of the trip was going to be like, maybe what the rest of my life was going to be like. I saw myself living in darkened rooms, searching for my keys.

Outside, the freeway was a grey curtain of noises. People were going places, getting to work on time, taking kids to school.

"I found it. It was inside the toilet paper roll. We can go now."

At some kind of surrender, I didn't fight the progress of the day. It was bigger than I was. I wasn't going to win. Maybe we would get there, and maybe we wouldn't. Maybe we would get back. I really didn't give a damn. This turned out to be a reasonable attitude, given the situation. At a vintners' convention, arrangements are always kind of iffy. As the winemakers assembled, tales of lost suitcases and missed departures were told. Arrivals at the wrong hotel, the wrong city, tickets left on benches at the station. But the grand catastrophe would go on; somehow at the appointed hour the spotless glasses would be out to pour.

"Tell you it's a professional liability. Most of these winemakers can't even remember their own phone number, much less what time their plane leaves."

Anthony and I worked his booth at the convention, poured his wine for the grazing tasters, smiled sexy smiles, and reassured them that, yes, they were saying something intelligent about the wine. Yes, they had the right to drink it. As the shadows of the day lengthened outside, the clamor settled down into the random last tasters, and we were free to swap our remaining wine. Here the good deals were made. Now was also the time to send out feelers about dinner—who would dine with whom in an elaborate political pecking order of prestige.

Anthony and I wound up at an Italian place with the right other winemakers and it soon seemed as though we were all old friends. Childhood secrets were told—confidences, hopes, and dreams. The chocolate-colored wine swirled in our glasses, as we sniffed and drank and sniffed and drank some more.

Time jumped and somehow we were back at our motel and eating again in the coffee shop. How could we be eating again? Some policemen came in for coffee, and Anthony became paranoid.

"You should go to law school. I'll give you the money. You should become a lawyer. I need a lawyer."

We left abruptly. It seemed like days later that the muffled sounds of noontime filtered underneath the drawn curtains of our room. It was time to head home. The convention was over. As we were packing up the Chevy to leave, I noticed an ordinary phone booth that seemed to ring a distant memory bell somewhere.

"Anthony, do you remember anything about fucking in that phone booth? Like last night maybe?"

"I don't know. I know I like that phone booth. I like it a lot."

I knew the journey home was going to be hard. Journeys were. We would have to drink our way up the coast in easy stages. Starting in bars at noon we could get to Hollywood the first day, Santa Barbara the second. Three days, and we would be back in the land of the familiar where Anthony had his ways. Hollywood was hard— the traffic brought out the need to get naked. At least we wouldn't be the only ones. Hollywood was crawling with mooners and streakers. Anthony was seized with the desire for clean clothes so we went into a laundromat, but he couldn't take the street life pressing in, the panhandlers watching the dryers with hungry eyes, the dealers opening shop on the hood of our car. The world was closing in on him, and I had brought him here. I, too, was part of the world out there, wasn't I? Awakening in the morning, I saw his eyes watching me like a cat's. There's nothing in a cat's eyes. They look through walls.

Suddenly I felt alone here. And vulnerable and unsure of myself and unattractive and a lot of things I hadn't been feeling for a while. I just wanted to get the trip over fast, but the pace of things was intractable, like trying to paddle in glue. It took us all day to get out of L.A. and when the cocktail hour rolled around, we were at some off-the-freeway bar in Oxnard, drinking martinis and warming up to a fight. Thirty drunken miles later we checked into a garish motel at the beach in Santa Barbara, unpacked our provisions, and proceeded to have at it. Anthony had taken a sudden dislike to the way I looked. There was something the matter with it.

"Of course there's something the matter with it. I don't have bound feet. Are you just noticing that?"

"You think you're real intelligent, don't you? Well if you were so intelligent, you'd know how to tuck in your shirt. And you don't."

Squaring off at the mirror, Anthony took the front of my black and gold silk shirt and tucked both corners back on themselves, so that the front of the shirt had the rigid appearance of a freshly made bed.

"There. Now that's a military tuck."

"Well, good. That's a big weight off my mind."

Why neatness in appearance should suddenly have become so important was unclear. Dinner now started to loom large also.

"I need to eat. If you're so tough, you can get me to a restaurant to eat dinner. I'll just leave that to you."

Buying into this, I drove us nervously around town, looking for that perfect place where Anthony could eat dinner. Boy, would I find a great place to eat, a place that would save us from this shitty turn of events, a magic place.

But the glass slippers would not slide on the puffy feet of the princess tonight. Too expensive, too crowded, too far to walk; and drunk and mad, we were at a stop light when Anthony got out of the car, announcing:

"I'm going to find a place to eat. If you were half the man you think you are, you would have found me food."

I sat there in the car, blessedly alone, in shock. Then I drove back to the Flamingo Motel and got my stuff and checked into the motel across the street. I was glad I had the car. But I was still fucked up. I loved this man as I had loved Donna and others, and I knew it was always going to be like this. Just one more time for the big emotions—up and then down and never any reasons for anything. Gestures. And real lives. I thought of my mother and her terrorist dreams. Why do that to yourself? To people you had feelings for. I just didn't want any more.

It was about midnight, and I headed down to the beach. It was an ordinary night with that calmness that all southern beaches have, that other language of reproach for the way we live. I didn't believe in God. And I didn't want to walk into the waves. But I didn't want to go on living the way I was. I wanted it to stop. And so I asked for help. I said "God, I can't do it anymore. I don't care what I have to do, but I want you to help me. I'll do whatever I have to do." And I just cried and cried and cried and stayed there under the blurry stars. After a while I felt calmer and walked back to the motel and went to sleep.

The next morning I went over to the Flamingo to pick up Anthony. Today was another day. Chances were he didn't remember the night before. Sure enough, he was almost cheery as he sat at the curtainless window looking out at the garish lawn chairs and flamingo decor. He also wanted to fuck. I guess that was his idea of making up with me.

"Is this your idea of an apology? Well, an apology is different. An apology is when you say 'Hey, I'm sorry I was an asshole and hurt your feelings last night.'"

"Me? Apologize? *Moi?*"

We drove north in a kind of burnt-out familiarity. At three o'clock we sat in a bar in Castroville and poured down a few martinis. At seven I was back at Luther's, without Anthony and with a bottle of Cuervo 1800 on the counter in front of me. I poured a tumbler full and drank all of it. Then I called Naomi and started pouring out all my miseries, blaming her for them, for not saving me from this shit, for being a coward in life. I ranted. I burst into tears. I think she hung up. I climbed the ladder to my loft and slept the sleep of the just. In the morning, the bottle of Cuervo was still there, but I knew it was over. I had no connection to it and never had. I didn't have to drink anymore.

I don't remember much about the following weeks. I know I went to work at the winery for another week. I know I didn't drink any wine. Soaked in the stuff and pouring it all day, I was without thirst. I wanted it, but it wasn't real to me. The will to do it was gone. Over a barrel of Zinfandel I handed Anthony back his keys. The keys to the winery. Keys to my heart. I drove from there to a twelve-step meeting—wine-eaten boots, wine-stained shirt, reeking of wine. Boy, were they getting a wet one. But nobody said a word. They just handed me a box of Kleenex and said, "Keep coming back." This time it sounded like a good plan. This time I didn't have any other place to go.

I couldn't imagine quitting drinking forever, but I knew I had to get back on balance. I thought it might take me a month to completely fix myself, maybe longer. A year was the longest I could imagine. In a year my whole life should be completely healed. To my surprise, instead of getting better, I started falling completely apart. I couldn't sit still in a chair; I babbled and cried at the drop of a hat. I couldn't sleep; I couldn't remember simple things. I could hardly drive. And to my surprise, those around me, instead of being glad I had quit, got huffy and annoyed. After several weeks of being a complete shit, Luther announced he wanted me to leave.

"I wanted to tell you before, but I didn't know how. That's why I've been picking on you so much. I think I want to live alone now."

I lay upstairs in my loft looking at my stuff, feeling paralyzed with fear. Where would I put it? It seemed like an overwhelming problem. But everything did. Part of it was the weight of having broken up my childhood home, and now I envisioned the remnant objects decorating Luther's dumpster. Carrying my household gods from friend's garage to friend's garage was not the way Niemanns were supposed to live. The enormity of the hole I had dug began to swallow me up. I woke up shaking from nightmares in which time became stretched, five minutes lasting five hours, a twisted version of childhood time waiting to get out of sermons and school. I called phone numbers of strangers from phone booths, shaking with hysteria and fear.

"Have you eaten breakfast yet?"

"Breakfast? No, I don't think so. But Luther's betrayed me, don't you understand, after I helped him all those months."

"Can you eat something and get to a meeting?"

"Well, yes—I guess so. I guess I can."

I ran to Naomi for support, expecting that all would be magically healed. I wasn't drinking now. I was going to be a good person; she would like that. She said she did. And invited me for weekends that turned mysteriously sour. I would arrive on Friday to find plans had been made. A straight couple from work for cocktails and dinner at some posh French place. They couldn't know we were lovers, which meant they couldn't know other things as well. Like that I was bouncing off the walls, for instance. I watched them drink the highballs of scotch, and sat on the sofa clutching club soda and twitching off to the kitchen for trendy snacks. It seemed like hours went by. The drive over the bridge, the parking place, the *maître d'*.

"And would you care to see the wine list, sir?"

Yes, they would, of course. The usual discussion ensued. The gurgling mouths and swishing glasses of the Laguna Beach Wine Tasters returned to me in a parade before my eyes.

"The Alexander Chardonnay? What do you think, Gypsy?"

"Try their Gewurtz, if you want a dry surprise."

My voice spoke from somewhere to my left, another voice than the one with the problems, the one whose cells were dying one by one. I would come to know this voice well. People would call it the voice of the disease.

I allowed my nose to brush the rim of Naomi's burgundy glass of Chardonnay, allowed the complex woody sweetness to sting. But suffering, a part of me remained motionless, outside in the cold, face pressed to the window of life, seeing only the fog on the glass. I did not pick up a drink like I would have every time before. As much as I wanted to be a part of this tableau, to belong to Naomi in her many delicious secrets—the wine among them—some new person in me said no and sat there alone keeping perfectly still, the way a deer keeps still when the sound changes.

This weekend scene was not unique. Somehow, every weekend was similar. Minefields and tripwires, drives to the wine country down memory lane. If Naomi joined me staying dry, we scarcely spoke, never made love. I called the program hotline wherever I was, tramped through hot tub retreats in Mendocino, searched out wrong addresses in storms on country roads to stay sober one more day. Like the ground settling after a quake, Naomi and I were seeking new positions. I could smell a struggle in the wind. There and everywhere.

I just couldn't seem to get along. Things were changing around me like a house of cards falling down. It was May, and spring hurt my eyes. The flowers wounded me, as if they were the vulnerable insides of the world, bleeding beauty. Everything hurt me. And everyone.

When Roma called me from Utah with the latest boomer news, I was more than ready to say *sayonora* to my whole life on the Coast.

"The streets are paved with gold out here," she said. "I made five thousand last month, and there's no end in sight. They're trying to raise this track across the Salt Lake, and frankly, I think it's going to take a while. None of the homeboys want to work the work trains, and so there's lots of jobs for us."

"The desert," I thought. "No wineries," I thought. "The kind of place where people put ice cubes in their wine," I thought. Utah was where I needed to be.

7
THIS IS
THE PLACE

WHAT IS A spiritual journey? To set out in search of something, confident you will find it or that you will yourself become its location. In those spring months I lay in my loft above Luther the Millionaire's mansion and read *Death Comes for the Archbishop* and dreamed of the desert. A place where the baggage of life falls away and there is only sky. It is the workshop for the last phase of an artist's life, the minimalist period, where thought is free to write its enigmatic own name. The desert has always meant this, has always attracted extremists looking for God's home or their own promised land.

Willa Cather's space, as I lay amid the ruins of my history, called me.

> Elsewhere the sky is the roof of the world; but here the earth was the floor of the sky. The landscape one longed for when one was far away, the thing all about one, the world one actually lived in, was the sky, the sky!
>
> Travelling with Eusabio was like travelling with the landscape made human.

When Westerners want to find themselves, they go look at the land; they travel. They find a mirror that looks outward and describe the geography of a certain frontier. Even today, like Major

Powell, we seek the blank space on all the existing maps, knowing, as no doubt he did, that the unknown river is in the mind, and all we seek is the empty space to discover it in.

I wanted to become my own story, as Dickens puts it, to find out who was the hero of my own life. I had told my story many times in bars, elaborating the fantastic, the grotesque, the dangerous. I had traveled in the manner of embellishment, knew all the side roads where one stopped at small wineries to taste, to lose days and weekends, to create a parallel life—a life of dreams into which my lifeblood and spiritual river was slowly draining away. At some point the two worlds merged, and I began to live in the other one. I had crossed the famous line. Sobriety brought me to understand this, but the map of my travels and its habits of thought remained. They were waiting for me everywhere. All I could think of was to outrun them and set out hopefully on the road to the desert lands.

Highway 80 is a straight shot from Oakland to Salt Lake City. All my possessions were in storage, my Chevy sold, and I was driving an inherited car, a Toyota with 12,000 miles on it. I was determined to drive it to death, which I finally did in El Paso, popping its toy tires like balloons in the freightyard, and stuffing its unforgiving interior with the possessions of the end of the line. For now, though, it was light and it moved fast—a thin shell hydroplaning toward Utah where God lived and money grew thick and green.

It got dark as I was driving through Winnemucca; slowly, the shapes hugging the Humboldt River darkened, and the river itself became a silver band, became a reflective steel rail before it disappeared into its own sound, into its domination of the night. The river, like the highway, was paralleled by rails running east. I had followed them over the Sierras through Truckee, past Sparks, and now at Winnemucca heading north. There wasn't much traffic, but I was glad to see a few freights, railpacks mostly, with ten units pulling over the ragged volcanic terrain. I intended to join that bloodstream, let it take my life, dominate my rhythms of sleep and thought, and put me among strangers in places I had never been. I wanted to go to the limits, the end of track, until I was absorbed, until the person I knew did not exist or had become one with her story.

I got off the road at Carlin, knowing it was a change point for crews from Ogden and Sparks. Gretchen had spent a lot of time here, and at first glance I didn't see how. A typical Nevada outpost, mostly gas stations, that thin veneer of commerce right along the roadway but no town behind it—nothing but the life carried in by the road. It had a railroad life also, but that life was sad now, a shadow of itself. In the bars you would meet the old men here who used to work in the roundhouse or as trackwalkers, but who had no jobs now to pass on to their grandsons and no one to understand the work they did.

It seemed like everyone lived in trailers. A fly-by-night state of one-arm bandits and hookers on wheels, like Waterbed Mary, the CB callgirl who operated out of her Dodge van in truckstops from Reno to Wendover. Ten-four goodbuddy. Put it on the Master-charge. Where nine-to-fivers come to play, to throw money at the machines, like the machines that eat their lives and dole out pay-checks, but this time there is a shot at the jackpot, a sucker's bet, but the only one they've got. A form of the desert, Nevada is, of course, a shrine. The silver dollar. The place where you go to touch money, to handle what it is you sell your life for and to experience the history of the country, what it was the white man wanted head-ing west. Gold in the earth, silver clinking in your pockets, a chance in life.

Intersected by interstates carrying long black limos with the win-dows blackened out, harboring silos and herds of sheep that sud-denly stiffen and fall in the pastures, this is a free zone where the rules do not apply. Scary Nevada, no place for a canary.

At Wells, the neon crossroads, I find a motel, pull in next to the blazers and campers and long American cars. I don't sleep well. The whole town is one big bar. My shadow self would love this town, love to carry a paper sack from the corner store and settle back into ease in a motel room, in front of the tube, later to drive wildly through unfamiliar streets to find a local bar and a friendly stranger and talk about the fucked-up world. A stranger to them and to myself now, I spend a night watching at my own bedside, watching this woman struggle with voices in her dreams, night-hawks descending to pluck out her eyes, motorcycle headed for the wall. The crash never comes, never comes.

This being a year of great floods, all the rivers had their strength, and the high desert lay saturated with impromptu lakes and wet mirages. The Bonneville Salt Flats appeared white and wet in a ghostly imitation of Lake Bonneville and previous geological memory. A trick of vision and you could see the land the way it was, and then its present form returns, the imposition of the familiar mileposts, billboards—welcome to Wendover where the West begins—the neon cowboy. What West? I thought. The wild West? I was coming from the West. Crossing into Utah, there was nothing. Nothing but the zone system of light on water, salt, and distant ranges. The highway followed the outside curve of the eastward range; it was starting to feel the shape of the lake, being forced to its conformity. The lake became more and more insistent, the road and the rails running beside it hugged the base of the mountains, and suddenly the lake was there—vast and chemical and still.

Nothing lived in it except the brine shrimp, tiny eyeless creatures harvested with huge nets. Evaporation pools trap the minerals for the two salt companies working each end of the lake. They use a strange and primitive chemical agriculture, their flat fields ruling off the water into different-colored sections; the lake itself bisected by the Southern Pacific track, one side red, the other greenish, according to the mineral concentrations. This happens because Salt Lake has no outlet; it is completely enclosed, a freakish fact of nature.

The road was skirting the lake now, whose dreamy presence created a blankness, causing me to float. The world was wet, clouds moving across its reflective surfaces like thoughts. In the distance an Arabian pavilion appeared to float on the water, its four globular turrets as white as salt, water lapping at its pillars. "Is this the Mormon Temple?" I thought, prepared by the desert dreamspace to believe anything. As I got closer, the image materialized into a bathing establishment eaten by the flooding lake, moated and resting in Venetian dignity as a roadside warning. Here lie the edifices of the world. All is changeable.

I located Roma in a basement apartment in Ogden, working the extra board and making hordes of money. Ogden had been a high seniority terminal for a long time, since there weren't many locals, and the only through freight run went to Carlin, Nevada—a distance of over 250 miles. Since brakemen get paid by the mile, a day's pay being 100 miles, a run to Carlin and back paid you five days' pay. Make one trip a week, and you still had a check for $2,000 every payday. The flooding lake, however, had changed the picture. The Southern Pacific tracks ran across the lake on a fill that rested on a natural salt bridge no one knew the depth of. As the lake rose, the waves began breaking over the engines of Amtrak, frightening the passengers. It was either abandon the track and go around the lake, or raise the tracks to keep pace with the lake. The Southern Pacific reasoned that it would have to pay crews even more money to run around the lake. This annoyed them. They decided to do battle with nature; it was more satisfying. They had won against the Salton Sea, why not the Salt Lake?

They put three work trains on duty seven days a week, twelve hours a day. They brought in their track-laying machines and maintenance-of-way work gangs. They quarried rock and started dumping. They raised the track three feet. The lake rose three feet. They threw old boxcars in as jetties. The waves broke against them, throwing salty mist in your face if you had to get off the engine. The salt crust dried on your clothes, stiffening them. The maintenance-of-way foreman got surlier and surlier. They were a ramrod bunch anyway, picked for their ability to push. This situation broke their hearts. You could dump rock for twelve hours and come back the next morning to find the lake had eaten it up again. It would be worse than before. They just got madder and kept dumping.

The Ogden homeboys didn't care to work these jobs. They were used to riding the cushions on that long run to Carlin, not eating granite dust and swatting salt flies for twelve hours. The salt flies, like the brine shrimp, were another freak of the lake's ecology. Where nothing else could live, they thrived. Tiny and swarming, they attacked by sheer numbers. You breathed them. They covered the windows in the engine, blocking the light. They formed a foot-thick carpet on the floor. Their juicy bodies slicked the track so that the hoghead had to sand for traction. The salt flies were joined, in their celebration of life, by the Brazilian spiders. These tiny creatures had been introduced by the railroad to eat the flies, as in the story. This they did, but not with sufficient rapacity to deprive themselves of a food chain. The two species achieved peaceful coexistence on the lake; the rusting boxcars shoring up the ruins were woven with ghostly webs as were the switch stands and anything left standing more than a few days. The crusted salt and droplets of waves were held like ornaments in these frantic and chaotic webs. It was their turf. We were the aliens.

Gretchen had moved to Ogden ahead of Roma, and she was settled in with some old head conductor. Roma was playing the field, and apparently they had some tussle about it, Gretchen saying Roma was giving women brakemen "a bad name," and Roma making disparaging remarks about Gretchen's sex life.

"People with a good sex life of their own don't go gossiping about other people's sex lives."

Well, I thought, if that were true, the entire town of Ogden was having a crummy sex life.

"If the shoe fits, honey, climb into the pumpkin."

Roma wasn't impressed with the social climate in Utah. She saw it primarily as a money farm occupied by barefoot and pregnant women ("teenagers!") and overstuffed boy-scout male chauvinist pigs. As Roma saw her mission in life to be the education of men, she had her work cut out for her. I would fill the bill as reinforcements, and with the speed of a drill sergeant she had me briefed on the markup rules exam and how to work the Ogden extra board.

"You've got to watch these crew dispatchers. They play favorites for the homeboys, and they'll cut you off right before you stand to catch a mainline run and call you back two hours later to catch a work train. Or they'll set you up to miss a call or just mark up someone they like ahead of you. Always know your extra board and always get the name of the dispatcher. It really helps to go out with the dispatchers, to tell you the truth."

"Well, I mean they can't do that shit. You can time slip 'em."

"This is Utah. I heard that they cut a boomer off in the middle of winter and told the guy 'I hope you and your family starve to death.'"

"It's hard to imagine anyone being that shitty. Why do they care?"

"It's a different world out here. A different world."

After I was squared away at the depot, Roma and I went out on the town to do some serious country and western dancing. This was the first time I had been to a bar sober, and I just wasn't sure about it. It was a typical roadhouse on the outskirts of town, a log cabin, bikes-outside kind of place. The kind of place I used to love. Now, I noticed the dirt, the smell of stale beer, sweat, and rancid tobacco smoke. "God," I thought, "what a toilet." Were they all that way? All those magic nights I used to have. All toilets?

Roma had a good time, though, yehawing and yelling bullsheyit, the way we learned to do in Texas. Roma could always amuse herself at a bar by picking some huge redneck to harangue about women's rights. You could tell that Roma was ready to wind things up when she started calling her adversary a Nazi. That was her exit line. The guy usually retreated at that point because other people would stare and gather around. Nobody likes Nazis. Roma didn't get to the Nazi stage until closing time, and it was three before we got back to her apartment. I had just closed my eyes when the phone rang.

"Niemann, run to Carlin, on duty 4:30."

As I drove down to the depot it was raining again. Ogden didn't look like it could take much more rain. The rivers were up to the top, not to mention the lake, and the whole town was at the bottom of a dam. I began to worry about Roma's basement apartment. The yard at Ogden belonged to the D&RGW, and their switch crews worked the trains. That's the Denver and Rye-o-Grande Western, as I was informed. All Southern Pacific crews did was get on their trains and ride. I was designated head brakeman so I could ride the engine and get to know the territory, and the sun was coming up as we headed onto the lake, the track just feet away from the water, now forming breakers with the north wind.

"Lucky it's a norther. Them southwinds are the worst. There must be fifty feet of mud on either side of these tracks, and nobody knows how deep this salt bridge goes. Engine go off the rail and it'd be years before they found you."

Hogheads are not a comforting bunch. They have lots of time on their hands to think about escape routes in case of disaster. They tend to brood about it. But this situation would have them stumped. There was no place to run to. Past the old trestle, a former solution to where to put the tracks, we head out into open water which now resembles the ocean Brigham Young mistook it for. The surf picked up. Waves sent salt spray against the windows coating them with crust. This was getting interesting.

The big danger was that the waves would eat a channel somewhere on the track and allow the high side of the lake to equalize with the low side. This would inundate miles and miles of track and create nearly impossible conditions for repairing it. The solution was for the railroad to either create a channel themselves or raise the tracks out of reach. The latter plan was in trouble. The right-of-way on either side of the track was so eaten away in some places it was hard to get a truck over it. And this was after months of work. There was a promontory halfway across the lake where the tracks skirted land for a while. The Southern Pacific had set up a work camp here for the track project. It was called lakesite and it consisted of a few trailers and a dining car. The nearest civilization was an army test site twenty miles away. We passed lakesite around seven in the morning, and the work train and track crews were standing beside the rails waiting for the last westbound to cross so that they could close their "window" and get to work. A window was a section of track that was being worked on. Like a window, it was either open or closed. It had stopped raining now, and the ground was steaming where the sun was. The track crew stood around in the little patches of sun, wearing their heavy coveralls and drinking coffee. Great bundles of ties lay on either side of the track.

Once off the lake, we started to climb. There was still snow in late May, and the quality of light had the clarity of cold weather. From here on in to Carlin it was all the hoghead's show. All switches were CTC, meaning the dispatcher in Roseville lined us in and out of sidings, and my job consisted of calling out the signals in a ritual with the engineer and checking our train behind us for telltale sparks from sticking brakes. The temptation was, at moments like this, to get comfortable. To kind of settle back and drift. That's usually when you went into big hole, when the brakes set up, and it was time to get out and walk the train.

This was a good run, however, and we got into Carlin around dinnertime. We made a zipper change at the depot, the outgoing crew swinging on as we swung off, trainman's grips hanging from our shoulders. Tired and dirty, we headed for the company dorms. Most of the regular crew had second cars at these remote terminals, usually big hogs with sprung seats and rusted underbellies. Comfortable old cars. The crew was mostly old heads, and they insisted on taking me to Wells for dinner and the slots. You just didn't move from one town to another on this run; you traveled from holiness to sin personified. I began to get the picture. Mormon Ogden— no booze, no gambling, no redlight district, no coffee in the depot. Carlin in the state of Nevada, and twenty miles away in Wells they had it all. What a set-up for a rail. No wonder the old heads were jealous about these runs.

It seemed like I was under a lot of pressure to drink.

"You want to have a what? You mean you're not going to have a drink with us? Well, you're no fun at all."

I was getting the picture that in Utah not drinking meant something different than in California. Californians are into health. Tell them that you've decided that food is bad for you, and you are now going to live on air, and they will look thoughtful and consider the proposition. Anything for health. But in Utah, not drinking meant you were being good, as in saintly. Anybody with even a hint of rebellion in them drank, even if they didn't like to drink. Now, to be considered a goody-goody went against my grain. I had put so much effort into being bad that this supposition was infuriating. Rails were also suspicious of a nondrinker because of the Company. You might be a fink. The Mormon rails, however, were double suspicious, since they assumed anyone who didn't drink would tell on them. Even people who did drink told on them, but anonymously. This telling on people was a big feature of the culture, like a social duty. So here I was in the role of a girl scout fink. Oh yes, and they couldn't place me sexually either, so that made me even more suspect. And I wasn't likely to turn up a sex partner in the near future, since sobriety had left me terrified of people. I couldn't imagine having sex with anyone. It would be like making love in a cafeteria with all the lights on.

This image of myself as an uptight, legs-crossed, potential fink annoyed me, but I had an understanding of how it came about. I was starting to be able to see how things worked. There were types that people expect to see, types they try to fit themselves into. If you don't fit into one, you are invisible. People can't tell what age or sex you are. If they can put you into a type, they will, and then they will see everything you do as supporting that role. I felt my personal history being reconstructed around me, as if I had been worked on by a moral chiropractor. I sensed I wasn't long for Utah.

Here you buy "set ups" in bars—mixers, virgin margaritas, all the exotic drinks. Then out comes the ubiquitous brown paper bag, airport shot bottles in purses, booze everywhere. I thought only alcoholics carried their own booze in brown paper bags in case the party didn't have enough. Just to drink in Utah, everyone was acting like alcoholics—the secrecy, the furtive pleasure, the remorse. "Wow," I thought, "far out." To go out nightclubbing meant "joining" every club that served liquor. These set-ups also cost as much as real drinks. I was paying for the illegality of fun, and I wasn't even drinking. I felt ripped off, outraged.

Well, I thought, I still have the gay life. At least I can do something that has the patina of stealth. But the scene here was, if anything, worse. I found nameless, lightless toilets with doors at the back—entrance through the parking lot please. Women sat in tight clumps at tables or huddled over beers at the bar, hawkishly surveying the empty dance floor. I would have needed a battleship to get through the ice here. Seven-Up wasn't going to do much, combined with my peeled self-confidence. I would spend hours searching for these bars, exploring dark parking lots, looking for the hidden address, and then stay ten minutes, counting them in exquisite vulnerability. Fun night out, huh?

It was beginning to dawn on me just how sick I was. I certainly hadn't expected it to take months to get over withdrawal symptoms. I seemed to get worse and worse. My mind wasn't working right. I couldn't concentrate or remember things. I had near misses in traffic, blanking out at intersections, losing my way in an easy town to know, driving for hours just to be moving, unable to sit in a chair—to sit still at any time. I felt an enormous pressure in my chest, as if every emotion possible had just doubled inside my brain and was going to burst out, destroying its human host. This explosion was likely to happen anywhere—in Denny's, on the freeway, standing beside the track with ten macho guys watching me. I also had no physical stamina. I was exhausted after being awake for three hours. It was a good thing I was on these do-nothing work trains and these long-haul mainline runs. Working as a switchman would have been beyond me, both mentally and physically. I probably would have killed someone.

Trying to understand what was happening and to find someone to talk to, I sought out twelve-step meetings. I was starting to get an idea of how dangerous a spot I was in—strange town, no friends, hostility at work, the only social life in a bar scene. But it seemed like meetings in Utah attracted only the lowest bottom drunks. There were very few young people. The prevailing climate of hypocrisy made it doubly hard to admit to being an alcoholic. It was better to stay in the closet, watch the deadly stillness in the clean streets, in the trimmed lawns and shiny new four-wheel drives, solid stone houses, and women hiding bottles in the basement, smashing them with hammers inside plastic bags, hands cut from wounds they will lie about or not remember when it's time to set the dinner table and wake up for the second day to begin for them. But alcoholic? Never. And the meetings were sad because the people really believed they had been defeated by the truth about themselves instead of feeling rescued by it.

All the women here seem to be married at fourteen, with four babies and one on the way. The men have the jobs, the power. Fat cows graze in the pastures, fences ruling off the land. There are social programs, clean streets, crosswalks that chirp for the blind, libraries with strange omissions on the shelves, and lots of souvlaki stands. People ask you the most personal questions about your life, and then if you try to deflect them, they think you haven't heard the question and ask you again. Are you married? Why not? Why don't you want children? Why did you leave home? Why do you want to work? Why do you want to do a man's job? Do you think you're a man? Do you go to church? Why not?

I finally started saying "Look, why don't you make up a questionnaire, and I'll fill it out. That way you won't have to stand here asking me all these rude questions."

This went over their heads. They would screw up their faces, tilt their heads, and say something like "You're real moody. You ought to find yourself a husband and settle down."

Could I talk to them? Where would I start? In the sixties, explain about how it was getting married in the sixties, how you had open relationships where all your friends took acid and went to bed together so you could change the world and stop the war. Explain about the acid—how you could spend hours and days looking at a shag rug, thinking it was God. How the two words for life were "wow" and "far out." How the most important thing in the world was to get as far away from your family as possible, because you didn't want them bugging you about who you were sleeping with, as if you could remember. How you took drugs all the time. And how it was OK for men to be lovers with men and women with women because nobody could lay a power trip on anybody about anything, because nobody had any answers because soldiers were bayoneting babies in Viet Nam and Watts was burning at home and we were going to start at zero. And so I could say, "Yes, I was married," but it wouldn't convey information here. It wouldn't mean I was "married" like you mean married. And I helped raise some kids, four with my husband and three with my woman lover, but that isn't information for you either. And about the job, well, that's a history course too, but the bottom line is that I am just here working. I'm single. I have been for a while. And even if I weren't I'd still be working. And I shouldn't have to explain it. I exist.

Curious, I began to read about the culture, the life of Joseph Smith, the goldwitch, and the phenomenally successful social network. The biblical landscape almost demands something like this religion here. Its map fits well. And Jesus was here in North America, Joseph Smith tells us; in the three days spent dead he traveled here to include us in history. The young goldwitch prophet, beginning to believe his own smooth con, becomes his own story and plays it well, plays the last act very well, And then the incredible migration west, and with such moral superiority to the goldrushing adventures. The Mormon pioneers were after something more to be prized than much fine gold, and sweeter than honey in the honeycomb. Their real hard luck was to be subject to historiography, being stuck with a verifiable past. Nobody inquires too closely into Jesus' miracles. Did the Red Sea part? We can't tell. Those are mythologies having the truth of age, of long believe. The Latter Day Saints have a bigger credibility gap, as the phrase goes.

On a journey of discovery, I had driven into a metaphor, a text imprinted on a landscape. I could see how it happened—the dead sea, the extremity of the location, its emptiness, the seagulls emblematic of the desire to reach the Coast. It was waiting for them, for its writer to perceive the text. What a vision.

But for me, the casting was wrong. I would have preferred Barbara Stanwyk for Joseph Smith. Bette Davis for Brigham Young. Then I would have stayed. My deseret. The woman in me was tired of this patriarchal text. My precious individualism was outraged by the place. The beehive. Where were the cultural rebels? What was all this sneaking around? Why were there no Hawaiian shirts in the thrift stores?

I bid in a job with Roma and the resident woman brakeman Frankie on a worktrain. We dumped rock all day trading off being the one on the ground with a radio, giving instructions to the hoghead on when to move. The other crew members did important things like cook elaborate lunches in the caboose. We began to barbecue. If we weren't careful we'd get ourselves run off our own job; we made it too much fun. Soon we heard that Maureen was coming too. Ogden was experiencing a cultural jolt—five women brakemen working out of its nepotistic, sweet thing ("We got a sweet little thing going here, boys") terminal. The response was different than in Tucson. The Ogden old heads looked on the influx of female talent as a pool for potential young wives. They thought we were here looking for husbands; the idea that we were competition for jobs never dawned on them.

Maureen arrived at the end of June and moved in with Roma and me. Actually, she moved into my closet; Roma was a little short on space. Within two hours, Maureen's closet looked like a college dorm room, covered with snapshots, souvenirs, and touches of home. As soon as the sun went down, Roma and Maureen were dressed to go trolling in Ogden's hot nightspots. In the past, I would have been with them. But now I felt frightened to go, outnumbered by the drinkers, afraid I couldn't find an exit line. I stayed home, went to bed haunted by fun. Fun I couldn't have anymore, flashes of billboards alongside the road, advertising tropical places, a woman in a bikini, a palm tree, a champagne glass in her hand. "Oh," I thought, "I can't go there. They drink champagne." I was getting the message all right—the subtext, the code. But I didn't feel the choice—to go and not drink. Impossible, I thought. I can't go there.

At three the party returned, hostages in tow, through my room, bumbling in the dark, into the closet for the night. Giggles, the story of Maureen's life, the snapshots shown, the sounds of happy drunks.

"Will you please shut the fuck up. I have the lights off. I have my eyes closed. You can assume that I am enjoying being asleep."

"Well, I'm sorr-ee. After all, I live here too."

"Could you just keep it fucking quiet. I'm first fucking out and I just might want some sleep, if you don't mind."

"Gypsy, you have really changed. I mean, you ought to think about it."

Incapable of handling this, I got dressed and left. Driving around Ogden at three-thirty in the morning, looking for shelter, the sleazy motel. No phone in the room, I miss my call for work. Maureen is next on the board, and takes it, hungover and happy from sex. Unfucked, undrunk, and miserable, I pondered my next move. On down the line seemed best. Why stay here and ruin all my friendships while I figured out how to function without booze? The process clearly was going to take longer than I thought, and it was going to have a lot more loneliness in it than I thought. I'd heard about Tucumcari, the loneliest outpost on the Southern Pacific system, and I decided to go there. It seemed like a good idea at the time.

8
CADILLAC
RANCH

TWO DAYS LATER I left Utah, driving the desert road toward New Mexico. After two months of constantly cutting me off the board and otherwise hassling me for being there, when the trainmaster's queen-bee secretary heard that I wanted to leave, of course she told me I couldn't leave. She liked telling people, particularly young women, that they couldn't do things. Well, I left; the agreement holds us thirty days. But they don't think we can read, or something.

Sweet highway, heading northeast. I could feel some of the problems blowing off my shoulders, hope on that center line, a new town, new place, towards more emptiness my bag of hurts hadn't filled up yet. Toward an unmarked canvas, an unwritten page. Toward a meeting with myself at track's end, country's end, as far in the future as I could push it.

Afternoon rain slicked the highway as I passed through small Mormon towns. I could feel the family closeness, knew that everyone was watching and being watched. A live soap. It got to be dinnertime, and I found myself at an intersection staring at Mom's cafe, a tawny brick building with a square Western facade and pickup trucks parked everywhere. Home cooking, the sign added gratuitously. I tried to remember the three warnings of the West: never eat at a place called Mom's, never play cards with a man called

Doc, what was the third? I ate at Mom's anyway. What the hell. The place was filled with families and men coming in after work. I stare at the local paper and wonder if I want to drive all night. One of the fringe benefits of being a brakeman—turning day into night. It's like living near the Pole; it's always daytime for a rail. On the map I find Moab, like the name, and mark it for my destination for today.

What I really want is to derail somewhere, not to go on with this pursuit of work, to come to rest so that the babble can stop, so that an overwhelming beauty can color me. There could be no further beauty than this country here, chocolate mesa fingers washed in lavender distances, streaks of green and rose, the grey highway following the contours of the land, Navajo sandstone bluffs turned on a lathe, saturation of color dependent on the changing light, a landscape continually repainting itself. I could have just stopped here, let the railroad find me, let my careening mind go on alone. I could have just stopped, but instead drove on, pushed the curtain of evening through the deeper canyonlands courting the swollen rush of the Colorado River. Hearing her now in the dark, I take only one breath of her swift presence, and then I flee. I inhale the icy ideas of her, get close to the great geographical imperative, the defining arterial fact of the Western states, feel her power, her tumbling mist on my face, and I turn away to the south. Like my own power, my own river of strength within, it is too mysterious and frightening now. Drawn to it, I turn away when I feel its presence near me.

The town of Moab appeared out of the silence of canyonlands like the neon blaze of Reno out of the high desert. Motels and hotels, kayak rentals and four-wheel trips, Americans playing hard in their two-week vacations. Ghetto blasters raging in the campgrounds till after midnight, sounds of drunken arguments centering on concepts of manhood, fights over fender benders in overcrowded trailer parks. I put in my brakeman's earplugs and sleep next to my car. I still feel peeled. Way too vulnerable to be in a herd of yahoos having fun. I want a library-like silence stretching from the Rockies to the Sea of Cortez. I find such a haven in Tucumcari, home of 2,000 motel rooms and 4,000 souls.

Tucumcari stands at the beginning of the panhandle and the

end of the canyonlands, where the erosions and canyons are shallow but still rust-colored, where there is more flatland and grasses and less gorge and riverbed. The Canadian River borders the town, forms amiably into man-made lakes, and continues as a warm desert stream, spending most of its energy underground. Cottonwoods and humidity mark its presence in the landscape. It being summer, the sky is dominant with thunderheads and dark slanting bridges to the earth, seen a few miles off but gone when you get there. Only a transitory dampness sinking into the fragrant sand. It can rain a few feet away, as you stand dry in the raincloud's cool shadow. The rattlesnakes thrive and grow long and fat with eating prairie dogs and mice.

Everything in the town was falling down: paint peeling, adobe crumbling, phones broken and unrepaired since Mountain Bell moved to Clovis. I found the dusty station and ghostly freightyard baking in the 100-degree heat and met the new trainmaster, a huge man bumped to this outpost as punishment and marking time until he could take his pension. His look was long suffering, but he was trying to change it into the hostility trainmasters were supposed to project. It didn't quite come off. It was just too hot. He went through the usual harassment interview and handed me the two-hundred-question rules exam. After I had sweated through it one more time, I marked up as a Tucumcari brakeman on the extra board.

For the first time in my life I was really alone. I checked into a seedy motel and paid by the week. The manager was an alcoholic who had come out here with his wife to try to make something work out. This was their retirement move, and they had taken on the motel sight unseen, with just an assurance from the owner that Tucumcari's fortunes were on the upswing. The second week I was there, a drunk driver drove his car into their living room while they were eating breakfast.

"It's a good thing it happened when it did, because any other time I'd a been sitting there on the couch watching the TV, and he'd have hit me sure as taxes."

The manager looked at me resentfully as if all this was somehow my fault. If only he had charged me more rent, his life might be better. I thought they were ripping me off as it was. My room was a dump, and I only spent two nights a week in it anyway, but I could tell that they resented my being there at all, using the swamp cooler or turning on a tap. They probably resented my being young and having a good job and having the freedom to turn up in a place like Tucumcari and leave again.

I didn't have a phone and couldn't get one unless I was willing to wait a month and pay an outrageous fee. And so I used my trainman's right to be called by a callboy who would knock on my door an hour before they needed me. I phoned Naomi every week from the only working pay phone in town, outside the 7-11 store. It was kind of beautiful sometimes, talking outside when summer thunderheads would come sweeping by in the late afternoon and dump a few feet away, filling the air with the smell of wet dust and static. Since there were three phones in a row you could also eavesdrop on other people's lives—one of the only sources of amusement in Tucumcari. The eavesdropping was different here than in Utah, however. There wasn't that disapproving edge, that stiffening moral cloud hanging overhead. Folks here were just plain nosy. They didn't want to be the only ones with their laundry hanging out to dry. The Tucumcari laundromat or beauty parlor was a hotbed of information.

"Did you say you worked for the railroad, honey? Why that other girl that does—you know Sandy Burnett—just bought a house on the eastside, you know the one. I gave her a perm just the other day, looks right nice on her. Look good on you too. Say I heard she had some trouble the other night, was drinking and driving that car of hers too fast through town, gave the trooper some lip, too, I heard. Don't tell her I said so, but you know this is a small town and not much gets by. Not much at'all. Where you from, honey? What does your boyfriend think about you bein' way out here?"

The railroad small world did me one favor out here, though, when I recognized Cadillac, the old head I worked with in El Centro, climbing off a caboose in the Tucumcari yard. Although I hadn't realized it then, he had impressed me because he was a sober man. Impressed me and made me feel slightly uncomfortable. Now I was just glad to see him, as if a cobweb feeling had been brushed away.

"I saw your name on the extra board. I figured it was you."

"Well you look right at home here. I thought you had a horse ranch and everything in El Centro."

"Decided to move it on out here. Say, I heard one of them Louisiana boys talking about you, saying women don't belong on the railroad. I told him the way it was. That he ought to be glad we got one that does her work. And that's just the truth."

"Well, these old boys here don't seem to want me to do any work. I had a conductor the other day order me to sit on the caboose. Said his wife would kill him if she heard he made me walk the train. I wanted to get off that crummy and get away from his foul cigar."

"Yeah, I know the one. God I hate a cigar."

The mainline run from Tucumcari was to Carrizozo, a distance of 180 miles. The tracks ran along the ridges of the Sacramento Mountains, averaging 6,000 feet. It was a roller coaster run, a hoghead's show to handle the air on a long train over such undulating territory. A lot of the new engineers weren't up to it, and it was common for trains to break in two because of problems with slack. This provided the train crew with their only exercise on this run—changing knuckles. There were no industries to spot, no cars to pick up, and the snakes were so bad that trainmen didn't usually walk their trains at every siding. They just wandered off a little into the desert and turned off their light, or hunkered down behind a tumbleweed and smoked. When the slack started to run, signaling she was starting to pull, the rear man would appear about twenty cars up the train, and swing aboard. When they had the Navajo track gangs in to replace the ties on this run, they spent more time killing rattlers than they did laying rail.

For a trainman, this run was a twelve-hour stretch of trying to stay awake and keep the hoghead awake. Since business was booming, you often got only eight or ten hours off between runs. As soon as you had your "rest" you were back on a train. Never the same hours of sleep, no pattern from day to day, week to week, month to month. Once on the train, there was no place to take a break, no stopping for coffee or meals. And nothing but darkness and desert to look at. Under these circumstances, people doze off occasionally. I was having additional problems with the schedule. I used to use alcohol to get to sleep immediately after a run, but now my body was on its own. Often I couldn't sleep and would end up having to stay awake two days or nights at a stretch, until I could collapse at the appropriate time for the railroad's needs. Railroad accidents get blamed on alcohol, but the true culprit is lack of sleep. The newspaper never reports whether the engineer tried to lay off and was refused, or how many twelve-hour days in a row he has put in. It was not uncommon for crews to work steadily for months with no days off—no time to get fully rested, pay bills, do laundry, put gas in the car. Legally, you die on the federal Hours-of-Service law after twelve hours, but there is no regulation about how many of those days can occur back to back. Twelve hours from midnight to noon is a long time after a month of it with short sleep at the home terminal and disturbed sleep in the substandard company dorms at the change point.

The company lodging at Carrizozo was a case in point. The buildings had been thrown together in two weeks, using the cheapest possible materials. The walls were so thin you could hear trainmen snoring in adjacent rooms, and when a crewcaller came to pound on a door to give someone a call, the whole row of rooms shook. Since this was happening at intervals all day and all night, it was hard to get undisturbed sleep. They had located the dorms, moreover, four hundred yards from the mainline which was on a grade. All day and all night you heard ten units of power opening up to pull out of town, it often seemed, directly through your room. The walls would vibrate with a continuous diesel throb, chug-a-chug-a-chug-a whirr, chug-a-chug-a-chug-a whirr, hmmmmmmmm-mmm, varoom. Objects would dance on the window baseboards. There were two ways to sleep through it—get dead drunk or get completely exhausted. The union complained about the noise level, and the Feds came by with a noise-o-meter and pronounced the levels acceptable. I couldn't imagine when they had done the testing. When there were no trains around, obviously. Or did this say something about all the levels the Feds say are unharmful?

At any rate, I wasn't drinking, so I had to get frazzled before I could sleep. And other than sleeping, there wasn't much for a sober person to do in Carrizozo. It was a mountain town of about 2,000 people and four eating establishments, two of which weren't open much. The other two catered to rails and were primarily bars. One of these was subsidized by the railroad to provide an open restaurant for crews at any time of night. The owner took the money and invested it in enlarging the bar. He was no dummy. He made a lot of money off the rails. Well, what were the choices? No moviehouse, no library, no gym, no twenty-four-hour coffeeshop, no bookstore, no pleasant place to hang out in at the dorms—just one big rec room with one TV set tuned to a sports or soft-core violent porn movie channel. No place to store bicycles or play an instrument or work out. Of course people went to the bar. You couldn't even listen to a radio in your room without waking up the whole row. And when the railroad decided to get punitive and crack down on drinking, did they stop subsidizing the bar? provide recreational alternatives? open a decent meals-only restaurant? Hell, no. They just hired spotters to hang out in the bar they subsidized to turn people in. The owner provided both the finks and the booze. Sober in Carrizozo, I sat in my room and read. I took up jogging and ran the dirt trails leading towards the base of the mountains. I played my flute over the hum of the laundry machines, sat on the fresh towels and tried to carve out some good space for myself, space that would bring my strength back, something that seemed far away and long gone.

The only benevolence around was what came from New Mexico itself, the landscape I passed through at different times of day or night. I can only say that it was never the same picture. I never got tired of it, I never felt I had been there before. It was the quality of the light and its constant subtle changes. I got lost in it the way I got lost in Monet's *Water Lilies* in its serene room at the Museum of Modern Art. Here ranchos needed thirty acres to feed one cow, and the land was for the most part undivided by fences, and the fences themselves were only wire stapled to mesquite posts, collecting tumbleweeds and blown debris. The small towns we ran through—Santa Rosa, Vaughn, Corona—were poor. But commonly a run-down stucco house or beat-up trailer would have a brand new horsetrailer in the yard, and beautiful animals munching hay under a lean-to. Their houses weren't much, but the horses traveled first class. The air was filled with the scent of pinyon, juniper, and mesquite, sometimes in bursts of fragrance released by a sudden rainstorm. A high-moving cloud would darken the greens of the trees, and the red-stippled soil would saturate and blacken. Then patches of light and dark would dance on the amphitheater of the rounded mountaintops.

It was looking out on this panoramic emptiness from the window of a moving train that I began my slow understanding of what serenity could be. My mind was a whirlwind, a spinning vortex of resentments, anger, and fear. These psychic tornadoes could spin themselves out here without encountering traffic jams or social relations. The other rails thought of me as antisocial. Aside from the small twelve-step meetings I attended in Tucumcari, this was true. It seemed like Tucumcari only had about six people in the program, and a lot of them were as new at this as I was. I went places with these people occasionally, and once I went out on the town with the other woman brakie, Sandy. The bar scene, however was too overpoweringly unattractive. No beautiful people in the fast lane here. Just balls-out, roaring, fighting drunks. Sandy and I tried to be sociable and picked up some construction workers from the project out at the dam. Like everyone else in the bar, however, they were too drunk to dance or talk. I got vertigo, wondering if I was going to get puked on in the middle of a two-step. And so I mostly visited the library or drove maniacally up and down Tucumcari's main street between its two poles of commerce, K Mart and Thrifty's. Peace came sometimes on those long mainline runs into the desert or when I was too exhausted by the crazy hours to have insomnia. Peace did not come naturally. Not for a long time.

I also developed a strange compulsion to buy things. I got fixated on what *Texas Monthly* refers to as the crowning achievement of Western civilization—the cowboy boot. I made a mental connection between this obsession and quitting drinking, but I thought of it uncritically in terms of expense.

"Well, I'm saving two hundred dollars a week not drinking, so I can spend that money on boots."

I didn't think, "Well, I gave up one obsession, so I better replace it fast with another so that I don't have to look at what's really bothering me." I hadn't gotten that far yet in self-understanding. So I bought boots.

What else was in it? What was going through my mind as I caressed the grey glove leather Saunders with a lizard toe and a slung-back riding heel, or the sandy-colored Tony Lama roper I had bought in Utah? Freud would say shoes are vaginas. In that case, sixteen-inch high-top black cherry goat Lucceses must make an internal journey as deep as the fallopian tubes and beyond. Not to mention the other possibility Freud was too hung up to mention. Up the waazoo, as it were. Hmm, I thought, as I rammed my hot swollen arches into some Hondo black bullhides with high red tops. Great idea, but too garish. You would have to be sixteen and a Boys Ranch cowboy to get away with wearing these. Painfully, I stepped on the boot tree, and began inching them off. Already my eyes were posting with incestuous haste into another pair—calm Kangaroo with a slight black patina, a comfortable foldability, butter soft and waiting.

I banked my first paycheck from the Tucumcari extra board, a relative fortune, and headed the Toyota toward the panhandle. The goal was Amarillo, 250 miles east; if there weren't boots in Amarillo, where would there be boots? I opened the windows and let the dry heat pour in, watching the arroyos flatten out and the blond grasses get taller. I knew I was on the outskirts of the city by the row of old Cadillacs set in the ground nose first, an example of Texas "ort" and by now a national landmark. I headed for a pay phone to check the yellow pages for boots, much like I used to call my connection from Salinas on the long drive up from L.A. I felt the same rush, the same need to possess the visualized object.

I knew I had hit the jackpot when I walked into a barn-like Western store in a nondescript shopping center, one of those it-could-be-anywhere locations. It was a boot library, with a corner (meaning a corner lot) for hat blanks. I was looking at around 2,000 square feet of boots, prices ranging from $150 to $800 a pair. I was looking at a lot of wealth, here. Boots are one of the acceptable ways to show wealth in Texas; they are primarily worn by men and are one of the few ways men can vary their dress. The wranglers, the denim jacket, the ostrich boots. The three-piece pinstripe business suit, the charcoal-grey lizards. The gimme cap, the t-shirt, the mulehide vibram sole workboots. Women don't wear them much, unless they need to for a specific reason—ranchwork, dating a rodeo star, or signifying that they have a male-identified power in the world. Dykes wear them—the well-dressed dykes you see in airports meeting knockout business women in pumps and heels. On the practical side, boots turn back snake teeth and foil red ants.

They are nice to have on while stepping in bullshit and keep broken beer bottles from shredding your feet while passing the time in Western bars. They make you feel safe and protected, the next best thing to a shotgun inside a Winnebago.

As with hats, there were dizzying choices here. Height, heel style, toe style, type of leather, ornamentation, customization, boot jewelry. The two basic heel styles were riding and walking. The riding heel is slung back toward the arch so that it will catch in a stirrup. This is a why-cowboys-hate-to-walk type heel. Today this style is predominant in Mexican boots, the extreme type having a slanted heel so thick that it nearly meets the arch of the boot. Then there is the height-of-heel choice, from one to two-and-a-half inches. Walking heels are shorter; riding heels are taller. In toe styles, the pointy toe most people associate with the Western boot is not really the classic. It was a style that became fashionable around the time of Hollywood westerns, but the round "Texas" toe is much more common. The toe can be plain or covered with exotic skin or metal tips. Some people like to dress up the heels of their boots with silver heel guards, a precaution against scraping the leather on the floorboard of your pickup truck.

The low-top boots are cooler, but they won't make you feel safe in tall grass. For work boots, the usual leather choices are bullhide, mule, cowhide, rhino, or elephant. Elephant boots would turn back a railroad spike. For show-off boots, you can choose anaconda, antelope, anteater, alligator, bullhide, camel, glove leather cowhide, black cherry goat, eel, elk, Gila monster, kangaroo, lizard, ostrich, ostrich elbow, pigskin, python, rattlesnake, sea snake, and shark. The knee-jerk environmentalist in me was having a war with the sex-crazed foot fetishist. I bought a tall grey sharkskin with a Texas toe. After all, I thought, sharks eat us, so fuck 'em. We eat cow, I thought, selecting some twelve-inch pointy-toe, riding-heel cream-colored Tony Lamas with brown lizard tips. No problem with bulls either, I thought, slipping on the fourteen-inch Saunders Texas-toe classics in chocolate-brown leather with tan overstitching. No problem at all.

The gay bars in Amarillo were harder to find. Most of them listed in my gay directory seemed to have been bombed out, leaving gaps in blocks of pawn shops and body shops, or they were boarded up, the nonexistent name doubly erased by signs of closure. Oh, brief candle. Haunted by the need to at least see one gay person, I finally found a seedy afternoon bar, a pool table, a few no-veins lizards on the stools, and one woman who looked like she could really kick ass. I drank a Seven-Up. I didn't talk to anyone. But it was enough. The hard-shell baptists and bulletproof cowboys could not obliterate me. I/we existed. If barely.

It was about ninety-five degrees and muggy. A thunderstorm was about to hit, and it was getting close to call time. Heading back toward Tucumcari, I drove through Clovis, a Santa Fe railtown as dusty and bereft as Tucumcari. Well, slightly less bereft. I wondered why I drove out here, to spin out from these railheads in crazy circumnavigations of nothingness. Was it to feel my difference, and try to piece together a police artist's composite of myself, a sketch of the subject from witnesses' reports? Perhaps their questionnaires were mine also. I surely came here to get away from Gypsy Niemann, last of the party-timers, and from her lovers and habits. And yet I felt I was running toward something also. But I didn't know what it was. Toward a vacuuming emptiness. Toward an idea of God that was something like that. Like a sandstorm. Like losing one's way.

I found my borders disappearing. The simplest questions were gnomic. Self-image, sexual preference, profession, family, history. I wasn't sure about any of them. That's why I came out here—to avoid confrontations, to let the information emerge gradually. There were no telephones, no hookups to anywhere. There was a small regional library, a cool haven opening the door to the past. I would read about my surroundings, about the Southwest. I would get my bearings for the new mythology I had to create for myself. I found Charles Lummis, early anthropologist who walked from Denver to Los Angeles following the Santa Fe road. Adolph Bandelier, who, with Lummis, chronicled the Canyon de Frijoles, found the puma hunting gods of the Anasazis; Mary Austin, genius creator of an inarticulate land, fitting syntax to the uncanny basis of Western beauty. And the penitentes, those sufferers in a common cause.

The penitentes were a Catholic brotherhood that grew in isolation from the church after the separation of Mexico from Spain.

They took their inspiration from the conditions of the place—isolation, the harsh retribution of the desert, and the immanent transcendence that seems to be waiting in the landscape. The penitentes took upon themselves the responsibility for their community's sins and, imitating the suffering of Christ, paid for them by beating their bodies with yucca whips and crowning their heads with cactus thorns. They hung a chosen member on a cross at Easter in a pageant of the crucifixion that went way beyond Hollywood in visceral impact. The sound of the flute accompanied their rites.

The power of this idea fascinated me. And it gave me a metaphor to visualize the increasing anguish of my state of mind. What were these fears that seemed to dominate my life? What was I being punished for? What was I running away from? Why was I so certain that it was horrible to be who I was, that such constant suffering was inevitable? I had the feeling that I was stuck in a repetition, that I had been reproducing some event over and over, that it was a painful event and I was doomed to play the same play forever, with ever greater intensity of feeling. I thought about the penitentes, gathering together a year's suffering, personally and for their village. A year's worth of meaningless, petty, repetitive suffering in a harsh desert that would repeat its conditions year after year. They could gather it together and throw it away and go on clean to another year. The imitation of Christ included them in a story that was greater than their story or perhaps was not. Perhaps that wasn't the point. They became included in the story, entered the hardness of the symbol, felt its thorns bite, and their suffering was represented. They became understood. They must have felt satisfied and at peace.

I wanted some such peace. Some such personal ritual. I wanted to find New Mexico wild enough and magical enough to be my text, to be the new world it once was. But there were Denny's on the interstate, and the penitentes' moradas were long gone, and ski lifts climbed the holy mountains, and there was merely less clatter here than other places, but no true magic land.

Warren Grimm was a conductor who sold guns as a sideline. He lived in an upscale mobile home with a perky wife who sold real estate and was a lot younger than he was. Warren was doing all right for himself and usually had a smile on his somewhat ashy and undefined face. Warren's face was kind of all over the place—there wasn't a hard angle about him anywhere—and even his felt rancher's hat partook of the general formlessness and flopped. Both Warren and his wife had a passion for guns and hunting, and they were always in line for permits to shoot rare deer and bear and whatever else gets shot by special lottery. When I told him I wanted to buy a gun, Warren explained the principle of good guys and bad guys.

"The bad guys all have guns and they don't mind using them, so you have to be willing to shoot them first, because you know they are willing to shoot you."

Warren advised carrying a loaded gun in the glove compartment and just easing it onto the seat if a cop pulled you over for anything. In New Mexico, as in a lot of Western states, you can carry a loaded weapon as long as it's not concealed. He also implied that if you were white, you wouldn't have any problem about it.

"Hey Joe, whatcha got that big pistola for?"

"Shootin' cans."

"Kinda big for shootin' cans, Joe. What kind of cans you shoot with that?"

"OH, Mexi-cans, Afro-Ameri-cans, Puerto Ri-cans."

Why was I at Warren Grimm's trailer buying a gun? I was told that as a woman, I needed a protection. Yes, there were snakes out along the tracks. Walking beside the train at night, you could hear them sounding off, and yes, you wanted a gun to shoot them with. But I didn't really believe that they would menace me, or that I could hit a snake in the dark anyway. The other implied threat was the presence of illegals on every train heading north. I had always seen riders, but down here we were almost a passenger train. They would hide in the toilets on the engines, under the floorplates, in the engine compartment, everywhere. It was a spooky experience to walk back through the line of units at three in the morning and find ten guys sleeping on the floor in each of them. I did think what if they attacked me? But how do you tell the bad guys at first glance in the dark? I didn't have Warren's infallible detection system. Besides, I think I thought that guys like Warren and some of the other rails with guns were the bad guys. I think they were the reason I was in this formaldehyde-and-walnut mobile home buying a *pistola*.

I settled on a Smith and Wesson airweight—a thirty-eight caliber five-shot revolver. The bullets weighed more than the gun did, and you could hide it anywhere. It was strictly a one-shot belly gun, however. Five feet was its outside range, and after the gun flew straight up in a Rockette kick, your chances of getting in an accurate second shot were pure fantasy. I must confess I felt a power rush owning this gun. Now I could shoot my nightmares. I was armed against the dream police. I was protected.

As Warren and I closed the deal, I could feel glassy eyes watching me. I was sitting in his living room on a floral couch, and I felt something furry brush my leg. Expecting a cat, I looked down to find I had brushed up against Warren's table leg. It had fur, and feet—hooves, actually. But then, as I began to look around the room, everything did. Of course I had noticed the mounted heads with horns. How could you not notice them in a mobile home? But Warren and his wife had not merely mounted the heads; they stuck the rumps up there too—banded butts with hanging tails. I began to have impure thoughts. I could picture Warren on a stepladder mounting his own trophy, while his wife threw down on him with her Browning nine millimeter.

"You want some tail, Warren? Well, tail is exactly what you are gonna get."

Then Warren's fireplace matchstick holder caught my eye. It was a dried and hairy bull's scrotum, hanging from a leather loop.

"Oh, that," Warren suppressed a giggle. "I was wondering what you were gonna say about that. It's what you think it is."

"Far out. I mean, where could I get one? I'd like to send some to my friends in California. We don't have stuff like that out there."

"Oh, we call 'em *bullies*. They're a kind of local enterprise, the slaughterhouse being' so close and all. You can buy them down at the gas station on the east end of town—the one that's closed down. Most people coming through town take one look and can't believe their eyes—that type of thing."

"Well, Warren, if it doesn't bother you, it certainly doesn't bother me."

Word got around fast that I had a gun, and getting on the engine or caboose became like the assembly of a posse. All the hardware came out and was passed around, with stories. At last we had something in common. As with stories, my little airweight grew in size. Rumor soon had it that I was packing a cannon.

"Heard you bought a forty-four magnum from Grimm last week. Good idea for a woman to have a gun out here. Did I show you my shootin' iron?"

Late August in the panhandle was the season of camp meetings and monsoon rains. As the summer wore on, I didn't make friends in Tucumcari and my loneliness intensified. The good old boy ranchers I worked with were friendly enough, but aside from cars and now guns, we had nothing to say to each other. Their efforts to find out what I was doing with myself were futile because I wasn't doing anything. Reading in the library wasn't something they could focus on. The word on me, as I later found out, was that I "had no social life at all." Well, it was true. The only homey space I found was a black-run diner, and I hung out there. They cooked things like "steak fingers" and okra soup, and every black person within two hundred miles stopped in regularly to gossip, and I kind of listened in on their lives. They were open and warm in a way the white Baptists weren't. And so, when the end-of-summer bust came for the extra board in Tucumcari, I had my Toyota packed—I should say stuffed—in a matter of hours. I could have held on and worked off the emergency board and probably have still made good money, but I didn't want the time off. What would I do with it? The truth was that I was still restless and blown around my detoxifying emotions which, like cloud horses, thundered across my psychic sky.

I called the El Paso crew dispatcher and found a brakeman younger than me in seniority was working in a place called Alamogordo. I bumped him and headed south. The guy's name was Angel Rios. I never got to bump him, though, because by the time I arrived at the depot in Alamogordo that afternoon, I also had been bumped, and they were trying to reach the guy who had bumped me to tell him he was bumped. This meant that there was going to be an overall scramble for jobs, and I decided to head down to El Paso and mark up as a switchman in the freightyard. I knew some people there from the boomer hotel in Houston, and also I had an offer of a place to crash from a Californian I had met in Carrizozo.

"Anytime you need a place to stay in El Paso, just give me a ring. Me and Chris got plenty of room."

I thought, "Why not?" If I couldn't work, it might be time to head home. Or it might be time to head back to that place beside the Colorado River that was waiting for me—those roseate cliffs in the back of my mind, the comfort of any icy river running through deep time.

9

THE PASS
TO THE
NORTH

EL PASO DEL NORTE was a famous place—a borderland, a break in the barren mountains running south into Mexico; the route chosen by the Rio Grande on its journey to the Gulf; a high, treeless desert restlessly containing twin cities, both on a boom. At least six hundred thousand people on the Juarez side; four hundred thousand on the Texas side. A university, industry, the immigration business, street life, illegal drugs, construction, an international airport, gay bars, straight bars, mixed bars, a racetrack. *Maquilladoras*—dual factories on both sides of the border, were sprouting like mushrooms. Gretchen's old head in Ogden described El Paso as "that hell-hole." The Tucumcari brakemen talked about it as an exotic city—very far away and full of the devil's temptations.

"You'all watch yourself down there. Take care they don't slip you a mickey."

But mixed in was an awe at the abundance of something for everybody.

"Now you go down to the Caravan East and you find yourself some good ol' country dancing. I used to go down there on my layovers to do my dancin'. That's all I did was dancin'. I would just drink Sprite."

The Tucumcari brakemen used to run all the way through to El

Paso and have a day's layover there before they caught a train back. They only worked three days a week, made lots of money, and got to see what was over the mountain. Not a lot of people in New Mexico did that unless the army forced them to. They tended to stay near home, and three hundred miles was like three thousand miles. The Chicanos didn't care to leave their extended families, and the white boys had to feed their cows every day.

The approach from the north was along a highway that skirted the Sacramento Mountains. From nothingness, the first outposts appeared; gas stations and cafes; then more gas stations; then carlots, bootstores, army surplus, discount jeans, C&W honkytonks, and shopping centers. After months of silence, it was the usual culture shock. Boots, I thought—boots and gay bars.

I found a cheap hotel and called Naomi from my room, the sun sinking over the twin smokestacks of the ASARCO refinery, and the paper shacks of little Jerusalem in Juarez bathed momentarily in pearly pink light. As Naomi and I got farther apart in miles, we had grown closer in affection, and in one of our 7-11 conversations in Tucumcari, we had agreed to try living together when work ran out and I could return to California. This time it was my idea, and I had been giving her instructions on how a romantic lover acts.

"Look, Naomi, send me little postcards at intervals, so that I get them when I get home from a run. Then you stay in my mind all the time, and I have secret conversations with you when I'm on the road. I get home thinking of you, and then—*voilà*, there are your few tender words in my post office box. It's a lover's box, really, since you are the only correspondent. Romance is about stuff like that."

She started doing that, sending little cramped notes to my box, the word *love* written as if under diamond-producing pressure, as if the whole story was there in that word, the whole awful secret that would ban her forever from the bosom of her Jewish family. Leaving Tucumcari, I had missed a promised postcard, one that was special, one that unfolded her affections. It rested naked in my abandoned box. Eventually, some bored or curious postmaster would reach inside and remove it, turn it over and read the numinous words and then ship it out to the dead-letter office. The worst case scenario. It seemed ominous to me. It bothered me I would never know what she had said.

Noami was strangely distant on the phone. I wanted her to come down to El Paso, spend some days with me, celebrate the city. She was peeved at me for suggesting this. More of my selfishness—my not thinking of her, of her life. "How can she be mad at me when she hasn't seen me for five months?" I thought. "Asshole," I thought. "Doesn't she know how lonely I feel?" I hung up the phone and looked out over the corraline humps slowly being darkened by the sunset. A huge cross, marking the intersection of Mexico, Texas, and New Mexico blackened in the fading light. The butter sun melted like a nuclear test on a far horizon, and I thought, "It's beautiful here. Why do I think it's beautiful?"

Later that night, I set out to find the women's bars. It seemed like I hadn't seen or talked to women in years. Just lean and scratchy cowboys with a thousand questions or endless monologues about horsebreeding or pickup trucks. The ecology of the range. The necessity for jimsonweed. Give me some attitude, please. I found it on Alameda Street in what looked like a trans-border hiking trail, blocks of upholstery shops, jukebox cantinas, body shops, wrecking yards. Poor people walking home on the sidewalks, carrying groceries, gangs of small children obviously out all night, playing breakdance bullfights with a piece of cardboard in freeway underpasses. I worried about my car, parked on the street, stuffed with all my possessions.

It was a Latina bar, noisy and crowded with butch-femme couples dancing the *cumbia*, everybody dressed up in some way, and an energy that moved in the room—volatile, capable of opposite moods. It was clearly unusual for an Anglo to walk in alone or to be there at all, in fact. I was lucky to sit next to a motherly type at the bar, a warm and inclusive person.

"I just got into town. Hours ago. I found this place in my gay guide. I don't know anybody. I work for the railroad."

She stared at me in disbelief. Clearly I was somebody who needed to be under a wing, needed to be clued in on the basics fast. Oh, lucky me.

"Is that right? You just got into town now, and you come here the first thing?"

She seemed to think that was incredibly funny. Pretty soon the whole suspicious row of faces at the bar opened, laughed, and came forward to shake hands, introduce themselves, and remark on this.

"Here, the first thing. Before you go anywhere. They don't have women where you come from?"

"Oh, hey, she works for the railroad, like Roberta. Hey, you don't know Roberta? She comes here sometimes, a real good lady. You can talk to her. And there's another one, what's her name up in Santa Rosa? Anne. You can talk to her too."

That was how it worked. The first night in town I knew everything about everybody within three hundred miles, but I couldn't let on that I knew until someone told them about me. Which, of course, would happen the very next time they went to a bar. Then we both would walk around with this mutual secret until the polite time had elapsed and we had decided if we liked the person's character, if we wanted to be friends. Then we would admit that we knew what we knew.

The next morning I called Jesse, the boomer who had offered me a place to stay. I hardly knew him; as a matter of fact, I had never even talked to him in Carrizozo. One day when we were all sitting mindlessly in front of the tube, waiting for our trains to hit town, Jesse introduced himself and made the offer. Out of the blue. I could tell he wasn't too sure about why he had done it when he answered his phone.

"Oh yeah, Gypsy—that's right, I did say that, didn't I. Well, there's plenty of room here, but not much else. This is all kind of a surprise. Did I tell you about Chris? OK—well then—I guess I have to tell you how to get out here. This is all kind of a surprise."

Jesse and Chris lived in an instant suburb on the east side, an enormous three-bedroom, ranch-style house with wall-to-wall carpets and no furniture. They had both left divorces pending in California, and the place looked it. Chris was the neat one—his boxes were arranged, while Jesse's spilled over with dirty laundry, stray cowboy boots, old pizza boxes. Beer cans were everywhere, as were gallon jugs of bourbon and tins of mothers' cookies from home. Chris had just bought a chow puppy that was busy chewing everything in sight. Also just lying around were pistols of various shapes and sizes, chrome-plated thirty-seven magnums, a twenty-two Derringer boot gun, a twenty-two target revolver. Shells were everywhere. Chris saw me eyeing the hardware.

"Have you been down to the yard yet? When you do, you'll know why we carry guns here. These homeboys don't exactly appreciate our being here working."

Chris was a bear of a man, Irish and husky, and I couldn't quite picture him having a lot of trouble with anyone. He did drive a flashy car, though, a black Cadillac El Dorado with California plates, and it turned out that the car, not his person, had been the subject of attacks.

"Sneaky little bastards. They smash your windows and ruin your paint job while you're out on a run. And the trainmaster just shrugs and says it's too bad. It's going to be too bad if I catch the mother-fuckers doing it. Too bad for them."

"It's those goddamn switchmen," Jesse agreed. "Your working buddies in the yard. But you'll do OK. I can tell you can handle it. I'm sure glad I don't have to work them switchers any more."

Sure, I could handle it. But I did already know the switchmen, probably the ones who were trashing Chris' car. I could see it. Southwesterners were hostile to strangers. Since the locals rarely ever left home, they couldn't imagine what type of person would do this. They thought all boomers were running from the law or deserting their wives and kids. Come to think of it, this was close to the truth. Also, violence was an acceptable way of handling things down here. It was the macho mystique, and the Hispanics, having invented it, were the most violent when it came to protecting what they saw as their turf. They had just gotten a toehold on the white man's railroad, and hardly any of them had untouchable seniority. Boomers tended to knock them off the high-paying extra board and onto the yard jobs. And so, any vehicle with out-of-state plates got trashed. Tires went mysteriously flat. Now, on the other side, it was true that some boomers were not too bright about how to behave. They came down in $30,000 mobile homes and parked them under the freeway overpass on company property. Or they drove Cadillacs. Their usual topic of conversation was how much better things were in California, Oregon, or Utah. How dumb the Texas brakemen were about their contract rights. How the homeboys didn't know anything about switching down here, what with the long mainline rides.

"Why, Jesse and me used to switch hundreds of boxcars a night on that Cal-P job. We'd work a list as long as your arm. Here these boys just shit if they have to set out a car. They get on the radio and start crying to the dispatcher and try to run the work. What work? It makes you want to puke."

This kind of talk tended to get you punched out in switchmen's bars. And of course the boomers wouldn't stay out of them. There were always a story floating around about how some skinny home-boy had made some boomer "do the chicken" the night before.

The El Paso yard was in the center of town, with highrise office buildings built over it, creating the infamous trainway, a long tunnel housing mainline track and yard tail tracks used to switch the lower end of the yard. It was cramped in the trainway with the tracks crowded together with crossover switches and interlocking signals. It was a bad situation for switchmen to share their working leads with mainline trains.

You would be riding the end of a long cut of cars, the engine out of sight, and have to ride deep into the trainway yourself to clear a low pot signal controlled by the yard's interlocking operator. You would get off the car and stand there in the semidark, feet away from a mainline train entering the yard, potentially shifting loads of swaying lumber passing an arm's reach away from your face. You got vertigo, wanted to lie down, close your eyes to get reoriented. But you had to watch your signal for the power switches to line up, so you could hop aboard your cut and start shoving back into the yard.

The trainway was also used by travelers from Mexico walking over the border or trying to hop a westbound. The little cubbyholes in the concrete walls were always occupied by a man with a bottle, who would flatten himself into the dark as you passed by, and you could feel eyeballs on your back as you stood in between the moving lines of cars. The fumes from the engines also hung in stagnant clouds, and whatever spilled in the yard found its way by gravity into the natural culvert created by this river of tracks. If a train derailed while you were standing there, there was no place to run. And, due to a little dip in the tracks, trains derailed there frequently generating "special notices" in the timetable but the same old problems for switchmen to work with. In Texas, however, it was not considered macho to object to a dangerous workplace, and people just put up with it.

The El Paso yard just hadn't been built to handle the volume of traffic it was now handling. It had been put together piecemeal, and the parts did not function harmoniously. To begin with, two separate railroads operated in the yard, and depending on the state of union rivalry, switchmen left traps for other crews or yardmasters favored one or the other railroad in granting permission to use tracks. The Southern Pacific shared the yard with the Texas and Louisiana, which it owned but operated under a separate labor contract. In the switchman's shanty, the Texas and Louisiana had one long table, the SP another. Working the yard, you always had to be on the lookout for other switch engines, and just because you made a lineup of switches for your crew's move didn't mean it would stay that way. Because you tended to get into a fast rhythm switching, this fact of life proved dangerous. The engineer would take a backup sign only to find some other crew had crossed over in back of him and changed his lineup. If the hoghead didn't constantly check behind him, he might find himself lined into another movement. More "special notices" appeared, but it was the yard itself that was the problem.

Before I could mark up, I had to make three student trips in the yard, which I did eight-on, eight-off. I still didn't have my strength back, and by the third trip the foreman just told me to go home and sleep, as I was just sleeping on my feet anyway. He was right, and I hit the floor at Jesse's and sawed wood for about ten hours—so I was told.

"Yeah, me and Chris just closed the door to your room, but we could still hear you in the living room. Sawing away. I thought, gawdamn, is she going to do this every night, but Chris said, no—you were just tired out. You sure were tired out."

Jesse looked at me. An amused and benevolent hillbilly look. But kind. I felt like it was going to be all right to stay here in spite of the booze and the guns.

In the morning I got called for the river job, a hauler that took cars from the yard to a small switching yard on the banks of the Rio Grande. It was a hot September day, with the heat starting at eight and building from there. We followed the rickety tracks through the poorer section of town, looking into backyard junkyards and raggedy laundry hanging on lines strung from windows to fences; but with animals, and children, and grandmothers, and life happening. "They are richer than I am," I thought, looking in on their lives. "They have families and relatives and time to enjoy life." I seemed to be on the outside of life these days, on the cold road outside looking into the lighted window at the ordinary life I could not have.

The crew were mostly Chicanos, switchmen bumped off the road by boomers, but they weren't uniformly hostile to me. I had poor seniority and couldn't bump anyone; also, I couldn't work at home. They could understand why I might be here, and they were certainly curious about why I was. The foreman and I started getting located in time and space.

"Oh, you went to Berkeley in the sixties, huh. I bet you were one of them hippie protesters when I was in Nam."

"Yes, that's right. Except I wasn't a hippie because I worked at staying in school. But I was a protester, all right. But a friend of mine told me that the real antiwar protest started in the army when soldiers started saying what are we doing there anyway."

"Well, soldiers don't get to say things like that. They just gotta do their job. I used to hate all you college kids when I was in Nam."

"Well, here we both are twenty years later, working the river job. And high school kids don't even know about Viet Nam."

The foreman sighed and let it go. It was true, that whole lump of outrage had been swallowed whole and the world was on to new problems now. He decided to lighten up and school me about the yard.

"You see that guy over there, riding the point. His name is Cesar. I'm warning you to watch out for him. He'll get you fired. We call him 'The Torch' because he likes to play with matches. He isn't playing with a full deck. Just be careful if you ever work with him."

When we reached the river we had to switch out some cars to make up our drag for the yard. There was a chain link fence that ran alongside the river and there were holes in it for people to climb through. Clumps of people were doing this all afternoon, dodging the green *Migra* Broncos that would drive up and down the fence chasing people back. Kids on the Mexican side would wade over and climb into a culvert on the North American side where the water funneled through an underwater drainpipe and spouted up in the middle of the river. It made a kind of water slide. The kids would do it over and over, mocking the border patrol and us as we worked, sweating, switching out our cars. I was standing in the yard talking to the agent, an older man with a lonely job, when we both noticed that my crew was going to make a hard joint on the track next to us. What we didn't notice was that the lead car was a loaded tanker with an open hatch—full of molasses. We heard the knuckles hit hard and both looked up to see a mushroom cloud of black syrup rise in the air and rain down in a torrent of fat sticky fingers.

"Oh, shit," we both said in unison.

We looked like caramel apples. Covered with molasses from head to toe. The crew was doubled over in mirth. You might say it broke the ice. They were going to have fun later at the switchman's bar with this one. But it probably was the best thing that could have happened to me. I tried to wash up some and spent the rest of the day trying not to lick myself off like a cat. I had molasses everywhere. In my hair, behind my ears, in my ears. When I got home I left my boots and socks on the sidewalk, and ran for the shower. Jesse gave me a funny look when he found the sticky heap of overalls in the kitchen.

"Well how was your first day of work? Looks like you got kinda dirty working in the yard."

"Later Jesse. I'll tell you all about it later. As my friend Wendy-the-Hooker said, 'At least this kind of dirt washes off.'"

When I went outside to retrieve my boots they were swarming with ants. Kind of a mild lesson, when you think about it. It could have been a tanker of sulphuric.

My motive for moving in with Jesse and Chris had been cheap rent, a free lunch. Jesse's motive had been a come-on. What we all got was something entirely different. The scene here at the rancho was not only heavy drinking but also a junk scene. Jesse was a periodic user, and Chris was his tight buddy, the one who took care of him and kept him from going over the edge. They both had histories in Nam, and I could hear Jesse wake up screaming sometimes, still in a personal jungle.

"Right at the end of my tour, they ordered me to drive one of those tractors around, the kind with a big umbrella, where you sit way up in the air. Like a sitting duck, I told 'em no thank you. I don't care what you do to me, but I'm not getting up on that tractor. So they sent me to Saigon for two months. It was like R&R. That was my punishment for refusing an order."

Jesse had been strung out, on and off, ever since the war. A lot of things went with it, rip-offs and jacking people up with guns. He would tell me these things, in that quiet gentle voice of his, and I would think "How on earth could this man do that stuff?" He would have to be completely different, a completely different person. I also wondered what I was doing living there. Of course, of the three of us, I was the one who looked the most fucked up.

Everything in my life was coming completely apart. I just couldn't handle it anymore. The yard shifts were too much for me; after nine months of not drinking I was still so physically wrecked that I could hardly work an eight-hour shift. It was like a prolonged recovery from a major illness. I had been sick once with mononucleosis, and I felt as bad now as I did then. This wasn't fair. I was supposed to be OK by now. I still had headaches, trouble sleeping, trouble digesting anything—still jumpy as hell. Every little problem was a major big deal, and I didn't have little problems. I had big problems down at the yard fighting off the antiboomer harassment, and I had big problems with Naomi.

We should have seen each other by now, had planned to, but every plan got canceled at the last minute. She seemed angry with me every time we talked. I finally got the picture that something was going on.

"I wanted to tell you that I talked to Rebecca last night about us. I thought she ought to know the truth."

Naomi tell a friend of hers the truth about us? This didn't sound right. Telling the truth was the last thing she would do. I got a bad feeling, an earthquake kind of feeling.

"What are you trying to do, seduce her? I just as soon you kept me out of it, if you don't mind."

"You always think the worst, don't you Gypsy? You just can't wish me well."

"What are you talking about. How can I wish you well when you're annihilating me?"

"It's always you, isn't it. Always about you."

"Well, yes. Goddammit. If we're going to live together, some part of it has to be about me. It doesn't sound as if you want me around. It sounds like you want Rebecca around more."

"Well, yes. I'm sorry it's come to this. But I do."

I hung up the phone. I looked down at my watch. It was time to go face the afternoon yard job. Then the glob of feeling lodged in my throat let go, and my soul lay down to die. Could these be my arms? Was it possible that this was my heartbeat going on? With the point-blank numbness of noon, I got in my car and drove down to the yard. To move anywhere was better than to stay in a room. It would be impossible to stay in a room.

I kept thinking, why now? Why, now that I had finally cleaned up my act did she want to bail out? It had been nine years. I couldn't grasp any of it.

I was on a regular job in the yard, which was good, but the bad part was that I had The Torch for a foreman, the one I was warned about when I first arrived. The railroad could be a sanctuary for people who couldn't make it in the outside world. There were some people you just worked around; it seemed every terminal had one. There were brakemen walking around who had plates in their brains, who were borderline psychotics. You wondered how they tied their shoes in the morning. And yet other brakemen would carry them, understanding that human failing was allowed to exist here. Once accepted in the yard, you could live here no matter what happened to you. At least that's the way it used to be. And so, I was going to have to handle Cesar today. And it was going to be hard.

Cesar had been a junior officer in Nam, and you got the feeling that he still thought he was there. He had that glazed and disconnected look, and he didn't take anything seriously. His other name was Teflon, because nothing would stick. Ordinarily the way switching works is like a team sport, like baseball. Everyone has a position and moves in relation to everyone else. There are standard plays, standard signs, things you expect other people to do. Cesar changed all that. He would announce a move, start it in play, and then inexplicably start doing other moves or start playing someone else's position. Since the team was spread out all over the yard, nobody could figure out what was going on. And then Cesar would turn up yelling at you for not being in position or for not doing your work. This "not doing the work" stuff was my flash point. I always did my work—that is, if I could find my work. If somebody else wasn't butting in and doing my work. Somebody like Cesar.

We soon collided at the crossover switch that Cesar had just decided to use instead of the sluff track he said he was going to use.

"Oh, are you going to do your job now, instead of making me do everything?"

"Look, man, if it isn't your job to throw that fucking switch, then don't touch it. OK? I'm not going to run after you when you change your mind every five minutes."

"I don't have to tell you what I'm doing. Just watch for car signs. Do you know how to read car signs?"

"Do you know how to read this sign, asshole?" I flipped him the "Fuck you and the train you came in on" sign. That was one of the first car signs we learned at Watsonville. Right after the "Officials on board" car sign.

Cesar couldn't believe it. I couldn't either. I was going over the high side. I had no control.

"Fuck you, goddamn cunt. *Chinga tu madre. Putana pendeja.*"

"Fuck your mother, too, you asshole. Fuck you."

We were screaming now, putting distance between us down the lead. "Fuck you. I'm the foreman. I'm gonna call the yardmaster."

"So go call the yardmaster. I want the yardmaster here. You fight with everybody. Everybody has trouble with you. Call the fucking yardmaster. You're fighting with the field man too. Why don't we all talk to the yardmaster."

I was shaking, and getting hoarse from yelling *fuck*. God, I couldn't believe it. I wanted to get out of here, move on, maybe go to Tucson where I knew people. Tucson would be easier. I could get away from this. But it turned out I was at the end of the line. Jammed up against the borderline, I finally turned the focus inward. I decided to take a look. That night I drove down to the twelve-step club instead of going home. And I grabbed the first person I saw there, an oldtimer who looked like the proverbial wino under the bridge. I burst into tears.

"You've got to help me. I don't want to drink any more. But I can't keep feeling like this."

He gave me a phone number and told me to call it in the morning. He said this woman would tell me what to do.

I found myself sitting in a garden with a tough little woman in her fifties. Her name was Maggie. She had a New York accent and a New Yorker's way of getting down to business.

"Listen to me. You're not going to Tucson. You're through running. If you stay in this pain, you will drink again. You need to have a spiritual awakening."

I looked around at the brown naked mountains and the freeway roaring with pickups and RVs. It hardly looked like the location for a spiritual awakening.

"I want you to write down your life story honestly. Don't hold anything back. And come back here and read it to me."

I didn't like the sound of this. I had a ten-year writer's block. It was my opinion, philosophically, that it was impossible to be honest in an autobiography. I had written a Ph.D. dissertation on this very subject. Furthermore, I didn't have a typewriter. It was too big a project. She was making it sound ridiculously simple.

"Just take a pen, sit down, and start writing. You'll be surprised."

I went down to the 7-11 and bought a legal pad and a pen. I went back to the club and sat down at a long table. I could see the brown Franklin Mountains out of the picture window. I started writing. When it got dark, I went home. The next day I was back writing. I couldn't stop. Memories would trigger emotions, and I would cry all over my legal pad.

At 3:30 in the afternoon, I pulled myself together to go to work. I had to deal with Cesar for eight hours, and it wasn't getting any better. The whole crew was fighting. Our engineer was off the extra board, and he had never seen anything like it.

"What is with this crew anyway? Y'all are yelling at each other all the time. This is crazy."

"Stick around. It gets crazier."

This was the afternoon that Cesar tried to kill me. We were shoving a flatcar to a joint on a track, and I was riding it. There's nothing to hold onto on a flatcar, and they have obsolete staff brakes that don't tie down fast. I was standing on top of the car, holding onto the brake staff and signaling the engineer to slow down. We had about five cars to a joint. Nothing. I gave another slowdown. If anything, we were going faster. I looked around to find that Cesar had cut me off and the flatcar and me were going to make a hand joint. I just got off when it hit. I could see the engineer was in shock. His mouth was hanging open in amazement. When I got back on the engine, Cesar was smiling. The water was glistening off the duck's back.

"What the fuck do you think you're doing?"

"It's OK."

"No it isn't OK, dickhead. It is not OK."

There was silence. Cesar stared off into space, his opal eyes tranquil and serene. He was looking up the jungle delta somewhere—innocent and at peace.

I got up the next morning and looked up Maggie. I was now going to read her my life story, tell this total stranger all my secrets. I thought she was going to feel sorry for me. After all, it was one long tale of love gone wrong. To my surprise, she asked me where I had been at fault. I was supposed to look at what I had done to retaliate. What decisions had I made that had led me to these disasters? How had I placed myself in a position to be hurt? I found that I felt better doing this. It made me less a victim. It also meant it didn't always have to be this way.

I was not going to walk away from this grief over Naomi. You don't walk away from nine years. But the size of my need to blame her was reduced the crucial amount. It was no longer a balloon filled with all the pain I had ever felt. I started to see where I had been at fault. Maggie rubbed my nose in it.

"Given who she is—not who you want her to be—is it possible she would have been better off not unearthing this part of her personality? Did you think about her in this? Or just what you needed from her? Selfish, self-seeking, self-centered fear. Do you understand it now?"

"I suppose she might have been better off if I hadn't swept her away. I thought I was being romantic. I thought I was rescuing her from herself."

"It sounds like she would have been much better off."

"Why is it so hard to accept this?"

"You are used to playing God. You need to find a power greater than yourself. You need to turn your will and your life over. Then you will get well. That's all I can tell you. I don't know if you can do it or not."

She told me to go home and ask God to remove my "defects of character." Then I could start working on being willing to have God do that. What was bothering me the most about myself right now was a bad haircut. But I decided to go through the motions of doing these things—mainly because I didn't know what else to do. I had run out of options. Everything I knew how to do to fix things went with drinking. It was like I was trying to learn how to write with my left hand.

To surrender was an odd idea. It ran counter to my whole approach to life. I remember an L.A. switchman saying to me, "You don't give up easy, do you?" *Easy?* I never gave up. Except for that night on the beach in Santa Barbara, I had never admitted to myself that I couldn't handle anything. Or anyone.

Now I was asked to believe that I was a part of the world, that I belonged here, that a power greater than myself would allow me to float. As other people floated, without my controlling them. As Naomi floated. This was hard. I had always brought an intensity to close relationships, as if that other person had what I needed to exist and could rescue me or destroy me. I never put that other person and myself in any larger context. Naomi told me I didn't wish her well. Apart from myself, I didn't. I felt like I needed her to survive. How could I wish her well, leaving me? A higher power that was greater than my desire would have to include her too, and her desires, her vector in life. There could be a larger context. And as painful as it was to look at it, that was where the truth was, and that was the direction true love would have to go.

These insights did not come calmly or easily. They came like a hurricane. I felt like a tree shaken to sticks by the storm. But I couldn't avoid them, and I couldn't hide my feelings from the world.

Jesse had been watching me go through all this, leaving every night for meetings and coming home and bursting into tears in front of the refrigerator. He knew something was going on.

"I don't know what you're doing, Gypsy. But you're sure trying hard, whatever it is."

"I just broke up with my lover. You met her. The one with the coats. And I'm just trying to stay sober. I'm just doing what they tell me."

Jesse had been out to California to go hunting and had stopped in at Naomi's house to pick up my winter coats. The thought of that connection reassured me. It made me feel less crazy. When the coats arrived, I was shocked to find sixty dollars in every one of them. There were four or five coats. It was a minor windfall. But of course it reminded me of the way it used to be. That sixty was for the half gram of cocaine that I would need when I went out drinking at a bar. I always had it with me. Last winter I was still drinking and using. This winter I was going to have to find another way to live.

On the border, the seasons changed almost overnight. One day it was 105 degrees; a few days later it was 50. During that short transition a desert wind arose and sent down brown clouds of "Texas rain" into the particulate air. Heavy strings of fire-red *ristras* hung from pickup trucks in parking lots along with velvet paintings of Aztec warriors and women with mountainous breasts. My blood thickened with the energy, and I had to be moving—anywhere. Starting out in the afternoon to drive, I headed northwest up the Rio Grande, just following the river, off the interstate, taking backroads.

I was intending to go as far as Truth or Consequences, thinking of staying the night, soaking in the mineral baths, perhaps getting a massage. The name, of course, intrigued me, and I had noticed it on maps with little comprehension of where it actually was. In fact, it rested directly below Elephant Butte Dam on the Rio Grande, the water project that turned the grand river of the north into the pacifistic brown ribbon I lived beside in El Paso. It was this river I followed through New Mexico, with its thick banks of willows and its heavy sickly green smell, retaining something of the feel of summer in its sluggish movements. The presence of the river re-assured me for some reason. I wanted to slow my blood to be in time with it. I began to notice wayside inns, how picturesque they were, how inviting. I even pulled off the road at one in Hatch, heard my tires crunch on the round river stones as I brought my car up flush in front. The inn was adobe with thick walls and Mexican tiled tables and the easy conversations of daytime drinkers. Time altered as I entered the room; it became a period piece and far away. I knew I had to leave. Could not even sit and eat. And soon I was driving again, this time with the knowledge that I was on some kind of a run. I passed geodesic domes and hippie houses; I was lulled with the impression of being home in California; the landscape seemed familiar. And this was not an altogether com-forting idea.

It became, if possible, even greener and warmer. I stayed close to the river and after wandering through farm country all day, it abruptly emerged into a naked terrain surrounding an enormous dam. Truth or Consequences squatted below its humpy shoulder, shopworn and pathetic. If a cure was to be found here it was of the miracle kind. Texans on vacation tended to be self-contained, and the town itself had little to beckon with. As I cruised its faded motels and spas, part of me rejected it and part of me found its place. The thought just lay there in a corner of my mind.

"No one would know. A place like this. You could buy a bottle and just check in."

As I heard these words under the surface of my consciousness, I realized that part of my mind was, and always would be, on cruise control. Heading straight for a drink. Wandering would turn out to be circling closer. Aimlessness would be self-deception. What was the difference between this kind of purposelessness and turning my life over, surrendering control? One was deadly, the other healthy. In the first case, there was a hidden agenda, which I could find if I searched my motives. In a surrender, I would have to release all expectations as to the outcome, I would have to let go of the results. But how to know? It was like a boxcar sliding up on you in the dark—the same skin prickle and body stepping out of the way. But how could you count on it every time? There were so many opportunities to slip. Somehow I realized that I would have to follow simple formulas. When I felt scared I could pick up the phone, or get to a meeting. So, having arrived in Truth or Consequences, I left again and drove the interstate back into El Paso, to the twelve-step club's evening meeting. As I walked in the doors, I felt relieved. I was safe for the moment. The liminal period was over, and I wasn't going to drink today.

One morning when I walked into our living room, I found Jesse sitting in a chair wrapped up in a blanket. He didn't say anything, and neither did I. I came back home later in the day and Jesse was still sitting there. In the same position. I went to a meeting that night and came home around ten. As I walked past Jesse's chair he said, "Why don't you ask me what I did last night?"

"OK. What did you do last night?"

"I don't know."

Jesse didn't know what he had done, but what the woman he was with had told him was enough to keep him in the chair. He figured that if he just sat there, it couldn't happen again. It suddenly dawned on me that Jesse was a blackout drinker. And that ever since I had moved in he had been checking me out because it rang a chord for him. Now I thought about the things he had said about himself.

"I was wondering if I was an alcoholic. But I don't think I am."

"Great, fine," I would say. And go on feeling sorry for myself.

"I stopped drinking beer for a week, and it didn't bother me, so I guess I'm not."

"Yeah, great," I'd say, deep into my own problems. The truth was that I really didn't care. I was so used to keeping people I knew at work away from me, that I couldn't really see them. Also, I wanted to keep what I was doing at the twelve-step meetings protected. I still felt fragile about it. The program was where I could be honest; perhaps the only place. And so I was indeed the perfect backdrop for Jesse to see himself against. I wasn't trying to convert him; I didn't even notice him. Until the chair. Then it all clicked in. And it gave me an eerie feeling about what I was doing here and how it all had come about. Out of the blue. A power greater than myself.

Jesse got out of his chair and checked into a treatment center for a month. I was amazed, and Chris was left holding the brown paper bag with the fifth in it. He wanted to be pleased that Jesse was getting help, but part of him missed his drinking buddy. Besides, taking care of Jesse had always made Chris feel together. Now Chris was alone on stage, the only one drinking.

"It's amazing about Jesse, isn't it? Well, I sure hope he makes it."

"Yeah, Chris, he sure surprised me."

"You know he's tried this before, but something always happens. But Jesse sure needed to get straight. I kept telling him."

Chris was working the road, and with Jesse in treatment, I was alone in the house a lot. Things were still tough in the yard, and it was beginning to sink in that the break with Naomi was permanent this time. It felt different than all the other times, and the difference was within me. The grief kept on breaking over me like surf. It felt endless.

One night when I was home alone the phone rang, and I heard a sick low voice threatening me. It was an incoherent ramble about beating up on women and wanting me to understand it.

"Who the fuck are you, and how did you get my number?"

"You cunts are all the same. You're all asking for it."

"Well, come on over, asshole. I have something for you."

Shaking, I got my thirty-eight revolver out of my car and tucked it under the pillow. Southern comfort. But it got me through the night. Some of the boomers' wives were getting obscene phone calls when their husbands were out of town on a run. It could have been that, or it could have been random. Whatever it was, I realized that I needed to find a haven for a while, somewhere where I could let my personal winter occur. Somewhere safe.

10

DOWN
THE LINE

BOUGHT a typewriter and brand new pickup—a granny gear, four-on-the-floor, plain-Jane Ford 150 shortbed with dual tanks, white on white. I had been listening during all those hours spent on the rails with ranchers. This was my first new car. It smelled new and it rode high, and I felt protected. A house on wheels. The new Western horse. I bid on a regular job that was going cheap on a work train laying track out of Alamogordo, New Mexico, about a hundred miles north of El Paso at the foot of the high Sacramento Mountains.

This work train was going to stay out on the line until it reached the end of the El Paso subdivision's territory. Then a Tucumcari crew would take over from Carrizozo east. All in all, they were looking at laying around three hundred miles of ribbon rail, replacing ties, and reballasting the roadbed. The maintenance-of-way division was in charge of the work. They used Navaho Indian work gangs who would stay out on the line for the whole project, living in company trailers and eating in an old Rock Island dining car. The company wouldn't pay them until the end of their tour and they would pay the chief. The idea was to keep them out of the available watering holes in the towns along the line.

This job was going cheap because it was twelve hours a day, seven days a week. The company paid for your room in the Desert Inn, so it was a chance to save some money if you didn't mind doing nothing but work. The Desert Inn was a decent enough place; you could get your rest here and get comforted enough to get up at five and go out into the winter morning to work day after day after day. I stayed here for three months, following the tie, steel, or ballast gangs up and down the line.

The first day of work I showed up at the depot at six. It was next to the park that ran alongside the main highway through town. The town was named for the fat, round cottonwood trees that shaded the park and became like old friends to the rails who watched them dress and undress through the changes of seasons. There was also a zoo in the park, abutting on the mainline, and it was a common joke to send some new brakeman out walking the train when you stopped in Alamogordo at night. The lions liked to cut loose with roars as soon as they woke up, and I could hear their muffled sounds across the park. The agent from the night trick was typing out the orders for the last westbound of the night. At eight a window would go up closing our section of track to mainline trains. Trains caught on either side of the window weren't going anywhere today. Our own train orders were waiting for us on the counter, giving us authority to occupy the main track after certain trains had passed. We would have to verify these trains, rolling them by outside the depot. This is the way I would see my friends for the next few months as they passed by on the mainline. Chris and, later, Jesse would throw off my mail. Mooning was also big.

I realized I was nervous about meeting the crew. I was going to be spending twelve hours a day with them. What if I drew another Cesar? About six-thirty the hoghead turned up, a fancy dresser with antelope boots and buffalo breath. I practically got loaded standing next to him. He kept saying things like "I'll wake up anytime now," and "I didn't see you in the bar last night." He seemed relieved when the track gang stumbled in with colorless faces and dark circles under their eyes; he obviously had seen them at the bar. They had probably spent all night going over the moves of the day before, and now they could all recapitulate last night.

"Hey Thomas, how're you doing this morning, buddy? You were doing all right last night, eh? How'd you do with that little blonde and her friend?"

"Hey man, my head hurts. How're you doing, man? You were still going strong when I left. What time'd you get to bed?"

I thought, "Oh shit, what am I going to do here?"

Then the other brakeman came in, a little solid Chicano guy named Angel Rios, the guy I tried to bump at the end of the summer. Angel entered the room like he was entering a bullring. A short little guy, built like an Indian, wearing an L.A. Dodgers porkpie hat, his dark face changeable from glint-eyed tough to cracked open with explosive laughter. From the moment he entered the room, he was sizing things up.

It was a free zone hour of day, the time before the day trick agent Raoul Rodriquez arrived, and the poltergeists were having their fun. Raoul was an object of mockery since he had been the agent at Alamogordo since the dawn of time and had developed proprietary attitudes towards his domain. Usually, he had the depot all to himself, with the other clerks under his thumb. Now he had to share his sanctum with a rowdy work train crew, bent on messing things up. Today, the extra conductor, "Father" Finnegan, was occupied in tying Rodriquez' order strings into knots and breaking off the tips of his carefully ground pencils.

"I am going to tell 'mithter Rodrigueth' what you are doing here," Angel said briskly. "He will be interested to know about this. I also have information for him concerning his hat. I think I know the man who stole it."

Rodriquez had appropriated an SP safety hat, one of the giveaways for trainmen that always fell into the hands of office people first. The operating crews would come in for their hats or jackets and find only extra-large sizes left, or that every clerk's kid had a hat but there were none left for trainmen. Raoul was proud of his clean new hat and left it hanging on a special peg in the office, from which peg it disappeared when the work train was using the depot as their on-duty point. Raoul mentioned its disappearance every day, as did Angel.

Having made his presence known in general, Angel now seemed to notice me. He came over and offered to shake my hand. It was a gesture displaying his big-heartedness.

"So, you're Niemann. You're the one who tried to bump me off this job. I've worked this job all summer, and everybody left me alone. Nobody wanted the work train then. But I don't care about the hours. It's work, isn't it? And you didn't get to bump me after all."

This was perhaps the crux of Angel's generosity. I had tried to bump him, and I had failed. Someone had bumped me first. That was good.

"Well," he said with an expressive shrug, "as you see, I'm back."

Then he cocked his head, listening.

"You hear them?"

There was the sound of the wind, the sound of trucks splashing the mud and water standing in the streets, the cold sounds of a winter morning coming alive and—muffled, like sea lions barking under a pier—the sound of lions roaring at Alamogordo. And Angel Rios ran to the green borders of the park, the roaring in his mind, and came back again to the room, eyes laughing, bringing a grander joke into the beginning of the day.

"*Mira.* Listen to them. Those roars—they mean something. Those lions want something, eh?"

He turned to Raoul, now arrived and pinning up the borders of his desk, demarcating this space "his" and that space "ours."

"*Buenos dias, Señor. No ha chochado?* The lions, they haven't had any today. *Mira.* Those roars."

Raoul, embarrassed by this in front of me, grabbed the order poles out of Father Finnegan's hands in mid-fencing thrust and ordered us behind the wooden gates, handed us our orders and threatened to call the "dithpatcher," to complain of our malingering. (Raoul had a distinctive Castillian lisp, broadcast daily on the radio and mocked daily by the train crews.)

"Esth Pee Alamogordo to the Cheef Train Dithpatcher . . . "

Raoul was always telling tales to the dispatcher, and this would escalate further his feud with the trainmen. Whenever he rolled a mainline train past his depot, Raoul would be on the lookout for any little excuse to make the trainmen stop and walk their train.

"Esth Pee Alamogordo to the Esth Pee 3881 East, over."

"SP 3881 East."

"Thir. You have a plug door open in the middle of your train."

And the crew would have to stop the train and walk it, cursing out Rodriguez and hatching some retaliation.

At times the dispatcher would intervene, telling Raoul to get on with his ratkilling and leave the hotshots alone. But Raoul would wait his chance to catch whomever he was feuding with on a dog train with no priority. That train was bound to have all sorts of defects while passing through Alamogordo. Come to think about it, Raoul was probably the one attracting all the mooning on through freight. He probably saw more bare rear ends than a San Francisco proctologist.

Orders in hand, Angel, Thomas, and I crossed the tracks and climbed up into the cramped engine compartment that was going to be our home twelve hours a day. I thought, "How am I going to sit in here with that blitzed hoghead and this junior tornado all day when I'm crying all the time, when I can't stop the feelings any more?" As we settled into our seats, Thomas leaned back and started to go into his rap about his hangover and all the macho drinking he'd done last night. He was throwing this up to Angel, playing *top this*. I thought, "Oh boy, here we go."

Then Angel reached into his wallet and pulled out a little card. It had the twelve-step serenity prayer printed on it. I had been saying it under my breath just moments before.

"You know, I don't drink anymore. And whenever I want to, I just read this."

He handed the card to the engineer.

"That's good. It really is. You know my wife keeps asking me to go to church and find religion, but I keep telling her—not yet. I'm not ready yet."

Angel didn't say anything to this, and I didn't know what to say either. Religion and not drinking were not hand-in-glove in my mind, but they were for a lot of people out here. It was the old "not drinking is being good" routine that always depressed me. It made me feel as though my life were over—that the hilarity and uproar in the bars was indeed the only alternative to a grim sobriety— crows dressed up for tea—and that whatever camaraderie I had managed to put together with the men I worked with was over too. I suppose this fear was behind my growing tendency to disapprove of them. They would never be able to understand just how afraid I was of the bar after work.

It was like being at the bottom of a well, and having the choice to climb out with a rope or a ladder. The ladder is rigid, but you can stand on it. It gets you out of the hole.

Angel and I were twins, in fact. I had quit drinking in February; he had quit in March. We were at about the same level of craziness in November—both hanging on by stubbornness and a prayer. And here we were together on the work train. Yeehaw.

The tracks we were repairing skirted the base of the mountains, which now were drawing snow, bringing out the red and green stippled tones of the earth. We bought winter coveralls, brown canvas jumpsuits with blanket linings, and rubber felt-lined boots. We would stand out in the high desert all day, throwing rocks at the engines, or prying date nails out of the discarded ties, watching the track gang sweat. This was our job, to shepherd the engine, which was being used as a plowhorse. I would go apart from the crew, and walk into the sagebrush and let rage take me, or sister grief. It was good to feel unconfined at this time. I would have done it anywhere—in a restaurant, in a switchman's shanty, in the middle of a switching move. But it was good to be able to have some privacy while emotions reversed my skin while I was wearing it. Then I would notice the cold and get back on the engine with Thomas to warm up for a while and let him start to tell me the story of his life. His life with his family reminded me of something a railroad son once told me about his dad.

"We knew he was home by his feet sticking out under the blanket on the couch. We were never allowed to wake him."

When it started to get dark, we would park the engine on a spur beside the mainline and head back to the motel. As soon as the door closed to my room, I would let the feelings out again; and, panicked, I would want to call Naomi, bail out somehow; the thought of the Desert Inn lounge, where everyone was except me and Angel, would cross my mind. I began to call strangers in the program from my room after work, would let these people talk me down, get calm enough to handle going out to a meeting where I would find safety for one more night. Then I would knock on Angel's door and take him with me. He would be holed up in his room, eating from the 7-11, with the TV on.

"It's good to get out. Without you, I would just stay in my room. I know I should get out, but I wouldn't on my own."

It snowed the week of Thanksgiving. Two maintenance-of-way foremen were having a jurisdictional tug-of-war, and as a result, nobody knew if they had to work the holiday or not. It was a three-hour drive back to El Paso, and rails with families wanted to know the day before so they could start the drive after work. One boss said yes, another said no. Our gang was the only one working—twelve hours in the snow—and we ended up moving that day, too, up the line to Carrizozo where we would be based from now on. We checked into our rooms, showered the muck off, and went looking for a place to eat our holiday meal. There were two places open—both bars. In the Outpost, people had been eating and boozing it up all day. It was a scene of destruction, and all there was left to eat were a few greasy chickens in paper bags. Angel, the Father, and I headed up to the Crossroads, the official bar. The Crossroads was a truckstop with pretensions to being Denny's. It fell slightly short, but we feasted on a thin slice of turkey with mashed potatoes and white bread. The Father's request for another slice of turkey was turned down cold by the waitress in a white t-shirt and lumpy polyester stretch pants. No free lunch in Carrizozo, my friend. Rails pay here.

When I went back to my room in the motel, I gave in to the urge to call friends in California, the party I would have been at if I wasn't here. It was a bad idea. I heard the laughing sounds, corks popping, a conversational roar. Life was passing me by. And to make matters worse, my drunken friends put Naomi on the line. I ended up banging the phone down in a rage; our worlds were tangential, veering off from each other into space. Light years would separate us soon.

"I just don't know what to do with you. I never did."

"This will never come back. Don't you understand this. It will never come back. It's the end of all of it."

What I'll never understand is why I didn't pick up a drink. Why I just sat there in my room at the Crossroads Motel and felt the howling storm inside, let it drive sharp icicles under my rib cage as I tried to breathe, let it go on its way. A true miracle of snowy whiteness, the New Mexico wind invading the Crossroads, the penetrating smell of pinyon burning in woodstoves, the indescribable loneliness of the West. I was powerless to go back or do much about moving forward. I felt every inch of my surroundings. I was there in the snowstorm, left with one thing—my sobriety. And what was that?

The brakeman dreams of hawks flying over the *malpais*, the broken land. And he is helpless before the rain-soaked scent of juniper, as he is before the remembered softness of his woman's breasts. The brakeman curls his fingers around the empty air. His room is filled with voices from his dream. The surfaces of the room seem cold and slick and mean. He builds a small fire with feeble phrases of the heart. Like stroking a cat, the brakeman repeats her name, and—bloodlike—the colors change. Later, on the rails, the brakeman rides the borders of his world. The engine clacks against cold steel.

Time had a floating quality, as though this period of time were more full of time than other periods. It was vivid, painful, and full of aesthetic awareness. I was trying to find a healing power, within myself and within the universe. I could not sit still, and being alone with myself was being alone with pain and rage. I picked up the Gideon's Bible in my room. It flashed me back to El Centro when I was just beginning this booming life.

I skimmed through the Bible looking for a poetic mantra—words I could say while running in the desert to get my emotions and heartbeat in synchrony with what was around me. I was drawn to the image of the tabernacle of the sun, its heat uncovering everything, the voice of day and night. Only later, thinking about what Alamogordo was—the location where modern death came into the world, the birthplace of nuclear energy—did I find this attraction to the Nineteenth Psalm uncanny. I would use the prayer in the same way I used poetry to channel emotions; running, repeating the words as I ran towards the base of the mountains, the winter smell of juniper and fragrant pine clinging to the sleepy houses, the snow cloaking the redwash peaks and the black lava filling the spaces to the west.

I had felt connected to the universe before—in playing music, in writing poetry, in making love—and I had tried to amplify it through drugs and ended up believing that the power came from the drugs. That connection packed up and left when I put down the joint, the straw, and the bottle. In truth, it had left long before, and the last days of drinking had been a futile attempt to get it back. I missed it then as I missed Naomi now; she was the last remaining symbol of something that would give me that power. A power greater than myself. I couldn't understand that the power came from within, and that I had to let go of the symbols before I could be in touch with it.

I felt emptied, like a shell washed up on the beach. When I ran in the mornings and evenings, some of the pain lifted, and I felt less alone momentarily. I felt as though I had been in a conversation with someone, with a part of myself I didn't know too well.

I was in the process of creating a conscious self-image. It had started in the beginning, when my physical body was in intense pain and I had to learn to care for myself somehow. My conscious mind was alien at this point, full of bad advice (a martini would fix this, you know) and recriminations (it's too late, fuckup; you'll never get it back now). I visualized my body—my physical self—as a small, round, out-of-shape bear, and I bought a teddy bear to take with me on my travels. I had set out for Utah clutching the arm of this bear, the brave brakeman, facing the unknown. I would talk to the bear—my body—in a maternal way, reassuring it.

"OK, bear. We know how you feel. We love you bear."

Now the pain had moved around. My mind was the most fucked-up part of me, not the bear. The mind was like a misguided chattering monkey. I could almost apply as a rule of thumb that if I thought X, I could assume it was Y. I had been using my mind for so long as an instrument of denial that I found it completely useless as an instrument of investigation. At best, it was like a nagging spouse. I didn't want to be left alone with it for very long.

Poetry was the only thing that seemed to help me. I would walk beside the tracks on the work train, reading Wallace Stevens aloud—screaming the poems aloud sometimes—and I would feel better, I would feel relieved. I read poetry for hours, wandering off into the desert next to the tracks, the Navahos and the steel gang working down the line, leaving me alone.

During this time a third part of my consciousness was starting to emerge. I think it was the person I wanted to be. It was a lion with golden furry arms and the restored courage of the Lion of Oz—androgynous, wise, protective, and thinking by love. It would talk to me about the other animals.

"I think you have a bear problem now. I think the bear feels lost."

There were, apparently, things lions just didn't do.

"I'm sorry, but that's not the lion way."

The lion just was there. It loved in an unattracted way. It loved everyone. It was like the sun. There were lions in everyone, and they knew each other and talked lion talk. Sometimes the lion seemed to be liquid, like an ocean surrounding land, seemed to be heavy like water, and ubiquitous—in our bodies, in the air, composing everything.

The feeling the lion gave me was the feeling of being held. The world seemed to be all rough edges, and the male world I worked in was friendly but nontouching. Looking in the phone book I found some new-age healers who did massage and turned up at their studio one night after work.

A flute meditation tape was playing in the background and an Indian bedspread covered the massage table. It was warm and smelled of incense and almond oil. A hippie-looking woman in a long dress came out from behind the curtain and watched me as I peeled off my blanket-lined jumpsuit and workboots. I lay down on the table and with her first gentle touch felt waves of emotions let go.

"Tell me how you see your body. Describe it to me."

"Oh, my legs are too heavy. I see my shoulders hunched. Tense. Blocked."

"Really? That's not how I see you at all."

"What do you see?"

"I see a powerful person. I see energy."

The warmth went through her fingers into the knots I had woven around pain. And I knew there would be enough here, out on the line, to get me through.

One evening I called my mother from my room in the motel. I needed to talk to her about what was happening to me. I needed to make amends to her. She came from a long ways off to hear me, traveling through her past, through conversations with people long dead, but suddenly she was on the line and I could feel her hearing me.

"Mom, I want you to know that I have stopped drinking."

"Well, that's good, dear."

"And, well, I wanted to let you know that when you were moving I was drinking a lot, and, well, I wasn't always kind to you. I'm sorry about that."

"Oh, you were all right, dear. I don't remember you being unkind."

"Well, I just want you to know that I'm changing things, that's all."

"I think, dear, that if you get to know yourself, you'll find a very nice person."

"Thanks Mom. I miss you. I hope you're all right."

"Yes, I think everything's all right here."

Her voice faded then, as if she forgot to hold the receiver close to her face. And the communication was gone soon, but I felt comforted by it. I didn't know if words could live anymore for her, but I had put the truth out into the world and it had existed between us for that moment. I felt that it did.

At Christmas a friend came out from California, and we set out to drive around northern New Mexico. The temperature hovered at around ten degrees, but the impending storm was waiting, holding itself back. We had the parks and monuments to ourselves on the eve of the storm. We drove to the sky city and the monument rock and the canyons where the people built twelfth-century condos and then inexplicably packed up and left, taking even the bones of their dead with them. These ancient places all felt the same. They were warm and calm, in the silty sides of broad canyons; there was shelter, light, and peace. They felt familiar, as if I had been there once before. "These are homes," I thought. "This is what home feels like. It feels like this place."

Round white dollar leaves on a cottonwood rattle in the wind. White sands from Lake Lucero, sifting through an hourglass of stone.

11

VERSIONS OF HOME

I SAT THERE in the cave in the Rito de los Frijoles, looking out a door. I was a woman lost in time, homeless, an alien in my own body. I can look into my eyes as I was then, and I can see a helpless blackness there: cornered animal eyes, ready to bite and claw. Weariness, a blankness in the right eye, a desire to lie down and sleep a long time, the eye out of focus, the pupil wandering upward, askew with the rest of the face. In the left eye is the fact of suffering, a blaming eye, bloated with despair, ignorant of the reasons, staring dead on at the worst.

In another picture my eyes are closed in profile, feeling the canyon wind, smelling the pungency of cold-released bursts of seedy smells, feeling the breath of warmth the sunlight casts into the coldest wind—a face as ancient as the stone surrounding it. In something like repose.

In February I returned to El Paso, and Jesse and I moved into an apartment by ourselves. He had chosen it, a place on the edge of the Western desert, a fortress staring out into space. It was a modern complex, unfinished, built like a fort around a central pool, terraced, empty of people. We were among the first tenants. We had no furniture, no pots and pans. We were both working the extra board running up to Carrizozo. It had been too hard for Jesse to go on living with Chris. He needed separation; he needed a safe place to hit bottom with himself, to begin his wrestling match with his angel truth. I was his protection; I knew I couldn't be that, but being in the same struggle, I would be enough. Living together, we both would get by. Looking out our window on this inexplicable view of the twin smokestacks of the smelter, high voltage wires, the slag pit and desert arroyos eroding down to the ribbon river, I could see the reason Jesse moved in here. From our window you could see the window of the room where he got sober, the recovery hospital. He was moving in across the street.

I kept on running in the mornings, but it was a different proposition here in El Paso. Other people were running too, but in little clumps, like jackrabbits. And green Broncos were cruising the dirt paths running down to the river, looking for them. It was the morning rush hour for "illegals" to get to work on the El Paso side. I would come back to the apartment and find Jesse in one of two places—on the floor in front of the TV or in his new waterbed. He seemed to be able to sleep sixteen hours a day. I could hardly sleep at all, perhaps because I was sleeping on the floor. On impulse, I bought a queen-sized brass bed with marble knobs and lace-trimmed sheets. Next was a seven-foot Chinese wooden screen, one foot too long to fit in my pickup truck. I think I was having an urge to drop an anchor in the sand.

Neither Jesse nor I cooked. I made one attempt when he came down with the flu and announced from his sickbed that "Mom used to make me a chicken soup at times like this." I went to the store and bought a huge pot, a chicken, onions, turnips, carrots, garlic, and flour, and returned home to chop and stew. Four hours later, the soup was simmering down to an aromatic, turgid brew, filling the rooms with nurture, when the phone rang and Jesse answered it. Ashen faced he dragged himself out of his waterbed, pulled on his boots, grabbed his grip from in back of the door, and said:

"Well, I sure do hope there's some of that soup left when I get back."

"I can't believe this. I just made you a soup just like Mom's no less, and you are going to Carrizozo for three days. I thought you were sick."

"Too sick to play, so's I might as well work. Sorry about the soup, Miss Gypsy, but you know the way it is."

After that it was microwaved potatoes and guacamole for me and McDonald's for Jesse, until we discovered Lucy's machaca down the street. Lucy kept us alive. We were both trying to discover what to do with ourselves without drinking or using. When Jesse didn't know what to do, he just stayed in bed and slept. Then he would emerge from his room and make an announcement.

"I've decided that I'm just going to be downright nasty to people from now on. That's how I really am. I really am a criminal. And then, if people like that—then they've been warned about what to expect."

"Well, what happened? I mean, what do people expect now?"

"Well, I don't know what they expect, but I'm tired of expecting things and having people flake out on me all the time. I think I'm going to change my approach, that's all."

Jesse was trying hard to get honesty figured out. It was supposed to be the bottom line for being able to stay sober. If you could be honest, you had a chance. He thought it was a way you were supposed to act. Like a role. There was no naturally honest way for him to act because he had quite a distance to go to catch up with himself. You might say he had looked inside himself and fallen in. It was like watching someone swimming in high seas. You saw his head above water and then he would seem to be swallowed by a trough. Then his head would reappear.

"I'm going to write down everything that I think. All my thoughts just as they come out. But you know it scares me. A person would have to be crazy to have the thoughts I have. I think I really am crazy and that's the truth. It's like I've been telling lies for so long that I think I am who I say I am. But I know I'm lying. It just goes round and round."

They never said getting sober was a picnic. I was struggling with how to be with people. How to be comfortable. How to date. The unpredictable hours on the extra board made it hard to make arrangements to meet someone, and, likely as not, the beeper would go off just as I was ordering dinner, and then I had to decide if dinner with this person was worth four hundred dollars or not. A hard choice on a first date. The bar scene made railroad life easy because the substitute for intimacy was always there and sex was always there—even if you couldn't quite remember what it was like the next morning. Now though, it was going to be eyeball to eyeball with another naked human being, and I wasn't sure at all that I was up to it. It was easier to stay marked up all the time and let the railroad jerk me around.

A typical day started with a 5 A.M. call for a slow drag, the TUKCY, better known as the turkey. The letters designated point of origin (Tucson), destination (Kansas City), and classification (Y = general merchandise, or whenever it gets there). I went on duty at the El Paso yard office and sat around for three hours drinking coffee while the switchmen screwed around with our train. We started pulling around nine. It looked like it might be a decent trip with hardly any meets. Then we scoop up our orders hanging at Desert station and find a meet order on a westbound.

EXTRA 8440 EAST MEET EXTRA 7236 WEST AT OROGRANDE.
EXTRA 8440 EAST TAKE SIDING AT OROGRANDE.

This order tells our train to wait on the siding at Orogrande until a westbound with the lead engine number of 7236 goes by us. We pulled into the siding and sat. The rear brakeman started walking up the train, and I got off the engine and took a nature walk in the desert. It was heating up fast. We could hear the westbound on the radio having air trouble. They were walking their train and bitching and moaning. We call the dispatcher. Could he let us go on to the next siding since the westbound had fallen behind? Chickenshit dispatcher today, afraid to take a chance, so we sit for three hours in the noontime sun in our iron box on the ore-slag roadbed. Finally the smoke and headlight of the 7236 comes into view, splashing through the pools of mirror water created by the sun and distance. I stand opposite our engine and roll him by as he rocks the tracks with hotshot railpacks heading west. It's our turn on the single track now, and going through Alamogordo I notice that the cottonwoods have turned leafy and green. It's a green order board, and a roll-by from Raoul.

"Highball Alamogordo, ESTH-PEE 8440 East."

At three in the afternoon, we are pulling our room keys off the board in the trainmen's dorms and heading off to the Outpost to eat steak and fries. We're there until about seven, listening to rails gossip and drink beer. The mayor runs the Outpost and it is the verbal bulletin board of Carrizozo, messages given and picked up, people's lives recounted blow-by-blow, what so-and-so did yesterday and what her husband thought about it. I got to sleep around nine and—what seemed like minutes later—was awakened by the crew-caller pounding on the door.

"Dalhart, on duty two o'clock. Talk to me so I know you're alive."

Bundled up in the face of the vicious wind, we stumble over to the Crossroads diner to get something into us for the potential twelve-hour day on a train, at least hot coffee and biscuits. Then, groggy and wishing we were asleep, we sit in the locker room at the tiny depot for an hour waiting for the sound of the ten units of power in dynamic to come throbbing down the hill. The floor is littered with tobacco juice, butts, coffee cups, and wadded-up train orders. The agent is a mean-tempered prima donna who considers sweeping floors beneath him, and his rookie flunky only works one trick a day.

"Trainmen are pigs. Who cares about their floor."

A TV is constantly playing the one movie channel, showing soft-core sex and hard-core violence around the clock. A little black kitten wanders in the door, and I hold her on my lap, stroking her matted fur.

At four the westbound rolls in, shaking the building and generating action in the shanty. The inbound crew swings off, and we climb aboard. I'm on the headend with the engineer, who is having a bad night. The whole cabin smells like a Greyhound bus station—that wino, oversaturated smell. After we get out of town, he turns to me and says, "Do you know how to run?"

"No," I lie.

"Well, just sit there and look like you do then," he says as he disappears into the toilet.

He stayed there most of the trip, appearing when we had to take a siding or do something complicated.

"Thank God it's not me," I thought. "Not anymore."

We watched the sunrise about thirty miles out of town and climbed off the engines at the El Paso yard office at seven. I got home and threw a stale plate of Lucy's machaca into the microwave and wolfed it down. By nine I was dead to the world. By three I was awake again, but feeling like dogshit. I just couldn't sleep long hours during the day. At 11 P.M. the railroad called me for a J train and another all-night was in progress.

By 8 A.M. we have progressed only thirty miles because about two in the morning we broke a drawbar and our train went into big hole. I was riding in the caboose, which was left sitting on the mainline behind about five cars. Then there was a gap of about five cars where the drawbar had snapped. We were going to have to get rid of the disabled car, which meant dragging it up the line sixteen miles to a siding where we could set it out. After we had set the cars in the siding I cut off the engines so we could go back and pick up the rest of our train. This left me riding the rear unit, and as I opened the door to the cab I realized that I had company. There were at least ten men sleeping on the floor. It was three in the morning in the middle of nowhere. I didn't want to be in the cab with them, so I rode outside. It was cold, and I wished this trip was over.

When we got back to our train, Logan, the head brakeman, walked up through the units to help me out.

"Goddamn, there's guys in all those units. Where's your gun?"

"I don't have it with me."

"Well, why the hell not?"

This mishap has put us way behind our meeting times with other trains, so we get sidetracked by the dispatcher to meet three west-bounds in a row. The last one goes by us about eight. I have walked up from the caboose and wandered out into the desert. I hunker down and smell the dew on everything before true colors can exist—the red spectrum just waking up—and I get my brakeman's reward. The job puts me here, where I could never otherwise be at these magic times of day, to smell the earth and the juniper and listen for a whistle or watch for the intermittent illumination of a headlight or wisps of diesel smoke. I see it in the distance, arcs of light, visible on and off as the freight train follows the curves of the land. I can hear it now, and soon the rails stretch and creak and all is noise and whiplash motion. In the minutes of the meeting of trains, I am taken away from myself in a breathless vertigo, steadying my eyes on the cars streaking past, looking for sparks or shifted loads. The caboose whisks past with a figure outline in the rear door, hanging on, enjoying the ride. Lights rise and fall in an arc. Highball. I can hear "wrong way" Mike LeBrun's voice on the radio.

"All black on the inside, SP 7551 East. How're you doing Hurley, you old skunk?"

"Sufferin' Pathetic, as usual."

"Swap you brakemen this trip. What'd you say?"

Wrong Way Mike LeBrun was a compact Cajun with cinnamon-red hair and a cinnamon-red beard and a volatile temper that was legendary. But it went with the package, if you know what I mean. His dust-devil explosions cooled off just as fast as they heated up and then Mike was back to his usual state of John Wayne orneriness—a state that turned courtly as soon as a woman appeared on the scene. I turned up extra on his crew one day and little electric tingles had started to happen. It started with a perception of difference. Wrong Way didn't look like any of the other rails. He was wearing clothes that fit him, for one thing, and though they were simple and well-worn, they looked expensive. He wore khaki slacks, a short-sleeved shirt, and wing-tip oxfords. His dress signified no affiliation whatsoever with anything. He also kept a distance with the other rails, particularly the boomers. You got the impression that after fifteen years, Mike might say "hello." Or then again, he might not. He was like a rock in a current; people just moved around him, leaving him alone. I thought he might be hung over because he seemed not to be where he was, was kind of stumbling around in the present tense. But when he turned around and fixed me with a pair of hazel, merry, feisty eyes, I realized that he could ground his mental helicopter in a moment, that he was perhaps the first really intelligent person I had met in a long time.

Mike started off our acquaintance by butting in while I was putting another unit onto our train. But instead of setting him straight about how I could do my work, I found myself watching the way he moved as he stepped in between the cars and hooked the airhoses together in one easy fluid handshake. It had happened so fast, I hadn't had time to get mad. I started to turn around and say something, but he was close to me and flashed a warm smile that was completely out of character with the rest of his face; it lasted seconds before the habitual furrows of disgust got his face under control again and returned it to a portrait of old head swagger.

"I think I'll ride the headend this trip. I'm tired of listening to old groucho go on. Scenery's better up here anyway."

The scenery had improved, actually. Almost overnight the brown clouds of sand blown out of Mexico had settled, the air had warmed, and violent bursts of color startled out of the gritty land. Spring had arrived, and the cottonwoods at Alamogordo were green. There was a definite restlessness in everybody. It was unbearable to be on a train all day. You wanted to travel off the tracks, to wander, to shed your skin, to change something essential about yourself. There was an urgency about it, as there was about the season itself. In a month it might be gone, replaced by the six-month summer of the Southwest.

On a siding at Three Rivers we were water bombed by another train. Wrong Way leaned over me to slide the window shut as the water balloon hit us, and there were warm splashes on our arms as they brushed—as our shoulders brushed—and we both were jolted with a mild electric charge.

"Hmm, that felt good," Mike said right away, leaning back in his chair.

"Yeah," I thought, surprised. "That did feel good."

I sat there in the cab and held the feeling in my mind. Turned it over and looked on its underside. No unusual fins or scales. A clear, strong good feeling. Spring. A flirtation. Well, why not?

I think I started sleeping with Wrong Way the week the wooden bridge south of Santa Rosa burned down. I say "I think" because nothing about that period of time is at all clear to me. I know I was working every day on the extra board, sleeping crazy hours, and spending most of my time waiting for a westbound in Carrizozo. I had a couple of eccentric affairs going, but nothing I felt very involved with. Besides, I was in and out of town like a yo-yo, leaving in the middle of dinner, in the middle of bed. I told myself I would keep things light with lovers for a while. I thought I wasn't ready to take up with anyone; I was still in shock from losing Naomi. "Love is where you find it," I thought. No heavy relationships. No commitments.

And so, when Wrong Way and I were stuck in Carrizozo while they fixed the bridge, I went along with it when he started offering me rides to the diner and back to the dorms. I kept a beat-up beach bike in Carrizozo so I wouldn't have to take rides from people. But I took a ride from Wrong Way and slid into the seat beside him in his gashog seventies completely nondescript American clunker.

"Are you an undercover Dick or something? I mean everything about you is invisible. This car looks like eight million other cars—has absolutely no signs of personality in it, no effort to dress it up in any way. Just like you."

Wrong Way was wearing jeans, no belt, a brown plaid Western shirt, businessman's socks, and black work shoes.

"You're not even wearing a railroad watch."

He reached in his pocket and pulled one out.

"That's right. I don't like to wear any jewelry. I hate wearing this watch. You know, I'm not really a railroad man. Oh, I've been out here a long time, and I can fix most anything that goes wrong on a train, but it's not what I really do with my life."

"Well, what do you do?"

"Oh, I search for buried treasure. And I give pretty brakemen rides in my car. You know it could get dangerous riding with me. I might want to chase you around."

The tease hung in the air. Wrong Way's ancient shocks hit the potholes on Carrizozo's residential main drag and bounced us off the dusty beige headliner on the interior of his white car.

"You know you could get some nice tuck-and-roll done over the border in Juarez. Class up this car a lot."

Our eyes met. Fire. Ball in play.

"Oh, I probably wouldn't know what to do if I caught you anyway. Probably just be confused."

We drove to the bowling alley which was only open certain hours of the week. It had been donated by a civic-minded patron and was the only nonalcoholic recreation available in the whole town. Wrong Way was going to meet some of his friends there and we played out the afternoon, knocking pins to smithereens and elaborately apologizing whenever our legs brushed against each other. Mike was fur up with the other guys—challenging them, mocking their ability to bowl, implying that their entire character was showing up now, and that he, as always, would win all bets. There was a lot of closeness in all this: punches on the arm, gestures, laughs, sweeping acts of generosity. And elaborate formality with me.

"Secrets," I thought. "This guy is all about secrets."

"Now, I have my own style of fishing," Wrong Way was going on. "I take this ranger with me on the bayou and I light a stick of dynamite and I throw it in. *Sacre bleu.* The fish float up. He says 'That's illegal.' I light another and I put it in his hand. I tell him 'Do you want to fish or do you want to talk?'"

Later, I ended up in Wrong Way's room, me telling him all about my life here, getting sober, living with Jesse.

"And we just moved into a new place—no furniture, nothing. I didn't even have a bed. I'd been sleeping on the floor for ten months and—"

"Speaking of bed, do you want to go to bed?"

Mike was sitting on the bed. He pointed to it.

"I have a bed right here."

I looked at him. It was a real question. The room dilated and gained humidity and heat. We both waited.

"Yes. I want to go to bed with you. But I don't feel comfortable here. The ears have walls."

"Well, let's drive then. Somewhere."

It was dark and we took one of the dirt roads leading up to the hills, past where I ran mornings, to a turnout marked lovers' lane. "Park here" it said. "This is the place to park." Mike cut the motor and we sat there a minute in the dark.

"I feel nervous."

"I feel nervous, too."

"Well you're the girl. The girl is supposed to feel nervous."

He leaned toward me and we started to touch. "He feels like me," I thought. "Our bodies know each other already and are dragging our minds along for the ride." His mouth was soft, responsive. "He's feeling what's happening," I thought. "He's not just going to perform a routine, to plug in some sex act." We were both trying to go slow. Not to rush. Or it felt slow in our minds while our bodies tried frantically to change places, to exchange skin. We threw ourselves apart on the seat, zippers and shirts undone, sweat and sex smells filling the car, windows fogged.

"I'm sorry I can't seem to keep my hands off you. But I guess you're acting like you want it, too."

"I haven't done this in a while."

"I haven't ever done this," I thought. "This is the first time I've ever made love."

"God," I thought, "what's going on?"

He reached over against me again. Launching pad. Countdown. He put his fingers into my jeans and started fucking me with them.

"I want you in a bed, lady. In a real big bed."

Things started coming unglued. There wasn't anywhere to go, but I wanted to climb through the roof, wrestle Mike LeBrun's soft and solid body to the floor of the car and fuck his brains out. I got his jeans down and my hand on his cock, and we both came that way, wrestling and kissing and getting arms stuck in clothes half off and bumping our backs and heads on the fucking automatic floor shift.

We threw the car doors open and staggered out onto the dirt. Mike walked around the car, checking to see if his legs worked. I just leaned against the fender, letting the dry night wind evaporate the sweat on my skin and feeling an entire shift in the world around me. I had gotten a break from the pain. It was gone. I hadn't remembered what it was like without it. I felt like I was doing everything for the very first time.

I didn't see Wrong Way for a while after that. On the extra board wheel of fortune, our encounters were up to chance. In any month I would rarely work with the same crew twice. Besides, he was married and there were rules to the game. No, I didn't feel right about it, but I wanted to keep this high alive. I wanted to pump it full of life. It was a fix. It fixed everything that felt wrong. I thought, "I'll keep it out of town. We'll get a meeting place in Carrizozo. I'll figure out a way to handle it." It was like being a teenager again, hyper-alive. I didn't need to sleep or eat. I read poetry all day on the train, driving my braking partners crazy.

"What's that stuff you're reading?"

"William Carlos Williams. He wrote about El Paso, about the bridge. Walking between the two cities, the sounds of life here."

"Is that so. Let me see that. That's really about El Paso?"

Mike and I would meet in the yard office, waiting for trains. We would maneuver for a casual look, sitting at the switchman's table, allowing ourselves one steamy glance, then covering it with a camouflage of conversation.

"This guy is pussywhipped," I thought. What happened to rocket man who blew things up? Mr. Dynamite with other men. Mr. Hide and Seek. Who faced down rattlers in old mining holes, outran soldiers when they caught him with maps and a geiger counter on their desert proving grounds.

I guess that was man-stuff. When it came to woman-stuff, Wrong Way was playing it close to the cuff. Pussy know how to bite.

"I just don't want anyone to get hurt. I mean I know I treat you like I don't even like you, but I can see it in your eyes, and if I can see it, others can see it."

"For God's sake, Mike, nobody gives a shit. They're too busy worrying about their own sex lives. I mean if you can shoot people in Texas and get away with it, why can't you fuck around a little?"

Mike had told me that in Texas the first one was free. If you kept on shooting people, you might have some explaining to do, but the first time was cool.

"Well, I gave my wife a 480 automatic for her birthday to keep in her purse. I'm thinking about that right now."

"Oh, God," I thought. "Here I am having a straight love affair, and I have to sneak around. I mean, how dumb can it get?"

And so I hatched the plan about the room. A kind of last tango in Carrizozo idea. The rooms for rent were above Calliope's antique store on the only paved street in Carrizozo. It was an old brick building, now the several shades of red New Mexico dust. High dirty windows overlooked the railroad depot and the dilapidated shops that formed the center of town. Beside the building was a small plaza, a courtyard garden cracked and dusty with a dry mosaic fountain in the center. There was no shade, and the concrete bench resting against the wall was little used, except by drunks at night. Even here you could smell the cat urine that emanated from the interior of the store.

The Calliope brothers owned half the town and lived as hermit outcasts. It was a clash of lifestyles blown up into Gothic theater. They looked like sweet nellie queens. They owned an antique store. What could be more normal? One of them was even a war hero. But the town and the railroaders never tired of gossiping about the brothers' sex lives. And during the long, cold war with the town, the Calliopes started letting their hundreds of cats shit and piss on things in the store. People still came in; they had to occasionally. And bargain-hunting tourists got into the store and into the piles of Indian rugs and blue jeans and Western cook pots and old brass beds before the full force of the stink hit them. Then they looked around and noticed the older man in the makeup and turquoise drag, but they were there already and besides there wasn't catshit on everything.

"How do you do, Gypsy. We haven't seen you lately. Is there some new romance been keeping you away?"

I knew the Calliope brothers slightly by now. After all, they were on the front lines. It was the least I could do to be friendly. Any outcast was a friend of mine. My picture of Dorian Gray was at home dressed in full leather drag, braiding her whips. Or God knows what else.

"Don't I wish. I think I went from alcoholic to workaholic with no in between. I have worked every day for the last three months except when I took a vacation to have the flu. Is it three in the afternoon? Well then it's time to go to bed for the day. You must know they only run freight trains at night, living so close to the tracks."

"Well, I hope you're having some exciting dreams then, dear. Something to make your life a little brighter."

"Well, I was thinking an apartment might make things brighter. Here in Carrizozo. Someplace I could stay besides the company dorms. What about the rooms upstairs?"

"Oh, well nobody stays in those. Not for the longest time. But you can look if you like."

We walked out the front door and Calliope pulled a key from his jeans. He opened a door onto a side stairwell. There were dusty mail slots with numbers. A roomy staircase led up to the second floor. The odor of cats was almost invisible here, except for what clung to his fantastical person.

"Is it just for you, or do you have a pretty boyfriend."

"Just for myself. But you never know; I might get lucky."

Sexual innuendo hung in the air as we climbed the stairs and entered a wooden-floored hallway containing eight numbered doors. He first opened a large room at the end of the hall with a window overlooking the depot.

"You can see all the railroaders from here — their comings and goings."

I wondered if he watched me and Wrong Way from here, or which rails he fantasized about, watching from these windows. I felt slightly uneasy in the room; it felt like a barracks, the single bed military and stiff. It was someone else's scenario.

The last room we entered felt cool and right. It was a large room on the courtyard side, and the high windows would let in the eastern light. A fine layer of dust lay on all the surfaces, muting them. In the breakfast nook, two benches faced each other conspiratorially over a small table. I could smell the morning coffee here, two people talking easily after sex.

I wanted this room left as it was, with the dust lying on the forties end tables in the particulate golden light. The overstuffed couches were ripe and sensual shapes. Their texture would be slightly abrasive to the skin and the warmth from the sunny windows would fall caressingly, like a cat.

An iron double bed stood in the corner, its thin mattress covered by a brown chenille spread. That would stay exactly as it was also. I wanted nothing here but desire, that eternal pauper, which can bring no impediments and still remain desire.

Calliope now gestured toward the bed, the surrealistic object of our separate visions.

"That's better, isn't it — in case you get lucky."

The overlapping images of desire breathed in and out through the room, colored the light of the afternoon, made the room a safe place, a place outside the city's walls. One could be free to come or go. One more secret in the house of cats. It would do for a tryst.

March brought a late storm broiling down from the north, giving you the bum's rush down dirt roads, tumbleweeds headed for the fence. We arrived in Carrizozo at midnight, and I had to hold onto the grabirons tight as I climbed off into the cyclotron. I found my beach bike on its side behind the shanty and swung aboard, the wind behind me filling my clothing like sails. It was so dark I couldn't see, couldn't see the snakes I worried about sometimes. Too cold for snakes tonight.

Inside the dorms, I looked for Mike's name on the logbook, took a key off the board for a room near his. Fuck the paper walls, the little dance with my crew.

"Going to eat?"

"No, too tired. Goin' to bed."

Tonight the storm was on the inside; my millimeter of natural patience had long gone into bankruptcy. Waiting the ten minutes it would take my crew to disappear, I opened the door and sneaked along the walkway like a cat on a fence. The sound of the knock seemed unnaturally loud, even over the storm.

Then the door opened. A world of another texture was inside. Things were in rumpled disarray; half in half out of sleep; quiet, half recognized. Wrong Way stood there in an old t-shirt and boxer shorts. He smelled like Wrong Way. He backed slowly into the room, the momentum was coming from me.

I put my arms around him in the dark. The first touch swept over me as profound relief. I was so reassured by it, as if an anxiety about a death had been swept away. A bad dream had been swept away. I touched the back of his neck, his shoulders, his face turned up toward me and I found his mouth with mine, felt his mind opening, spiraling, and I followed it through the magic portals, the world growing smaller beneath us, Mike LeBrun moving gently in my arms. Friction. Tiny cell explosion. Slow motion. The wet sand absorbing millions of protoplasmic light flashes, each wave a rim of slow fire cartwheeling to the beach. The sound of the wave's recession. The moment before the next crash.

I moved around his body with my mouth, touching him lightly, randomly, so that each place would be waiting for the next to touch, would start to turn towards it, so that all the diameters of the body would feel, would awaken sensually. He felt like my double, as sensual as I was, as responsive. I wanted his cock now, in my mouth, wanted to take him to a big edge, a slide on the Big Dipper into the Southern Sea. Gasping, he pulled out of my mouth, and swept me under him onto the bed. I was a lion now, a lion spirit going for the back of his neck, tooth and claw. And then, feeling the whole weight on me pressing me into the bed, I took him inside, surrendered to the fuck, brief intense waves of pleasure hitting the seawall.

Opening our eyes, it seemed the world was deadly still, the storm, the mainline trains all still. Listening.

We fell apart on the bed, sex over so quickly. Time now for words.

"Sexy lady. How do you know how to love a man like that?"

"Well, I'm from L.A."

"Well, it kind of makes a man want to go there. Sexy lady and a dangerous lady."

"I thought you were an outlaw. A rocket man. I thought you liked it dangerous."

"I'm in bed with the dynamite; I'm holding the fuse, and I got the match lit too."

"I know it isn't OK here. But I could rent a room. It would be private. It's a way around."

The offer hung in the air. Early light fringed the dirty windows. It was growing colder.

"I don't know. I think it's better just to let it ride. Say, are you this friendly with all your conductors?"

And how to say no, it is only you—the other lovers don't matter, in a way they don't exist. This is something created out of ashes. It has never existed before. It is the purest love you have ever known.

"You know, you ought to teach other women how to love."

"What makes you think I don't?"

"Well, does that mean you're a pro?"

I guess you could say Mike and I had a communication gap. I would tell him the truth, like about me and Jesse being just friends, or my having love affairs with women, and I would watch him think I was lying. He would look at the words like a sculpture in an art show, walk around them and nod, agree even, whatever was called for. But he never believed it for a minute. He was such a liar himself.

Perhaps *liar* is a harsh word. Wrong Way created fictions and lived in their world. As a treasure hunter, it wasn't the prize he was interested in, it was looking for the prize, exfoliating some secret from its iron hat. Always a desire for a greater wildness in the world outside; looking for something metal that was lost, something valuable that existed long ago. He was a self-taught historian of mischance. In the driest and most landlocked spot in the country he dreamed of sunken treasure, the Spanish gold routes, deep mountains of water. He had a version of a true North American virus: goldrush fever and prospector's mistrust.

For the treasure was hidden in the people here. The idea, so prevalent in California, that you could change your life, that life could begin several times, was unknown here. The high school years were the Golden Age. After that, the desert wore people down. The material culture, when it became at all overscale, turned garish and dominated the landscape. The desert is actually very fragile. It was hard to see alternatives. Nature was not kindly; shelter was important. And Mexico pressing against the borders reinforced the worst in North American values. They want what we've got don't they?

I walked into the El Paso public library one day and found an edition of Mary Austin's *Land of Little Rain* with photographs by Ansel Adams. It was a perfect book. A counterpoint collaboration of two geniuses in love with their subject. Prose that was photography and photographs that spoke to you. It gave me goosebumps reading it. I wanted to steal it, but instead I brought it back. A harried, middle-aged woman librarian was sitting behind the checkout desk, dishing out snappy comments to a teenage helper. I handed her the book and asked if she had a copy of the new biography on Mary Austin. She looked up at me in shock.

"Who are you?"

"Someone who loves Mary Austin."

The woman looked at me with a helplessly truth-telling gaze.

"She changed my life."

I wondered what could that mean, here on the borderline. Her library a beachhead of what would have to be remedial culture, with so much of the population learning English and the rest defending its fortresses. How was this changed person living now, here, with this secret? What could it mean to have your life changed and have to live in isolation with it?

I suppose that was my question also. It had certainly happened to me. Wrong Way would wonder at my being here: "ending up here" was his phrase. I could tell I didn't compute. My words were failed messengers, arriving at their destination wearing foreign dress, conveying their opposite. The distance was too great. Words, in truth, do not travel well. Living and eating and sleeping and working with someone is often the only way to communicate.

Wrong Way would give me advice.

"Why don't you play the game? Wear a dress, go to church socials?"

I would stare at him in disbelief. Did he think I just didn't know what to do? That I had grown up on Mars, without television? He also believed that "inside every woman there is a little girl" and that "what every woman really wants is a knight in shining armor."

"Hard work keeping it polished," I said. He didn't get the joke. I decided not to tell him what I saw in him, the receptivity, the femininity. He wouldn't take it the right way. But I felt it. He was as bisexual as I was. That was what I liked about him. I had started having vivid fantasies about making love with Mike, but we would be two men—sometimes a jailfuck scene with Mike the dominant one, fucking me in the ass, telling me he was going to make me his girl. "God," I thought, "this is wild stuff." But of course there had to be some truth in it, some deep private truths for both of us, finding their space to be on a highballing freight train, in a room traveling in between locations, strangers on a train, strangers in a dream.

Sometimes the hard-shell homophobia of the Southwest just plain wore me out. All year I had sat through movie after movie in the trainmen's locker room in Carrizozo, the only alternative to being there a blizzard or a heat wave outside. Waiting on our train, this was where we sat. With the good old boys spitting brown tobacco slobber into their paper cups, I had seen women bludgeoned, chased, yelled at, terrorized, power fucked, cut up, gang raped, mocked, belittled, and generally used—on a daily basis. Nobody but me and the two other women brakemen ever noticed this. The other trainmen were kind of bored, sort of amused. Then one day the movie *Deathtrap* came on and we got to the scene where Christopher Reeve gives Michael Caine a sweet little peck on the cheek. Grown men leapt to their feet and rushed out the door.

"That's just disgustin'. Seein' that just makes me want to puke. My Gawd, I can't stand it."

Somebody might be protesting just a teeny bit too much, don't you think? Just a teeny bit, maybe?

The call I'd been waiting for came at 3:30 in the morning, the crew dispatcher's voice like a shot of adrenalin, erasing the fact that I'd only been asleep four hours.

"Niemann, on duty 4:30; you're with conductor LeBrun."

"Jackpot," I thought, flying into the shower and letting pleasure steam onto my back, mirrors fogging up with lust. I pulled into the parking lot and stopped with a crunch as my snow tires spun on the dirt. They were baking bread again across the street. The sweet yeasty smell. I had parked next to Mike, and I liked the way his jeep looked next to my truck. It was automotive love. "God," I thought. "I'm really from L.A."

I joined the crew in the conductor's room, a small space containing log books, job advertisements, timetable bulletins, a standard clock, and union bulletin boards. Mike was there talking to another conductor, and we gave each other studiously cool nods. Then the other brakeman walked in, the survivalist from under the freeway overpass. This guy was a boomer from Oregon who had moved down here with his family in a mobile home and parked it under the freeway on company property. He was a husky blond haired blue eyed neo-Nazi fanatic. The type of guy you could picture belonging to the Aryan brotherhood or some other bloody right wing terrorist group. He was a bible-thumper too—and intelligent, with a biblical rationalization for all of his white male supremacist power-grabbing opinions. You know, a relaxing kind of guy to be around. Particularly if you were female or brown, or—God forbid—black. Gossip had it that he had forbidden his wife to turn on the air conditioner during the day while he was out working. If he had to endure the heat, so did she. She was also supposed to answer the door with a loaded gun in her hand to protect his honor. I bet they didn't have too much company. He didn't let his son go to the public schools—they were too left wing. In Texas they were too left wing. And he was in some kind of court battle about it. The kid had to drop and do pushups whenever Dad Survivalist didn't like something.

"Kids who do dope should be shot. That would take care of the problem."

"Well, what about mistakes? Don't you think you learn from them?"

"My son doesn't need to make mistakes. He just needs to do what I say."

I could picture the headlines. Survivalist found with Ninja star through his heart. Son held for questioning. "I was protecting my mother's honor. Somebody had to do the son of a bitch."

Pretty soon the Survivalist and Wrong Way were talking fire-power, and out came the hardware right in the conductor's room.

"Well, of course I have an Uzi at home, but I carry a Beretta nine millimeter on the road."

Wrong Way was unsnapping his nondescript Samsonite suitcase. Inside were some t-shirts and a nine millimeter German Luger.

"This will stop anything and blow a hole the size of a dinner plate. Now in extreme cases, you can lock in this." He extracted a long metal military looking object from under his socks.

"Thirty-two shot snail drum."

He jammed it into the bottom of the gun and held it out to the Survivalist. I lost my cool.

"Don't give him that thing; he's a religious fanatic. He thinks they should shoot schoolkids for smoking dope."

They both turned towards me with childlike surprise. What was she weirding out about? Back to the guns and man talk. Wrong Way was reminiscing about the time he and a buddy destroyed a car with machine gun fire.

"Took that clunker out on the property and let fire with all we had. Pile of scrap in five minutes. Sure was fun."

"God," I thought, "I think I'll go back to my truck and get my gun. What if the Survivalist and I have to walk the train? I'm not meeting that dude in the middle of the desert with no pistol."

I walked back in with my new pistol, a gun Jesse helped me to buy, a Smith and Wesson thirty-eight with a four-inch barrel. You could hit things with this one.

Mike and the Survivalist were discussing how to load an auto-matic so that you wouldn't leave fingerprints on the shell casings.

"Rubber gloves. It takes time, but you won't be sorry."

This time they noticed me come in.

"Nice piece," Wrong Way said softly, caressing the barrel of my gun in his calloused palm.

I felt sexier then. I had a nice gun, a nice little piece. I was part of the club. The crew clerk came by in the carryall, ready to take us to our train, and Wrong Way turned to the Survivalist:

"You ride the headend this trip."

I saw his blue Nazi eyes deepen and a thin smile start. Fucking bible thumpers sure have a nose for sex.

"Sure thing, Mike. If you say so."

I waited in the caboose for the air test, sun risen by now, the carmen taking their own sweet time. We would pick up Wrong Way on the fly as he rolled the train by leaving town. As we started to pull, I opened the window and watched for him. A hundred and twenty cars, long old train, but at last he was there, hooking aboard.

"Highball Mac, everyone's on."

"Highball, here we go."

Act four, scene three. The lovers have a chance to converse at last. Why, then, by ten o'clock had we talked about caves and poetry and Wrong Way's days as a dynamiter for government seismologists and the old roads up there in the Organ mountains but not about us, not a word about our love affair? Because there was something Wrong Way didn't want to say, but not before we made love.

So picking ourselves off the bed in the caboose, radio chattering to empty ears ("You're breaking up Mac. Got a bum radio."), Wrong Way looked at me and sighed deeply.

"Well, you were saying all that about honesty and stuff. I guess I got something to tell you. I didn't want you to get that room because I don't want to hurt a lady's feelings."

"A lady's feelings?"

"A lady in Carrizozo. It's sure my fault. I don't know what I had in mind."

"Well, was she at the dentist or something, that day you were chasing me around. What did you have in mind?"

"Well, I guess I wasn't thinking about what was going to happen. I just wasn't thinking, is all. I won't blame you for being mad at me. I think they should have a place like AA for people like me to go— sex anonymous. I just don't want anybody to get hurt."

"Well, I'm fucking getting hurt. Don't touch me. I'm going to have to take all this in. You are really amazing, Wrong Way. I think I'm starting to understand why they call you Wrong Way."

"Well, there's the right way. And then there's my way."

In Carrizozo we swung off the caboose and joined the Survivalist in the locker room. It was around dinnertime and he asked Mike if he was going to eat.

"Oh well, I suppose so. You want to go eat, Gypsy?"

"Why not?"

One big happy crew, off to eat at the Crossroads.

We all ordered steak and baked potatoes. It was survival food in New Mexico. You wanted to see what it was you were eating. The Survivalist was up to something with Mike, as if he were trying to pull him away from me, to establish a male confidence that I was left out of. I felt the tug, like a kelp bed sucked by the breaking surf. The Survivalist was talking about his upright way of life.

"I plan to grow my own food, build my own house, and educate my own children."

Mike looked at him in vague agreement. I could feel him inching over to the Survivalist's side, away from me. In public he couldn't take my side anyway, and the Survivalist was putting up a big umbrella.

"Of course a man has to keep to the straight way. You can't give in to temptations. All of them boil down to lust, one way or the other."

Wrong Way didn't say anything. I couldn't believe he was going to take this. But I guess this was what it was all about. These were the words walking around on the surface of this world, and what you did in private you kept silent about. Well, I wasn't going to keep silent—in a theoretical way, of course.

"Well, what about the lust for power—like you're having right now? It seems to me that the desire to be right all the time is a kind of lust, don't you think?"

The Survivalist fixed me with a superior gaze.

"It's not just me saying this. The Bible says these things."

"Well, you should take it on a talk show. My Bible has never said one word to me. Not one single word."

"You're being silly."

"No, you're missing my point. The Bible doesn't say anything. You interpret it. And you interpret it the way you want to. That's lust."

"Well, I think we all know what I mean by *lust*."

Wrong Way just sat there, waiting for the next move.

"Say, Gypsy, I wouldn't eat that coffee creamer if I were you."

"Oh really? Why not?"

Holding the little packet in the air and allowing a thin stream of the powder to float down towards my plate, Wrong Way lit a match. There was a silver blue flash as the powder ignited.

The Survivalist and I watched, spellbound. Wrong Way the trickster, the coyote.

"Now if you had a gum wrapper, I could show you another one."

"Well, I guess you can make a bomb out of just about anything."

"Just about. You'd be surprised at what a lot of ordinary things are made of."

I was thinking about the Survivalist, what bothered me about him so much. Why I wanted irresistibly to fight with him. He was a man who believed in his fictions, who saw the world as being real, firm, black and white. He was willing to shoot what he saw, to get in there and rearrange the nuts and bolts of things according to what he saw. And he was capable of it. We were natural enemies. And I knew he would win because he was incapable of understanding what fictions were.

Our argument began again and went on and on and on. I hadn't met anyone out here with such developed verbal skills; I couldn't pin him. I would push him back to his unquestioned first assumption, and he would wiggle out like a greased pig with yet another oration. He refused to grant me any points at all. Wrong Way had settled back and was watching the show. After several hours, we were talking about shooting each other. And I realized that my own philosophy was going to do me in. I saw that I was the Survivalist; we existed within a power greater than ourselves, connected. Brother Survivalist was a cardboard figure of myself set in a Western movie front. Struck by this idea, I spoke to him as if he could understand this.

"You know, if we were enemies and I had to shoot you to save my life, I wouldn't be sure that it was you, and not me, that I was shooting."

The Survivalist knew his line on this one.

"Well, I would know. I would be sure."

Wrong Way pulled his chair closer and reached in his jeans pocket. He pulled out a primitive looking little gun with a broken pearl handle.

"Look at this little stinger. Antique Derringer, a lady's gun. Even says *Lady Luck* on the stock. Had to have the bullets made up special. Could you imagine this looking at you over a hand of cards?"

Wrong Way gathered us in, the so-called real and the magical soldiers warming at his fire. We passed the lady's gun, handling the bridge object, the ancient artifact owned by the emperor of the games. And so we left the Crossroads diner and proceeded to our separate beds. It was a windy night, but a warm wind blowing summer and sameness in the air. I had a lot to think about, and I would dream about my father, Carl Niemann, and all his photographs of the desert.

"Where are the people?" I used to think. "Why does he take all these pictures with nothing in them?"

"Landmarks," he would say about his scientific work. "For the next traveler along the way."

Things went on this way for a while. I found myself feeling lonelier than I used to be, and I started searching around Carrizozo for another lover to even out the balance of power. I started hanging out in the bars for the company I hadn't needed before. It was funny. Because I wanted to be with Wrong Way, I started cruising everybody else. I drank my orange juice and watched the tequila bottles staring back at me from behind the bar.

Tonight it was dinnertime, and I was alone as usual. It was a slow night even for the Outpost—a few tourists on their way to the races at Ruidoso, a few hardluck miners who seemed to spend most of their time shooting pool, and a couple of rails. I knew where Wrong Way was. It was a Saturday night; you either ate here or at the other place. My doubles pool partner, Mario Villaseñor, was getting lubricated and his daughter, the bartender, was giving him a hard time about it.

"No coaching, Mario. You let her make her own shot."

"I ain't coaching her. You just keep track of what you do. I don't need no babysitting. See what happens when they grow up?"

"You really have thirteen kids?"

"Yes, I am very macho man. Thirteen children and ten grandchildren."

"Quit bragging, Mario. You know who did the hard part."

Mario's daughter's words seemed to float behind a plate glass window. I felt cut off from everyone in the room. The sounds in the bar were becoming cacophonous and random. I realized that there was nobody I really knew in here, in the whole town; nobody I could really talk to.

The jukebox was playing "Waltz Across Texas," and one of the rails asked me to dance. It felt good just to touch someone, to pretend to be close for the length of the song.

"God, you make me feel like I can dance. You sure do hold me like I was a man."

But it wasn't working for me, and I knew the old solution was gone as well. I saw a succession of failures in all the things I would try to do that were like a shot of booze. I couldn't even want them anymore.

I went outside into the gusty May night. Dust was flying and I could taste the grit in the air when I wet my lips. My bike was leaning against the cafe wall, the ugliest bike in Carrizozo, so ugly the kids wouldn't even steal it. Carrizozo itself was a little like this; a rugged, weather-beaten place surrounded by forty miles of broken black lava, but with a clean soul inside it.

I wondered if it was time to go home, to head west, back to my easier society. The street was dark and the dogs ran after the bicycle and barked. But nobody came to their doorway to look. The Calliope brothers' store was dark also, but a single light showed from a window in the back. I wondered about their life then, wondered what sadness it was. My own still unrented room was dark as it had been for years.

I could imagine it clean. The windows washed and refracting light. A desk with a typewriter and papers stacked on the couch and chairs. Books lay in piles beside the quilt-covered bed. An enormous Chinese screen showing cranes flying over a golden sky gave the room definition. It was my room. An Indian rug, two grey hills, lay on the wooden floor. The woodstove hissed, as resinous bubbles formed on the burning pinyon, filling the room with warmth.

I would have unusual visitors here, people from dreams, people from the past, people who were only a word or phrase. Perhaps they could be persuaded to talk about their lives, to tell their side of the story, to be at home in it for a little while.

I understood that I would rent the room for myself, then, either this room or another. That I would write things there. In the meantime I could hold the room in my mind, in the center of myself, and I could go there when I needed to.

I rode over the ruts and gouges in the road, wheels humming, mind humming, carried by the wind.

12

A ROAD
TO RIDE

B Y N O W I had nearly eight years working in the craft as a brakeman/switchman. I had worked every type of braking job there was from one-day turnaround locals to mainline runs. I'd been on work trains doing every kind of track work. I'd been a switchman in small working yards knocking out hundreds of cars a night and pulled pins on the crest of giant humpyards. I'd worked tower herder jobs and retarder operator jobs, learned the map of tracks in five giant yards, been over thousands of miles of track from Houston to Oregon, worked fifteen different terminals, worked with every kind and race and age of person—old heads and rookies, good people and people with no morals at all. And I'd come to respect the craft and understand the life that went with it, its history and how people lived with it.

And now things were changing, not just in me, but in the life of the railroad as well. I was just a leaf floating on a larger whirlpool of economic, political, and social changes affecting the whole nature of the work and the workforce. I had been among the last railroad workers hired, period. Since that time I had been swept from place to place as one of the *nouveau* boomers in a race to catch up with the job. But the job and the rules of the games were always changing just a little faster than we could change. Huge switching yards were virtually closed down overnight. Rumors would circulate.

"They're going to run everything the southern route, switch it all out in Colton, Tucson, and Houston. Everything else will be shut down."

"Hell, I've seen 'em just plain run business off. They just about asked these truckers to come in here and take over the perishable business. Growers aren't going to wait two days for a switch. Company's in the real estate business anyway, not the railroad business anymore."

Switchmen from the Oregon humpyards would drift south, end up in L.A. or El Paso, only to be cut off there six months later. They would move their families depending on some trainmaster's assurance of work. And why not say there was work if you needed bodies that week? If you jerked the workers around enough, maybe some of them would quit, and that was objective number one in the new ballgame.

The political climate was right for a war with the union, for radical changes in working conditions, pay rates, craft distinctions, crew size, and operating conditions. Everything was up for grabs. The Southern Pacific itself was in corporate limbo from 1979 until the ICC turned down its merger plans with the Santa Fe in 1986. The uncertainty about whether the SP would take a bankruptcy dive hung over all the contract negotiations. It was one giveback after another, undoing a hundred years of labor agreements. And it was hard to explain what all these givebacks represented, hard to defend them to people who didn't understand what railroad life was like.

It seemed like the right to breathe was becoming negotiable. For instance, labor agreements gave you the right to an agreed-upon place where you went on and off duty. If you didn't have that, the railroad would define your home as wherever you quit working that day, and they would want you back to work eight hours later. You would think that a home, or someplace you could think of as a home, was a basic worker's right. You worked; then you went home. But the railroad didn't think so. According to their logic, you had time off, not time at home, and labor had to fight for defined on-duty and off-duty points (or home and away-from-home terminals). Deadhead pay was the penalty pay the company had to forfeit if they put you on or off duty anywhere other than those points. It was a day's pay extra, and it seemed like a lot until you started being jerked around like a pingpong ball, sitting down to Thanksgiving dinner and winding up in El Centro. Then it hardly seemed enough. Well, deadhead pay was soon a thing of the past. Now you got the time you spent deadheading added to your day's pay, which was no incentive for the company to make an effort to get you home.

There were many other changes: crew size; use of radios; elimination of train orders, herders, and cabooses; adoption of a new rule book; rest restrictions on the extra board; a two-tier wage system; the installation of "talking" trackside hotbox and dragging equipment detectors; random drug and alcohol testing; and a buyout program. And a reign of terror to induce employees to take it.

Essentially, the railroad wanted to dump all local freight business and run short cabooseless railpack trains from port to destination with a minimum of switching. They would like to run these trains with two crew members: an engineer and a co-engineer. The goal was to completely merge all crafts, so that anyone could do anything. Systemwide seniority was a step toward this idea since it created a mobile labor pool that would take up the slack wherever business needed extra workers. Now the goal was to cut the labor force protected by union agreements. The new federal regulations allowing random drug testing provided the means to this end.

The terminal superintendent in Tucson announced a personal goal of firing thirty percent of the workforce—people he suspected of being drug addicts and alcoholics. Suddenly, I was not the only person drinking orange juice at the bar. Any accident, no matter how minor and regardless of responsibility, was followed by a trip to a clinic for urinalysis. Legal intoxication was not the guideline followed in dismissal. Any reading for alcohol brought dismissal. Given the railroad lifestyle and the fact that it was impossible to predict exactly when you would go to work, this meant that you could never safely use alcohol. Some traces might be present even though the person would not be legally intoxicated. Traces of marijuana might remain in the system for six months, and a trace was enough to get you fired.

Even though I had nothing to worry about personally, I deeply resented the company's approach to this problem. They were just using the testing to fire people. They didn't address any of the underlying problems like the exhausting hours of work, the ratty away-from-home lodging places, the lack of recreational alternatives in such places, the lack of counseling benefits on our medical insurance, and the stress that their own pressure created. Rails were going to quit drinking and find that they were getting a bum deal in life, and it was going to get bummer.

The new contract the UTU was negotiating turned out to be a fuckover. Union big-wigs—slick fast talkers with iridescent three-piece suits—parked their Cadillacs in front of the switchmen's shanty and handed out big cigars.

"Don't worry boys; we'll take care of you. You should see what other railroads are having to accept."

Other railroads where? In Mexico? India? Poland? But the union leaders knew their men. It was just the junior people that would be hurt; the ones with seniority would get even more money. And who cared about the junior men? They should have to pay their dues. When the railroad ran with a short crew, they paid seven dollars extra per man and also paid into a fund that would be divided up at the end of the year according to how much you worked. Obviously, the trainmen with seniority got to work and also got to collect the most for those who didn't. Short crews were only supposed to run under special conditions and only when "protected" men weren't available. As a general thing, they were supposed to be phased in by attrition.

Of course, once the agreement was signed, the company and the union reached a hip-pocket agreement that allowed the company to run lots of short crews. So called "rest restrictions" limiting the availability of brakemen working the extra board were instituted. Returning from a trip to your home terminal you might have to wait sixteen or twenty-four hours before you were eligible to work again. And when you became eligible, you often had to wait even longer before a job was actually called. In the meantime, while you sat on the board, the company ran short crews.

Graffiti such as "UTU Sucks Cock" started to appear on caboose walls.

In place of a brakeman, every other train crew member was supposed to get a radio. The art of handsigns and teamwork was being phased out. One person with a radio could do a lot of moves that formerly took several persons. It wasn't as safe, however. Radios malfunctioned, and there wasn't another person backing you up with signs. You also got more careless about knowing where everybody was. You just assumed that everybody could hear your moves and would be in the clear. But radios were not easy to carry so that they could be heard, particularly when you were riding cars or doing some work. Now, along with your lantern, you had a three-pound radio to hold onto while hanging off the side of a freightcar.

Radios were also going to be used in place of train orders. The old way was to have station agents copy train orders from the dispatcher and hang them up for crews to grab off order boards as they passed that station. Now you would get your running authority directly from the dispatcher by radio. That meant the agents were no longer needed and the railroad could close all the little train order stations, like Raoul's. A lot of the railroad had already been converted to power switches and signals controlled by a CTC operator, but train orders were used over a lot of track that hadn't been upgraded yet. Now that track was designated DTC, or "direct traffic control," territory. Train orders were out and, with them, another area of expertise.

Reading train orders was not easy. There were twenty-five distinct forms of train orders according to the purpose of the order. Everything from orders to meet trains, to wait until certain times before proceeding, to authorize work extras, to inform trains of times of work being done, to advance trains to the next station, to change parts of an order. The orders were written with telegraphic briefness. Each word was crucial; which train was named first was crucial. Actually, everything was crucial since the information concerned which train would go where in meeting another train. Any error in an order invalidated the entire order so once you scooped the order up, you then went over them minutely and compared interpretations with the rest of the crew. The results were interesting. Not everyone understood how to read train orders.

EXTRA 8330 EAST HAS RIGHT OVER EXTRA 8557 WEST ALAMO-GORDO TO CARRIZOZO.

This order gives the first train the right to the main track between the points mentioned but not at the points mentioned. At either Alamogordo or Carrizozo, the first train must take the siding. Both the dispatcher and the train crews had to be experts on train orders or there could be real trouble. Switching over to DTC made it easy, just like the electronic cash registers make it easy for people who don't know math to make change. I wonder if it isn't being made too easy. Train orders made you think. They were part of the craft.

I suppose what was happening was that the craft was changing into a job—something that was fairly simple and that you could train people to do. Railroading as a craft wasn't something you could learn in a classroom. A lot of the old heads hadn't ever studied the book of rules; they just memorized them. They had a shortlist of the rules which they worked by, combined with twenty years of experience. The experience was the crucial teacher. The old-time conductor had absolute authority on his job; and he had to know about the equipment, the track, the needs of the industries he spotted, the character and habits of everybody he worked with, what the danger signs were of something going wrong, and what to do if it did. You would be riding in the caboose with an old head and he'd pick up on a sound you never even noticed.

"Goddamn if they haven't fixed that frog yet. I keep tellin' 'em they're going to have a train on the ground right there someday. Didn't you hear that click?"

Put the two-man crew on the headend with nothing to do but ride and stay awake and they'll never hear that click, never notice the shifted load forty cars deep, never smell the overheated brake shoes before they're burned off. The brakemen now care less than they used to because they have less responsibility. Funny thing is that if the job's too easy, you can't trust people to do it right.

A craft has a life of its own, a world of its own. It's self-regulating and self-rewarding. Trainmasters would come and go, but the switchmen would remain working the same yard for twenty years, and the weight of their experience kept things moving smoothly. There were bad jobs and good jobs, and the old heads got the good jobs. All you ever were was a switchman, but a switchmen with thirty years could bid in a herder job if he wanted to take it easy. The company didn't promote you, but the craft had promotions built into the seniority system. When the company eliminated the herders, it was part of a push to homogenize all the jobs. What you did when you went to work on day one would be the same as when you quit thirty years later. This concept would destroy a craft. It would take control out of the hands of the switchmen and give it to management. And management was notoriously unstable. They changed their policies every time car loadings fell off a percentage point. Operating crews were called rails because that's what the railroad ran on. The crews were the continuity that kept things going, year after year.

Along with short crews, the company also wanted to run without cabooses. There were numerous safety rules requiring somebody to be at the rear of the train to observe the trackside detectors, to observe the train, to walk the train whenever you stopped. So along came rule revisions eliminating those requirements and trackside detectors that transmitted information by radio. The company envisioned short, cabooseless railpack trains highballing from coast to coast with a two-man crew. The reality, we knew, would be the same old heavy, mile-long Southern Pacific trains with crummy power. On the railroad, Murphy's law applied. And you could add to it. "When it goes wrong, nobody will fix it."

Trainmen felt pretty strongly about losing the caboose. After all, it had formerly been their home. They used to live in it, cook on the coal stove, sleep on the bunks. Each conductor had his personal caboose that went with him if he changed jobs. To a homeless profession, the caboose was at least a symbol of home. It represented the brakeman's craft; it was the conductor's territory as opposed to the engine, which was the engineer's territory. The famous "conductor's valve" on the caboose was the last word in any dispute. If the conductor didn't like what the engineer was doing, he pulled the air and stopped the train. Kind of like a presidential veto power.

Why was this arrangement important? Consider this situation: a heavy rock train was leaving Ashland on the Siskyou branch and climbing up to the steepest descent on the SP lines which began in the middle of tunnel thirteen at the crest of the grade. There was a dip in the ascending grade, and the cars bunched up, causing an air hose to kink behind the engine. For some reason the hose stayed kinked when the slack pulled out, and going for his airbrakes in the middle of the tunnel, the engineer realized that all he had were the brakes on the engine. He threw it into big hole, but the kink kept the system pressurized. Since they were in a tunnel, they couldn't call the caboose. On the caboose in a tunnel in the dark, it was hard to tell how fast they were going. But they were clearly going over fifteen—way over fifteen. The conductor pulled the brake valve and jumped. He knew even an emergency application probably wouldn't stop the train on the grade. But at least they got an emergency set. The runaway train, now in emergency, took the twenty-five mile curves on that three percent grade at fifty and didn't jump the track. A happy ending. But what if it had been a cabooseless train?

The old heads had grim predictions.

"When I see one of them cabooseless trains, it just about makes me sick. You just wait until one of them things breaks in two on Donner summit and it's winter and you're fighting six feet of snow to get back to where the knuckle's broken, and before you can get to it, the air bleeds off those cars and it's *sayonora* Sam all the way to Roseville. Can you imagine a freight car coming off that hill into Roseville, all those grade crossings, all those people? Bound to happen someday."

Aside from the major disasters, the everyday operation was going to be a lot more dangerous without cabooses. A trainman in a caboose can spot trouble before it gets serious—a shifted load, a smoking brake shoe, a kid who's picked a risky place to ride. People try to run grade crossings all the time, and an engine crew has no idea what's going on more than twenty cars back. You could be dragging an automobile behind you for miles and never notice it unless it ruptured an airhose.

When you do any work with a train, you don't just go in one direction. You might go up the line to pick some cars up and than have to shove back to make a set-out somewhere else or to get around your train to go in the opposite direction. All this maneuvering is usually done on tracks that are crossed by grade crossings and automobile traffic. Having a caboose that you can shove at the end of a train gives you control over stopping without having to signal the engineer. If you see that maniac who just has to cut in front of you so he won't have to wait for the train, you can pull the air. Otherwise, you are out there with a radio hanging onto the side of a freightcar while these idiots drive straight for you. And believe me, they do. I have been in the middle of an intersection, with fusees down, waving a red flag, and had people try to run me down. So don't figure people will stop, because they won't.

Engineers hated cabooseless trains for other reasons. With the long trains SP ran, it was hard to fit into sidings to meet other trains. With no caboose, the engineer didn't know when he was in the clear and so he had to pull all the way down to the signal and hope he fit.

The company really put out some slick propaganda on the caboose issue. I read an article in *The Wall Street Journal* that was supposed to be informational. It was practically written in baby talk. It used phrases like "the little red caboose" and "in the old days." The message was that cabooses were cute, and gee, they're part of American Wild West history and all, but hey fellas, this is now and we've got technology and we don't need those overpaid oldtimers in their overalls waving at kids from the little red cabooses anymore. And the public thinks that well, they must have a gadget that does it all by now. But railroading is still a primitive artform involving ten thousand tons moving at sixty miles per hour with only minimal control over stopping.

13
NORTHLINE

MY UNION GRIEVER assured me that the new agreement wouldn't hurt my job.

"You'll be workin' better than you ever did. And at the end of the year—that productivity bonus."

Two weeks later I was cut off the Eastline extra board. I moved over to the Northline extra board that ran from El Paso to Lordsburg, New Mexico. I wondered how long I could hold onto that. It was just as well I moved, actually. Now my chance encounters with Wrong Way would be confined to the parking lot. The railroad giveth, the railroad taketh away.

The Northline run was a long flat haul across the low southern desert, and the July monsoon rains were starting to humidify the static dusty air. The Northline was all CTC—no switches to throw and nothing to do but get on and ride. It handled all the traffic on the Sunset route across the country, so there were lots of trains to meet and lots of time spent waiting in sidings. The rear brakeman had a good many walks in the desert to look forward to, had a lot of time to think.

With the rain and the saturated earth came the snakes out of their holes, looking for refuge on the warm ballast beds of the roadway. With the desert a lake, we had to walk the ballast too, swishing knee deep in tumbleweeds and sliding around on the loose scree. One morning around three a scanner got our train, one of the new talkies at a spot that had already won the name of "malfunction junction." What the rules called for was an inspection of every bearing on every axle for overheating. The brakeman walks the train and marks each wheel with a chalk that has a high melting point. If the chalk melts, you found your hotbox. Actually, you can smell a hotbox. All that reaching down was making me nervous tonight, reaching down in the dark where the snakes like to snuggle up. The third or fourth car I marked I saw a snake next to the wheel. It was a dead snake. Some other brakeman had found it first. Now I really wanted to inspect this train. Halfway back, I met the conductor, Clothesline, who was walking up from the caboose. As we were talking, Clothesline reaches down and picks up a stick.

"Snake over there."

He casually ground the rattler's head into the sand with the end of his stick, still talking about his exwife and passing up the chance to blow her boyfriend's head off one night in his trailer.

"I had that bastard dead to rights, breaking into my trailer in the middle of the night. You want these rattles for your guitarbox? The Mexicans say it makes the music sweet."

Rattles in my pocket, I head back for the engines, checking the other side of the train. About twenty cars from the headend, I see what looks like a six-foot snake emerge from a large bush and crawl across the ballast toward the train. I get the shakes—my lantern is bobbing around in my hand—hot bulbs and all. I rock the snake, and it coils up and starts striking at the heat of the wheels. It hits the underside of the train. It had to be a good three feet from the rail to the car. The bastard is six feet. Fuck the hotbox, I'm leaving. I climbed down the embankment and gave the angry snake a wide circle. This was no time for pride. As I scrambled back up the ballast, I gave every bush a roll by. When I got back on the engine, the hoghead is in a snit.

"What took y'all so long? We didn't have no hotbox. Damn detector's been stoppin' trains all night. Damn rules anyway. You just coulda stood in one spot and I'd have pulled up and shoved back and we'd be gone."

"I just didn't want to miss all the fun, Low Water. We have a lot of fun out there in the dark."

The rattles, by the way, do make that guitarbox sound sweet.

The town of Lordsburg was even more desolate than Carrizozo, if such a thing were possible. The first night I caught a Westbound into town, the only movie house was burning down. I looked around for the good things about the place. Well, I had a whole empty locker room to practice my flute in, a step up from the laundry room, and the acoustics were nice. There were also nice flat dirt roads to run on which headed off into the desert. If I waited until six, I could run five miles without getting heat stroke. The little drawback to this plan was again sharing space with the snakes. They were also waiting for six o'clock so they could head out to look for dinner without getting fried. One evening I jogged right over a rattlesnake. We both jumped a mile and then recovered and threatened each other. He curled up and rattled; I threw my rock. We both cautiously moved on. I had been far away at the time, holding in my mind an image of my cabin in the Santa Cruz Mountains. It was the room again—the home space that I mentally furnished with a rug, a woodstove, and the winter time of year. As I ran I went there and I could feel myself starting to be at peace. I also started to change my running prayer to bring out the feminine side of my god-consciousness.

Goddess, lady, let me walk with you this evening. Let me be with you in your peace. The sun, your brother, lets his head recline upon the pillow of your yellow hair. Your sandy breasts turn violet in the intermediate light. Lady, come into this your perfect body. Breathe with me, enter my blood. Come to me in dreams tonight, and let me lie with you and your outrageous lover. Between your milky breasts I sleep. The blood of a childbirth bleeds into my dream, and I awaken with eyes washed clean. A creature of your luminous demesne.

It took about a month for me to be cut off the Northline board, and I again found myself on a work train based in Deming, New Mexico. On my days off, I would escape the August heat by driving up to the Mogollon Mountains above Silver City where I found hot springs, cliff dwellings, and moments of peace. Often I would just drive the dirt mining roads until I came to a place by water. I would sit next to it for a short while as if it were a person I shyly wanted to kiss. Then I would turn around and drive back to Deming. There was no destination. Just the desire to be moving through a loneliness that gave the landscape an intense beauty. The purple spaces; the indistinct forms of the humped high desert; the shock of water releasing acrid bursts of juniper, pinyon, mesquite, and sage. Bands of greenery following underground waterways. Seeps. Sulphur springs. Mineworks. Distances. The mind's own movie opening before you.

If I thought I was unique in my struggles to live a new life, I had only to watch my brother, Angel, fight similar battles with his problematic actors. Unlike me, he had not left home. He remarried his last exwife and moved in next door to his mother-in-law. He was determined to triumph this time. He was going to straighten out everybody in his life and show them how he had changed. With alcohol, you see, dreams came true. It was possible to get what you wanted—a shot of booze, and the predictable suspension of disbelief. It happened every time. But now when Angel's desires came true, they were themselves and not his desires. It wasn't the same at all. Now the wife he wanted back appeared too fat, too spendthrift. The mother-in-law was nagging. The children ungrateful. And fellow workers potential trouble, people to be controlled somehow, people you had to have an angle on.

Angel had always used his brains to fight with when he could. He would set people up to fight each other and then sit back and watch them, taking each man's measure. This was the way he'd managed to survive. Now he was being asked to drop his guard, to ask for help, and to give up resentments. No wonder he stayed in his room. It was the only hard shell left. And, as if drawn to this kind of struggle like a shark to blood in the water, crazy Cesar started in after him. It was as if he couldn't get away with milder forms of error anymore. The minute he took a wrong turn, some giant allegory appeared to shove his nose in it. Angel's ante had produced a full-scale battle with an unscrupulous nut.

Angel drove a blue fifty-six Rambler classic with candy-apple paint and a fuzzy hanging from the rearview mirror. It was a pride and joy. He came home from a trip on the Northline to find the windshield smashed. Three times. Like mine, his company mail never made it to his mailbox. A mysterious voice would call the crew dispatcher and lay him off the board. Always sneaky shit.

He knew it was Cesar, but he couldn't catch him at it. And now he couldn't just retaliate without knowing for sure.

"Why don't you just trash the trainmaster's car? That way we might get some protection in the parking lot."

"I'm just going to watch and wait. One day he will make his mistake. And I'll be there when he does."

The stress at work was hitting everybody hard. Anything would do as an excuse to fire you. Six days off for not having a timetable in your back pocket. A week off for not knowing the rule of the day. A week off for not padlocking the doors of the engine when you got off to take a coffee break. Officials hiding in the bushes, spotters in the bars, uncertainty about the contract givebacks. Camaraderie was gone—what fun there could be in doing the work was gone. Everybody was afraid for their job and worried about the house payments, the car payments, the fancy RV they bought when business was on a boom.

About this time the company sent around rules instructors to give classes for promotion to conductor. Just as they got to me, the instructor left town.

"Oh, they'll be back in two weeks to finish up."

A month later I decided to just write the exam. It was hurting me not to be able to bid in conductor's jobs, and with the short crews, a brakeman was becoming an endangered species. I had to brave the guardian of the cave, the trainmaster's secretary, to come in on my time off and work on the test—four hundred questions on every minute detail of train and engine operations. She didn't make it easy for me. I'd come off a run, having been up all night on a train, and find her ready to disappear for lunch.

"You'll have to come back in an hour. I can't let you stay in my office by yourself."

I'd like to see that bitch work all night and then hang around for an hour while someone went to lunch. In an hour I could have been through a plate of machaca and dead to the world. Needless to say, I did not speed through the exam. A lot of trainmaster's secretaries were like this—particularly hostile to women trainmen. Being kiss-ass drag queens all their lives, it irked them to see women playing by other rules. Not that I didn't respect them for doing their work, but I didn't respect them for any reflected glory they got off some manager. And I tended to let them know that.

"Well, why don't you try riding a freight train all night and then standing around all day waiting for somebody to powder their nose. I wonder how you'd feel about it."

"Why, I get up early and go to work."

"Sure you do, Betty—sure you do."

I passed the test, though, and got my conductor's date. The first thing I did was bid in a conductor's spot on a work train picking up ties just outside of El Paso. Now I had to decide if we could throw that switch or not. On a work train you work with the track gang foreman. You both get authority from the dispatcher to share a section of track for a specified length of time. The problems have to do with understanding what the limits of that authority are. The track gang tends to be more cavalier about red absolute signals than a train crew is. The foreman might want you to go do something, and you have to figure out if you have the right to all the switches included in that move—whether you are going to run out of time before you get done and where you can put your train to get in the clear. Whatever goes wrong on a job, they always fire the conductor. For instance, our hoghead was routinely running ten miles over the limit. But you can't just get on the radio and tell him to slow down, because that would bust your whole crew. You can say code things like "It's riding kind of rough back here, Joe." That means slow the fuck down. If you really want to push it, you can always pull the air, but I was a long way from pulling the air at this point. I didn't want the reputation of someone who gets in power struggles with engineers, because from then on it would be war—the girl conductor trying to prove a point. I decided to shine it on and talk to the guy after the run. If that didn't work, I'd dig in somewhere. Basically, I didn't care if I did get fired. I wasn't making payments on the American Dream.

I saw a lot of the American Dream working beside the interstate arteries that carry the speeding dreams. My image for it is a Chevy Blazer pulling an Airstream, that silver bullet you live in on vacations at the lake and after retirement when you join the Winnebago tribe that parties from park to park. It's also a handy place to have to live in when your American Dream wife throws you out of your just-paid-for house and files those divorce papers. This was the story of a lot of rails who spent just too much time out of town making the money to buy this stuff. They got more and more ingrown and sculptured by their job, and it became harder and harder to fit into the surrounding society.

The railroad had its own style, and it accepted a lot of eccentricity in its brotherhood. Sometimes it was hard to tell the rails from the bums, the switchmen from the guys who lived under the bridge. Show me a switchman, and I'll show you someone who picks up junk. These guys would scavenge anything—wire, old clothes, hats, railroad spikes, other people's lunches, stray lumber, angle irons, tie plates, anything. On the job you switched out a lot of loading docks and passed by a lot of backyards. It was a gold mine for scavengers. The crew would be talking in the engine, and suddenly a switchman would dart out the door and return hauling a cable or a hammer or a brown paper bag.

"Stop under the bridge on the way back, Joe; I want to put a few things in my truck."

Their bachelor houses became Dickensian fortresses resembling the industrial environment they worked in.

"Heard the health department was after Tennis Shoe again. Told him his backyard was a health hazard. How he can stand himself, I'll never know."

Tennis Shoe was a case in point. He was unquestionably a very wealthy man, divorced, and with the seniority to hold any run he wanted as an engineer. He was an older man with wild long hair and wore large greatcoats and navy peacoats that looked like they had thousands of miles on them—and not all the miles by Tennis Shoe. He moved very fast for a big man; you would look around and he was off the engine rooting around in some dark pile by the side of the tracks. Minutes later he was back in his chair with either a new specimen or a snort of disgust.

Tennis Shoe carried a large suitcase into which he made frequent forays in search of nourishment. Food also fit into the category of desirable objects to pick up, and Tennis Shoe's lunch consisted of his own refrigerator's leftovers plus the perfectly good stuff that other trainmen had thrown away. The food was preserved in old mayonnaise jars and other mysterious containers, all of which were visited during a night's run. Tennis Shoe munched continuously, screwing and unscrewing jar lids, and wrapping and unwrapping amorphous materials. There were lots of smelly cheeses and milky liquids.

The sheer combination of odors—plus those emanating from Tennis Shoe himself—was overpowering, particularly in the enclosed space of an engine compartment. He also liked to run hot— kept all the windows closed and the heater cranked up full tilt. A lot of engineers are like this; they get down to shirtsleeves and simulate Florida in January in their engine space, not at all considering their brakeman who has to be dressed to go out the door into the storm at any moment. Storm or no storm, however, I had all the windows open when riding with Tennis Shoe. Father Finnegan once told me a story that says something about eccentric rails and their cameo appearances in normal life. The Father had run into Tennis Shoe at a Parents-without-Partners dance in El Paso and described him as looking like a dapper Southern gentleman, dressed in an impeccable white suit, and quite popular with the ladies. He was a Fred Astaire on the dance floor—highballing down the East-line in his smokey attire—to be transformed by stardust on the parquet floors after midnight. Another Cinderella story.

Summer's heat, the monsoon rains, the Sunland racetrack skirting the west side of town—large puddles make lakes on the dirt roads leading into the hills. I come off a run with Clothesline, hotpants conductor, and go to Juarez to eat, to end up on the town with an Alabama chicken farmer and his wife. He tells us how he hates big-assed women, the stripper shuffling through a *cumbia*, thinking of her kids at home. He orders beer, *ceer-vee-sa*; hates Mexicans who speak Spanish. He likes us. We speak English. His wife has a soft heart for the teenaged whores, wants Clothesline and me to spend the night. Juarez is lit up like noon at midnight, money turning lights on all over the world, and everybody drunk except for me. I am the dancer, also thinking of home and the parking-lot struggle with Clothesline, who thinks this scene is bound to turn me on. And I wonder if I can go out in the world anymore.

Later, another wave of influenza swept through town, the border bringing commerce in everything—money, drugs, and bugs. For a month, I cannot work. I am too sick. The blankness of the apartment stares back. Jesse and I microwave potatoes for meals, eat Lucy's machaca, stare across the brown mountains into Mexico, the "little Jerusalem."

In the engineers' shanty in the El Paso yard I see the writing on the shithouse wall. "Gypsy Neiman eats pussy." "Shitheads can't even spell my name right," I think. "They should be glad somebody eats pussy around here." I hadn't found any volunteers. Was it a hanging offense? Did they think your lips would fall off? I crossed out my name, wrote "your mama." And I thought about the Watsonville wall: "Chuckie dives. No muff too tuff for Chuck." Well, that was California, home of the brave.

In November, still sick, I decide to go home. I can tell Jesse is afraid, talks of moving too, doesn't want me to leave him on his own. But the work isn't here and the fever has softened me; I no longer want to push or fight or make money or stay out in the desert alone. I can stay up three hours at a stretch and figure easy stages, driving the backroads, going slow.

Jesse helps me carry my Chinese screen down to my truck. It barely fits, protruding into the cab.

"I'll send your bed home when Chris gets his boxcar from the company. No problem sending it home with his stuff. Now you get out of here before I get mushy. God, I hate to say goodbye."

"I'll see you when you get to visit your folks. Maybe you'll come back to the Coast yourself."

"I'm just not ready yet. I'd just better stay away."

Jesse left before I did, heading to work, his beat-up pickup disappearing out the gate of our condo complex. He was sure a gift from out of the blue. I hurry now, unable to stand the place. An hour later, I was down at the yard with transfer papers in my hand.

"Put down Watsonville Junction, switchman's extra board, it's always wide open and I've been here sixty days so now I can go home."

"OK, Niemann." The crewcaller gave me an almost fatherly gaze. "I guess we can't hold you. Have a good trip home."

And I am swiftly gone, turning up the Rio Grande, the fall *ristras* a deep red, hanging in heavy strings from the back of farmers' trucks. I have choices to make at Las Cruces, to go south to Tucson and L.A. or up the Rio Grande and west on backroads skirting the Mogollon Mountains. I want to know their boundaries and curiosity takes me north. In Socorro I have to stop; the fever is back and I need to sleep now. Socorro is poor and Hispanic and it's getting cold. There are wood piles on porches and several old trucks and cars for parts in most backyards. Socorro lies on the banks of the Rio Grande, but the landscape is higher and more desolate than in the south. To the east lies what the Spanish called the *Journada del Muerto*, miles of black lava flow, in the days before highways nearly impassable. The lava cut the horses' hooves and was home to rattlesnakes and cactus. The idea of crossing fifty miles of this seems impossible. Struggling up sharp outcrops and fissures, how could horses cross it at all? At night the moonlight is absorbed by the rock, creating a strange matte surface without accustomed reflection. The silence is also different here as if sound, like light, cannot echo. It is a blanket of darkness thrown across the middle region of the state, and Socorro sits on its edge, just scraping by, as it always undoubtedly has. It doesn't have the feeling of a place gone into decline but rather of a place that has always been marginal and poor.

I sleep as if I'm dead. Wake up damp with the fever gone for a while—time to get on the road. More choices—to go up to Albuquerque and west on the interstate or to pursue this mountain road. There really is no choice, although my reasoning seems odd. I want to hide; I feel weak and vulnerable. The interstate is naked and impersonal and fast. It would feel like an airport, and I wouldn't be in New Mexico anymore—I would be on my way to L.A. I would already be in L.A. in a sense. The two-mile strips bordering these huge arteries should incorporate into their own state called Interstate. East of the Rockies they would belong to New York; west would be L.A. The truth was that after two years in the desert I was afraid to go back. I would do it slowly in stages, I kept telling myself. Perhaps I would never go back at all.

West from Socorro the road climbed slowly behind the shoulders of the black range, the Tularosa Mountains, the Gallo Mountains, and to the south, the Mogollon range, the heart of the most magical wilderness in New Mexico. The backside was gentle and covered with yellow range grass with black lava outcroppings and wavering thunderheads with their daily indecision. A storm was hovering, the edge of winter about to move in. I bought roasted pinyon nuts for the trip, and the floor of my truck filled up with the little brown shells. I saw no one on the road. I felt the presence of the mountains and was glad I came this way. I loved them. They had been my moments of gentleness during the past summer—the few hours in which I had felt caressed and happy. One day walking upstream beside the Gila River I had found a hotspring bubbling into the cold water. There was a kind of pool scraped out of the river mud, and I lay in it, warm and cared for while the frigid water tumbled by. A fisherman was making his way along the bank and saw me in the river.

"Kinda cold to be swimming, isn't it?"

I smiled a secret smile.

One-horse towns were strung out every fifty miles—Magdalena, Datil, Quemado. I passed only two trucks all day. It was a roller-coaster road contouring around the foothills curving west, past outpost stations of the New Mexico Institute of Mining and Technology. Past Magdalena, the landscape flattened out into a high mesa called the Plains of San Augustin, and I came upon the first of a series of giantine radar screens, oversized satellite dishes laid out in intervals against the now lunar landscape and called, with scientific simplicity, the Very Large Array. Windmills for tilting. Somewhere near here was the White House ruin I had read about in Charles Lummis, a place he had described with love, a place he had thought beautiful. There was a White House canyon and a rancher's barbed wire fence, and I knew it had to be here, but I couldn't push myself to find it—had to just feel its presence hidden under the blanket of yellow range grass and pine.

At Quemado another decision. Up highway 32 to Zuni and the interstate or along the backroads to Holbroke and the tip of the White Mountains in Arizona. I felt the tug of Tobe Turpin's trading post and a woman selling fiery tamales out of the back of a truck in the parking lot, but that would be the last of the country. I kept on to Arizona, conscious of the difference between the states almost immediately across the state line. Suddenly there are "ranchos" and painted white fences, Chevy Caminos and Blazers and big white American family cars. Wealth is here: shopping centers, stores, gas stations, beside-the-road curio shops, apartment complexes, planned communities. Green pastures, lots of gringos, few Hispanics, Indians tucked away. Segregated Arizona—a place for everybody and everybody in their place. Suddenly I just wanted to drive fast; just wanted to get home.

I started thinking by time miles, three hours to here, two hours to there—the L.A. freeway thinking. The mystic blanket of New Mexico time is gone, dissolved like Prospero's magic in thin air. It occurs to me it's been a long time since I've been to a twelve-step meeting and that I'd better get to one.

Sick and pushing it, running with an approaching storm, Flagstaff appears out of the blur of the interstate. I find an expensive motel, need the plushness to sink into, the illusion of care. Flagstaff is roaring with tourists on their way to the Canyon, making rivers of cars and busses turning left; international travelers with cameras and in clumps. The town itself is hippie hip: surplus stores, coffeehouses, holistic medicine, craft stores, expensive tourist stuff, marketable Indian artifacts. It was Berkeley without the books. Books were hard to find out West. Even Western writers like Larry McMurtry hardly made it to the shelves. Homogenized chain stores dished out slick titles decided upon by New York marketeers. As hard to find as homemade music or hens' teeth—another culture lost to the satellite dish.

Oh well—you find what you find.

Motels were hard places for me still, the sense of being in a danger zone, between locations, not accountable to anyone, with no one knowing where I was. The lounge was always down the hall. There always was the lounge. I woke up and it was dark and a storm was shaking the walls. I called Roger, as I usually did when I needed a steadying voice. He was always up at three in the morning, swimming in a room with music and books, his mind feeding on rare ideas. After the call, the panic swiftly returned. This was going to be a hurricane. I turned to the book called the "Big Book" in the twelve-step program. It contained stories of alcoholics told by themselves and written in a style best described as no style. It was an odd experience reading the Big Book because although I had read it cover to cover many times, I had no recollection of many of the stories. I think that most of them were uncannily unmemorable unless they specifically applied to you at that moment; then you read them as if for the first time. It might take years, but eventually all the stories would find their unique application to your life. It was a browser's book, a book for terrified browsers with the four o'clock shakes. You picked up the Big Book when you didn't have anything else.

In the morning I had the usual feeling of well-being after sweating out a fever the night before. Things were all right today; the fear had receded. I felt good enough to get on the road to Barstow if not Las Vegas and the Dam. The Grand Canyon and the river makes up or down choices necessary when driving across the West. You are always aware of it, the routes it offers you that conform to its route, its unalterable shaping of the land. I bow to it now, its difficulty, letting the storm decide me to go south, the rain slanting into the windshield, forming little waves on the front of the truck. I choose the desert—the Mojave, place of shapes and canyons, oases, hot springs, and testing grounds. The bottom of the Colorado, the bottom of the Sierra Nevada, the junkheap of L.A., Barstow was a desert junction, filled with gas stations, motels, and chain foodstops. I checked into a motel and ate the worst Mexican dinner I'd had in two years—everything covered with black olives and sour cream. But I felt at home here because of the sound of the hump.

It dominated the town, the protracted dull scream of metal clamp on metal wheels slowing boxcars down as they rolled off the hill into the receiving yard, the Barstow Santa Fe hump. Barstow was the big classification hard for Santa Fe's east–west traffic, a sister yard to the Southern Pacific's big yard at Colton less than fifty miles away. One thing about being a rail—you are never away from it. You wake up in big cities hearing some town-job's whistle at 3 A.M., and you're home; you're on that crew in your mind; you know what that job is like; you can picture the diner where they eat breakfast at four, and the city is yours; the night is yours. Driving along an interstate, you pass a through freight, and you know that train: where it's been, where it's bound. Who made it up and where. You know the switchmen's lives, you know the change points for the braking crews, you know the container yards where it will end. The yard at Barstow was like a lake behind a dam, collecting the rivers of tracks running into it. In Barstow, the sound of the hump sang me to sleep, hearing the cars roll off that hill—an ace, a deuce, two aces. It gets to where you're grateful for a night at home in bed.

The following day brought me home to the place I'd left two years before, to the land of six hundred wineries and to the shipwreck of my past. The rain I'd been dodging since Flagstaff dumped on me now. Three weeks of it without break. I was still sick and taking antibiotics and sleeping on the couches of my friends who all lived in the mountains, huddled around woodstoves all winter. The years in the desert had spoiled me. I never got warm. My cabin in the woods needed work—needed to be dug out from under the redwood loam that was in the process of digesting it, the interior cleared of junk and debris from careless tenants and the fallen parts of the trees it was hung upon. I wanted that room I had visualized in the desert. I wanted to open that door.

I suppose it was strange that I had left El Paso the way I did in the middle of a sickness in a rush to get to a home that did not even exist. But this is the way it is for people just getting sober. The idea seemed imperative. I felt I would just get sicker if I stayed where I was. I just got out of bed and knew I had to leave that day. And now I was here, still sick and trying to get sheltered and warm.

I had never met my tenant; in my absence people had come and gone and handed the place over to their friends, the way it goes in the mountains. I was cleaning out one of the small cabins on the place, a room constructed by attaching tires to two redwood trees and hanging the structure between them. In a storm this semi-treehouse swayed like a boat on a rough sea; the beams bowed and creaked and little tree mice used them for highways. Termites and scorpions and banana slugs lived there too. This used to be OK with me, but now I wasn't so sure. Finally I got it clean enough to sleep in, and bought a woodstove that would keep me marginally warm. In the morning of the first day living there, my tenant was at my door with a present. Three magic mushrooms, a little mushroom family, newly sprouted.

"These have your name on them. They just came up."

He held them out to me and I took them in my hand. It seemed to be like this with my sobriety. Like Angel's fears materializing with operatic gusto, these mushrooms were a product of my mind. They were my last reservation. I had thought, "Well, I can take mushrooms again someday. They're not really drugs. They're spiritual." And here they were, being offered—with my name on them.

I handed them back. Not that I didn't want them, but I wanted some other things more. I wanted the real miracle to keep working in my life, the spirituality, if they's what it was, that has to live in ordinary life if it's to do any good. And if I didn't find it sober, OK, then, I wouldn't have it. I would live without the sound of music in my life if that were necessary. Whatever happened, I wasn't going to take anything. I abjured rough magic.

Perhaps that's why, once I created the room I had created in my mind, I could not live in it. Not yet. Like Angel, I was trying to master my past, to have something back the way I wanted it to be. But living in Lompico, up in that dark box canyon, was only a reminder of how alien to my former self I had become. I couldn't live up here with the low-bottom drunks and dopers anymore: their pit bulls and dobermans and guarded houses with high fences to hide the plants, and their threatening looks when you met them at night on the only road in. And it sure was hard to get off the mountain at night to go to a meeting, and that dirt road was a mean mudslide after a rain. I couldn't imagine how I used to think it was fun to coast down it in my fifty-six Chevy, drunk on my ass, tearing the shocks off the frame and cracking even the leaf springs—hell, I never noticed. And even more unmanageable were the feelings that the silence and isolation of the woods turned loose in me. The long careen had stopped; I was laid off and the crewcaller no longer bothered me with midnight calls; and I was back home, wasn't I? Well, why didn't it feel like home? Waves of grief came out of me there, sadness for everything in my life, a renewed shock of loss hit me like a nightmare bullfight. They were my feelings, and I was at home. But home had changed. It was simply gone—no longer here or anywhere.

Home would have to be an entirely new idea for me, an idea whose seeds were barely in the ground yet, a place I'd never smelled or tasted.

I thought about Jesse in El Paso, and I wondered how he would fare with all this. I wondered that any of us could get sober, could come through all this illusion. If I had known what it was going to be like, I wouldn't have had the courage to try.

And something inside me opened like a petal against a warm wind, and it was OK that I had been alone and cold and unable to love and that it might be so again and that I would never know anything, really, about this brilliant and inarticulate world or about love, other than to feel its heartbeat shadowing my own, sometimes, leaving me shaken and poorer and content.

14

SHASTA

HUNKERED IN under the rain in the redwoods, I did home things and waited for spring. I wanted to clean up the cabin so I could photograph it. I knew I wasn't going to settle down here, but I wanted images of home. I was creating a set for the story of my own life. Looking through the lens I looked into a window framed by redwood leaves and saw a brakeman's lantern by the bed, a polished mahogany desk with a banker's lamp—green halo of thought—a typewriter, photographs of the desert, a web of chlorophyll green behind the backlit windows in the sun. A treehouse, hole-in-the-rock hide-out from the world, warmed by a lamp and protected by a huddle of giant trees, tall mothers whose faces are high above, talking, whispering in the wind.

Periodically I drove down to my storage space to visit my "stuff," impediments of my past: moldy ancestral portraits, boxes full of books, sports artifacts, the wardrobe of other lives. I thought, "You are a fucking failure in life. Still in storage. When is it going to end?" I started sorting through the objects. My life passed before my eyes and into the junk heap. The gatekeeper started following my car, carrying his scavenger's box.

"You throwing this out? Mind if I help myself?"

Naomi's pictures floated to the top of the heap, carrying the magical immanence they always had. Ripped hemispheres of the face, left brain gazes looked back at me from the dumpster.

"I'm not gay; I just love Gypsy." "I'm sorry. I just can't face it. Can't face it. Too hard."

One morning I lay in my loft bed looking up at the cathedral of trees. Little mouse sounds scuttled along the barky beams. I had spent a week jacking up the sides of the house to get a level kitchen floor, but it still resembled the mystery spot. It was spring and termites were beginning to drop out of the walls. I hadn't been able to write. I woke up in the middle of arguments with people long gone out of my life, on to new dialogues of their own. Why was I hearing these reruns? And it was spring, time for boomers to arise and pack, to buy hot bulbs and new straw hats, seamless elkskin gloves and guitar strings. I felt a weakened pull to go on the road. I thought "I'll stay inside the state. Just boom California, follow the seasons and the crop runs and the stories. Just stay inside the state." It was all I knew how to do. Switch keys and two-dollar lantern. If I wasn't a rail, what was I now? Since I didn't yet know, I clung to the old, called the dispatcher and marked up on the San Francisco Coast extra board.

I got a room in the Western Addition district, close to the commute depot where I would be working the peninsula passenger trains. It was a marginal neighborhood. You found little gram plastic baggies on the street, and the mom-and-pop corner grocery store carried mannite for cutting cocaine and whole shelves of ziplock bags. Groups of men roamed around at night, smashing bottles and emitting loud sounds of swagger and boast. Cars seemed powered by rock and roll. Coming off a run, I often got home late; had to park blocks away and walk to my room, fingers clutched around a roll of pennies in an old sock.

Commute brakemen had an easy, mindless job. Call the stops, open the doors, shepherd the hordes, highball the engineer. It was like pulling pins on the hump, an ox-like physical routine, but packed in the train with dress-for-success sardines. My fellow-brakemen advised me to get my punch, work as a conductor.

"You ought to go get your punch and get out here with us. Don't let them give you any bullshit. You can handle it."

I went down to the ticket office and asked for a punch. The agent handed me one through the window, and some ticket stock. Then I went over to the trainmaster's office to get some harassment—maybe a rules exam. To my surprise there wasn't any. They were short of conductors that week.

"You want your punch. Go pick it up."

"I already did."

"Well, you're qualified then. Go for it. Good luck."

On a passenger train, the conductor was it. You had to make sure you ran by the rules, and you had to handle the people and all their problems and enthusiasms. And you had to punch the tickets and collect the money, making change and watching who got on and off. Three-minute stops. My first run was Good Friday, and all the ticket offices were closed.

The other conductor tried to cut me in. A crash course lecture on getting a system.

"Well, always take your time when you're handling money. Remember they won't fire you for going slow; they'll fire you for making mistakes. Always put your twenties away separate, and get yourself a leather wallet like this, a fast one, and keep your ones and fives in it. Make change out of your wallet and put their money in your pockets. I put ones in my right pocket and fives in the left. Twenties go in the back pocket. Never make change out of your pocket. I use a coin changer and put their coin change in my jacket pocket on the side here. I keep my hatchecks in my right jacket pocket and keep nothing in the left, so that I can put used-up hatchecks in there as I work the car. The one-ways and the round-trips go in my left front pocket, in sequence. Always remember to grab them in sequence.

"Now, when you punch them, don't punch the return—and use the going section as a hatcheck. Fold it to the zone they're traveling to. Fold it all the way over for the last stop. Put your conductor's receipts in your shirt pocket, in sequence. That way you don't have to sort them out after work. Open the doors for the brakeman at the last stop. Nothing to it, Kid. Good luck."

My first run was kind of a blur. There were hands in pockets and counting out change. Rows of mouths moving and the train lurching and surging as I checked my rate card and divided by two for the senior citizens, stuffed bills indiscriminately in bulging pockets, learning why you never make change out of your pockets as wads of money drifted to the floor past rows of hungry eyes watching. The helper conductor was taking care of me, working three of the four cars as I struggled to control my one. After what seemed like ten minutes I heard the brakeman call out "South City" and it was time to clean up the hatchecks and arrive. I gave him a glazed look. A flashbulb went off.

"You'll appreciate this later. Kind of a memorial. Everybody's first run."

"It was over so fast. I'm stuffed with money. My punch is jammed with paper circles. I can't do this three more times today."

"Oh, this was the worst. You did good. And it's good you're out here. We need more women and brown people; not just these old white guys. It's good for the public to see it."

I liked it when the little old ladies would come up and shake my hand.

"I thought I heard a woman's voice making the announcements. You keep on. We'll show 'em."

Yeah, I thought. You still don't see women doing things out in the world much. And this wasn't even a physical job. It was just a traditional job. It took people back to their histories, their nostalgias, and here was a new character playing a new role.

"Well, oh my God if that isn't something. A girl conductor. What do I call you? A conductorette?"

"This worries me. It really does. Round trip or one way?"

I tended to brush off these paper pushers like medflies. After all, I had been harassed by the best.

I started to feel a part of the city, a part of its daily tidal surge. Shoeshine men would shout "Hey Muni" at my brown uniform; Japanese tourists would ask directions to Esprit. The depot was at Fourth and Townsend, a South-of-Market warehouse district home to leather bars, the flower market, and artists' lofts. Suddenly I was not a body-snatcher pod anymore. I was conservative. Booming certainly gave you a crash course in the sociology. But it was hard to start to relax and let the guard down. And so, I volunteered to answer phones at the San Francisco Sex Information hotline.

The hotline had an intensive training course that tried to desensitize the volunteers to anything they might hear on the hotline. The idea was not to make judgments on any behavior that was between consenting adults. We were there to provide information, referrals, and to listen. Gradually, I began to feel the straitjacket straps coming off. They didn't call it Bumfuck, Texas for nothing. One day I was on the phones and answered an out-of-state call. A wronged, determined woman's voice informed me that her traveling salesman husband was a bisexual. She wanted to talk about his betrayal. His lies. His affront to her sexuality.

I found myself really feeling for the guy. Straitjacketed, needing to find out about himself, family responsibilities, an anguished reach for freedom.

"Is it OK for a person to be bisexual?"

"He should have known. He shouldn't have done this to us."

"What if he found out about it later? What were his options?"

"We had an agreement. He broke our agreement. Our fidelity."

"Is there anything he could have done to explore this, that would be all right with you?"

"I don't understand how he couldn't have known. He deceived me. Tell me, how could a person be that way and not know it?"

"If some crucial part of you can't exist if it's known, then you can't afford to know it. That's why I asked you what his options were."

"I just don't understand this. Thank you."

The hurt and determined voice signed off. The relief map of the country returned. Rivers and volcanos, escarpments separating town from town; people living in clumps, watching one another; the steel bands of the rails connecting them. Oh well, my brother salesman — good luck.

Railroad work was definitely not booming this year. It was the famine pattern — a few month-long booms, enough to get the gossip started, and then a bust. You would be doing well to cover a month's rent — certainly not first and last. I had seen it like this before, and I knew how to play it. But my heart wasn't in it. Not completely. A conflict with railroad life was starting to emerge. Eight years of booming, barely hanging onto an extra board, had made me a leaf on the water. Every time I heard "Oh, you can work here year round" I waited for the other shoe to drop. It was like trying to predict the movements of a sandbar. And it was getting worse, not better. The company was closing yards, abandoning branch lines, and rerouting traffic on a continuing basis. The old seasonal patterns of rush work no longer applied. There was no predicting what the company would decide to do next. They didn't even know. And being among the last brakemen hired, I was at the end of the whiplash slack. And I was starting to know it didn't have to be this way. The railroad was cutting me off the extra board every other week, but I could choose to stay, to do other work, to begin my life.

If I had been writing, I probably would have stayed. But I was a brakeman; I had those muscles and I needed to use them. The railroad was like a bad love affair. I bitched about it, but I always went back. I called up Jesse, who was home visiting his folks. I knew he'd understand.

"Jesse, I'm going booming. I need help getting my stuff back into storage."

"What took you so long? It's August already. I'll be over in the morning."

California was burning as I drove north past Sacramento. The river of its name flowed calmly here in the upper San Joaquin valley, its force domesticated by the Shasta Dam, below an abrupt climb into the Cascades and Dunsmuir, my destination. Ash from the fires was in the air, making the valley's humid heat feel even dirtier, and the river had been sucked up by summer into a thin blue strip between the swollen cheeks of the river bottom. The longest run out of Dunsmuir came this way to Roseville, running through the country of peach orchards, nut farms, yellow fields with black earth furrows, bell peppers, prune trees, tomatoes—all the sun-drenched crops. At Roseville there was a humpyard, and crews changed for the run over the Sierras to Sparks, Nevada, or down the valley to Fresno and L.A.

Dunsmuir was a tiny, old-time railroad town, wedged between the cascading Sacramento, which fell 3,000 feet in about seventy miles, and the steep walls of the canyons. It was halfway up the mountain wall and was a railroad outpost and little else. The tracks paralleled the river. I looked at a room in the old hotel which fronted the depot in the center of town. Fifty dollars a week and within calling range. But the air conditioning was in the hotel, not in the rooms.

"Aw, just leave the door open some," the stubble-faced day clerk advised. "It'll cool right down."

I could see me in my Hollywood sleep shade, sleeping all day after an all-night run, the winos shuffling up and down the hall. Like hell I was going to leave the door open. Instead, for a lot more money, I found a cabin at weekly rates. The owners loved me. I was a working person. I wasn't here to drink beer and pretend to fish. I was also railroad. That made me one of the family.

The family feeling was big in Dunsmuir. It meant that when you were in the post office writing a postcard, two or three people would be looking over your shoulder reading it. I was eating dinner out one evening and got up to get the coffee creamer off the counter. I turned around to see the three big guys in the booth next to me leaning over the top and pawing the book I had left on my table. They saw me looking at them. They smirked and hee hawed.

"It's *The Song of the Lark*," I spit out. "You are being very rude. Why don't you mind your own business?"

The three faces just stared blankly back. It was as if the family cat had just recited the *Declaration of Independence*. No, it hadn't happened. No. They went back to their redneck mumble. Like the hull of a ship passing over the fatal reef, it made hardly a ripple on the surface of the water.

My first day in Dunsmuir I had a premonition of all this in my obligatory conversation with the local trainmaster, known by all as "that asshole Schmidt."

"Everybody's probably told you what a butthole I am. Well, they're right. I'm the biggest butthole you'll ever meet. So let me tell you right now if you're thinking of fucking with me, take your best shot."

I'd taken my best shot in the third grade when I took a swing at Stevie Tyler behind the bungalows on the Boys' Side. He punched me back right in the nose, and I decided I wasn't going to fight with boys anymore. The thought of taking a shot at Schmidt seemed very remote.

"Look, Mr. Schmidt, is this really necessary? Believe me, I'm a good employee—I know the rules; I protect my job; you're not going to have a problem."

"You got that right. I can tell you definitely I am not going to have a problem. And just maybe nobody's ever really watched you close before. Well, I'm going to watch you close. And let me tell you it's a small town here. And I know what people do and what they say. Now, I see you've had a lot of injuries on the job."

"Well, a skinned knee once. A bruised thumb."

"Well don't try that here. I'm warning you—don't get hurt here."

"You know the rules, Mr. Schmidt. You have to report even minor injuries."

"I'm not telling you not to report them; I'm telling you not to have them. Do not trip. Do not get dust in your eye. Do not bruise your thumb. Not in my terminal."

I was getting the picture. The Dunsmuir mutiny. I backed off. Lie, I thought—flatter. He may bite.

"OK, Mr. Schmidt. Whatever you say. I'm here to work."

"Well go mark up then, and no missing calls either."

It was berry season and they grew beside the river. I'd wake up early and go for runs on the railroad right-of-way, carrying a berry basket, and let the air and the smells and the warming solitude sink in like sun after the winter. The railroad was its usual brutal, disruptive self; but I was being nourished here in spite of it. I liked hearing the river in my sleep. And the presence of the mountain drew my eyes as I might watch a sleeping lover, the way its shoulder looked from over there, catching a glimpse of a mood passing in a dream, a storm, the fear of a storm. Mount Shasta was visible from all directions. Running to Klamath Falls, we traveled around its flank, the glaciers reflecting the moonlight like a mirror for light. Once over the summit of our run, we tracked its telescoping presence behind us all the way to the Falls. A presence always there. I could see how people came to call it a guardian, a place of power. It made me feel safe. I looked forward to seeing it every day.

Things started happening to make me want to settle down. One day as I walked the train on a doomed run back from Klamath with a dynamiter in our train and bad dynamic braking on the engine,

I found a chainsaw lying on a lumber car, thrown away by a lumberjack because it had a broken starter rope. My first thought was "great—now I can cut wood for the winter. It was meant to be." Mount Shasta was like that. You started seeing things in terms of gifts, of providence. A rosiness descended on intentions. People I didn't even know had been offering me places to stay. They seemed to feel that, obviously, I was meant to come here, so they would assist with the details. I gave a hippie-looking hitchhiker a ride up the mountain one day because he was carrying a big bag of groceries. He invited me to see where he lived.

"You're wearing purple. That's the color of the mountain."

We kept driving up and up. Finally we were at the trailhead. He put the groceries in his pack, and we started up the trail. At a big meadow, he paused at a spring and fished a quartz crystal out of the sand.

"I put these here and other places."

"Far out. I like the small kind," I said, pointing to the carat diamond ring I always wore.

"Wow. That's funny. That's a funny thing to say."

We walked up to his camp, a mountain tent under a windswept juniper, a crystal stream with crystals bubbling through the tufted tundra. Wildflowers out on a spree. Trail mix, marijuana, and books on God.

"Doesn't anyone bother you here? And all those other people living here. Aren't there nosy rangers? Where are the obnoxious people?"

"They don't come here. None of the above. Nobody bothers us. We kind of coexist."

I found myself thinking, could I live here and take calls on a beeper? How long would it take me to get down the trail? Silly thoughts, ridiculous thoughts.

"I know a cabin on the mountain where you could live. Do you want me to take you there?"

"I don't know. Yes—I mean, I'll have to think about it. I'm a brakeman. I probably couldn't stay here all winter. I mean, I couldn't work. I'd feel like I was losing something if I just sat around. What an idea."

"Yeah."

When I got back to my room at the motel, I found myself thinking seriously about living near Mount Shasta. The railroad would be unreliable as usual. The company wanted brakemen immediately when they needed them, but they didn't want to pay for the privilege. So they tried various means to circumvent our contracts. Schmidt's method was to cut the extra board on Tuesday and call it back on Friday to avoid paying the brakemen's guarantee. Normally I would have just left under these conditions, half because of the money and half because I got so angry when trainmasters tried to weasel out of our agreements. Now, though, I just stayed around Mount Shasta on my days off and went to some meetings. It was hard for me just to stay put, to not drive off the mountain to Roseville to go shopping or to find some other destination I had to go see. But I had heard something at a meeting and it spoke directly to me. Someone said that whenever he felt compelled to do something, he tried very hard to do nothing. At least for a while. To get some time between the desire and the action. This effort would make the next compulsion weaker.

And so I tried to do this, to not get in the truck and drive, to stay around town and get a few things done, check the oil, go to a hotspring.

"Say, lady, did you know you had a nail in that rear tire of yours? Good thing you decided to have it checked out."

OK, fine. I was getting the message. I drove up to Weed to a hot springs resort and checked in. The masseuse was a crisp older woman with a European medicinal air. She didn't waste any time with small talk.

"Why have you come to the mountain?"

"I came here to work. Down in Dunsmuir. Railroad."

She sniffed. I clearly didn't know why I had come. Perhaps the mountain knew.

"You are tense here and here. It is from holding the shoulders. You should not wait too long about this. Do not wait until you are old. Perhaps when you were young it was not all right to have breasts, yes? Well, that was then. It is all different now. Now is a new day. It is good to be near the mountain."

She pummeled me into a noodle and then she left. I hobbled in my crisp white sheet into the scalding bathtub. She was right. It was not all right to have breasts, not on the railroad, maybe not ever. What was going on here? I wondered if I could move in here, pay by the month? I lay on the deck, wrapped and steaming, smelling of arnica massage oil. Mount Shasta was doing its purple thing in the descending butter light.

It might work out, I thought. I could rent a cabin, substitute teach, and work the railroad whenever they called me back. I'd get by. But what about the silences? The ghosts and the fears and the lack of a rush, the inexorable movement of water on its way somewhere, the large circles of freight cars going south, going east. Arrival frightened me. Being anywhere frightened me. I thought about the casting pond in Golden Gate Park in the City. I found it one day on a run, hidden in Eucalyptus trees, covered with lily pads, or clouds that looked like lily pads. After running I sat on a low concrete bench and let the water become my mind—resting, thought asleep, napping. The lion voice began to talk to me.

"You can love Naomi again if you want to. Without ever seeing her again. You can have that love forever. You choose to hold onto the pain."

A little old man wandered down to the pond's edge. The lone caster. I wanted to cry. I knew I couldn't hold onto this thinking. How did you get to live here? Anywhere?

Anger decided me, in the end. My war with Schmidt. I was tired one morning after nursing another limping piece of junk over the summit from Klamath Falls. It was Tuesday morning. I was cut off.

"Godamn Schmidt. I'm sick and tired, and I'm not going to take this anymore."

"You'll work next weekend. He always does this."

"He does it because he knows he can get away with it. He knows we'll mark up whenever he calls us back, and he can have his crew for the weekend. We all ought to take our two-week callback every time. Then he'd have to honor our guarantee. It's another screw job."

The crewcaller just looked at me and waited for my psycho wrath to pass. He'd heard it before. He'd hear it again.

"Well I'll take my transfer papers then. It's a short enough season as it is."

"OK, where to then?"

"Make it West Colton. Might as well go for broke."

West Colton was the last resort. Gossip had it that "You can always work Colton" because nobody could imagine being happy doing it. It was a smog-filled sinkhole on the refuse-filled outskirts of the L.A. basin. I had worked into it on trains before and sat in the switchmen's locker room and listened to right-wing tax protesters orate on the invalidity of paper money. Colton was also the scene of an act of mayhem in which a switchman with a shotgun took an elevator to the top floor of the yardmaster's tower, stepped out, and blew the yardmaster away. Everybody was of the opinion the yardmaster had it coming. That story was extreme—even for railroad gossip. It said something about the place.

When I called the Colton crew dispatcher, though, I got a highball on work.

"Come on down; you can hold a regular job," he said.

That was what I was looking for, and so I took a last long look at the tumbling Sacramento River, the woodsy depot, and the tall trees. It was hot here. Why was I going to the desert? I told myself I'd stop for a swim at Delta on the way down to the lake. Little rewards to get me out of town. But arriving there, I kept on driving, the camel hump of Mount Shasta rising like a moon behind me as I drove down and down, following the river and the rails south.

15
END OF
TRACK

PAST THE Sacramento Delta and the Bay, the
California rivers were sucked dry by irrigation
and the summer heat. I passed Tracy and the
valley towns I'd switched on the west side hauler,
past Fresno where I'd spent those long nights
not drinking. Every minute not drinking. Things were different
now, I thought. They were moving—wildly, it was true, but moving
somewhere, toward something. As I entered the web of freeways
feeding into L.A., I thought of the other map I knew, the tracks
feeding into L.A. down to the port of Long Beach, out toward the
desert and Colton. The L.A. yard was limping along now, grass
growing on the hump where I'd spent the rainy winter pulling pins
on the midnight shift. It had gone the way of the Portland yard,
the Klamath yard, the Oakland yard. Roseville to the north, and
Colton to the south were the big operational switching yards now;
and everywhere else, temporary little switching yards would be
opened and closed experimentally, sending waves of switchmen
bumping out on the road and other waves of dumped brakeman
in search of someplace to work. We were getting to be like the
freight itself, except that we had no destination. Like the thief that
always comes, there would be the phone call at 12:01 and the two-
week paycheck to get home on. Wherever home was.

And so, like all the southbounds, I was headed for Colton, the space-age yard with motion sensors on the tracks, all power switches in the yard, herders and yardmasters in towers, and ant switchmen on the ground carrying out some small part of an overall plan. Yard of the future. Why did I think of it as some vast, dead sea?

I parked myself for the night in a shoddy motel with an expensive facade (casino carpets, a bed that shakes) and decided to call and markup in the morning. The winds of Colton and the winds of my own history rattled and shook the aluminum windows, sent Santa Ana positive ions into my synapse dreams. A feeling of the familiar was everywhere here. I'd gone to college in Riverside, the next orange grove town up the line, and I remembered the grade crossings and the freight trains throttling through the darkness—signifying danger, excitement, another world than my world of books and family pain. I remember being vaguely aware of the yard at Colton then, of something happening there I had no knowledge of. Or ever could.

In the morning I called the yard. In two days the situation had changed, apparently. I could hold the switchmen's extra board, but there was no guarantee of how often I could work. There were strategies with a yard board, however, that could get you work. You had to bid in jobs every shift, and you might hold them for a day or two days. Then you would be bumped, but you kept bidding every shift. Another plan was to find someone younger than you who was an aggressive bidder. You then bumped him every day, following him from job to job. Since I didn't know the jobs or the board, I found a younger man and bumped him. I would be a ground herder for a yard work gang.

"Don't I need to qualify in the yard? Work some student trips?"

"No. The guys will help you out. There's nothing to it."

I found the work gang on a small spur track under the main tower. The scale here was vast. The top end of the yard held receiving tracks for mainline trains. These tracks led into the hump, under which bowl tracks fanned out like a delta. There was another tower at the far end of the bowl tracks and then tail tracks where the outbound trains were made up, inspected, and highballed out of town. About two miles away there was another yard—Old Colton, where reefers were stored. The tower herders threw all power switches in the yard, and you had to ask permission from them to make any move. I had to call the tower to get us out of the spur and up to the top end to fix rail.

"SP 3450 calling the A Yard Herder."

"I don't know you. Where's Lopez?"

"I bumped Lopez."

"Another damn boomer. And a woman yet. Don't even bother to learn the yard before you bump on a job."

"You got to work to learn the yard, pal. You going to throw the switch or you going to give me your opinions on life?"

Any man, faced with not working or bumping on a job, would bump on a job. But being a woman and doing this, I was making myself a target. Boomer, woman, and uppity. Well, it was all true. After eight years, I'd paid my break-in dues. Besides, this was my place. L.A. I was born here. I'd had about enough of this boomer bullshit.

The Hispanic guys on the work crew just smiled their gentle Spanish smiles. Later they offered me lunch—homemade burritos and jalapenos, sacks of them. They always had the best lunches and always enough to pass around. The work gang worked slow, creeping up and down the rails, and I started to relax a little. It was still a problem getting God in the tower to let us in and out of the rails, but not the problem it was going to be on a real switching job. I had a bad feeling about this place, the whole thing—the smog, the heat, the snarly feelings crackling through the supercharged air, the sterile emptiness of the yard. Miles and miles of track, ghostly boxcars floating down the hill, booming crashes as they hit deep in the bowl, smoke from engines rising above the tops of the cars. But no people. I couldn't see a single switchman anywhere except the pinpuller on the hump, trudging like a convict to the crest and dropping the pin, trudging back to the next cut. The one lone worker in a huge mechanical terrarium, lunar landscape, no human sound.

That night at a meeting, we talked about anger. I was thinking of the tower herder. The guy next to me started to talk.

"Well, yeah man, I mean I still get angry, man. I've fought people since I got sober. I've stabbed people since I got sober. Some dude starts talking dirt in front of my wife, man, it makes me mad."

He brought his tattooed fist down on the table hard. The circle of steely eyes didn't flicker.

I was sorry I had brought the subject up. My teeny little problems with the tower herder—I hope I didn't forget and say "fuck" in front of this guy. Then I noticed the other tattoos. Jail tattoos. They all had them. Five prisons in the area. Oilfield-looking dudes with pointy-toed boots. I started to think maybe I'd live somewhere else; commute out here to work. I was just going to be too damn lonely here.

I had a friend in Hollywood with a big house, and I moved in there. Right off La Brea and Hollywood Boulevard, street of broken dreams. My plan was to commute out to Colton to work and sleep in my truck if I had to work shifts back to back. In Hollywood at night, police choppers raked the rooftops with searchlights and sounds of beating blades. Car alarms went off every fifteen minutes and continued wailing for hours. It was like a tropical city in a war zone. I wondered how anyone could sleep. Luckily, I worked at Colton most nights; but coming in from the desert in the morning, I hit the legendary L.A. rush hour traffic jam. Bed, when I finally got there, obliterated me in seconds.

The best jobs at Colton were in the bowl, coupling up tracks and doubling long cuts together to make up departing trains. Bowl switchmen had two goals in life: to work two-and-a-half hours a night and to play poker. One man took the radio and went out and did the work while everybody else sat in the shanty and played cards. Then they traded off. They all were thrilled to see me walk in the door.

I don't know why I expected it to be different. I suppose it was all this time on the job. I'd had enough of these scenes, nobody talking, the grunts, the exclusions. I think it was also the contrast with Mount Shasta, the welcoming I had begun to feel there, the softening of my desire to be on guard. There were no women here on the ground. Not one in all of L.A. There was one woman switchman here, a black woman, who was restricted to working the tower. Everybody gave her a hard time on the radio. She told me she was glad to be off the ground. Too many hassles, too much harassment.

Same old scene in the locker room. I'm at the end of the table, reading a book. The topic of conversation turns to sex, meaning they want to talk about their dicks. But there's something queer about that. So first they have to do some faggot bashing.

"You know that driver in L.A.? One with the long blonde hair."

"The faggot one?"

"Hey, man, I saw him from the back one time. And he looked good, you know what I mean. I says, 'Hey baby, what's happening?' He turns around and winks, man. Blew me away. I thought he was a chick."

"No faggot's getting my stuff, man. I'm saving this big piece of meat for Miss perfect thirty-six."

"Yeah, well, what's ten inches long and white?"

"What?"

"Nothing. Ha ha ha."

"Hey, man, I was out behind the engine taking a leak and a carman tried to couple me up to an airhose."

Then this new guy comes in and sits down. They keep on talking about their dicks.

"Hey, why are you guys talking about cocks? Are you queer or something?"

"You missed the first part," I said.

The guy who walked in was my foreman. They called him Rambo. That's because he wore combat fatigues and had a ten-inch survival knife strapped to his thigh.

"Why do you wear that knife out here?"

"Protection. Walking these tracks, I like to have my knife."

"Funny, but I've never felt threatened walking around out here. And besides, there's nobody hanging around the yard. In fact, we're in the middle of the desert. There's nobody around anywhere. And the place is lit up like San Quentin."

"I just like to be ready. That's kind of my motto. Be ready."

Rambo had this other annoying habit of whispering on the radio when he was coupling up tracks. You could hear the engineer asking him over and over for signs. He would whisper back something barely audible, as if he didn't want to part with any information, at any time, to anyone.

One night he turned up without the knife.

"Goddamn officials took it away from me. Said it was a concealed weapon. Well, this ain't."

He reached in his jacket and pulled out a stun gun and started waving it around the shanty. Not much interrupted a poker game, but this did.

"Get that thing outta here. Quit fooling around. You'll have the officials down here on our backs, and then we can't play cards, see. So put the goddamn thing away."

I went out to my truck to sleep. I'd done my shift in the bowl, and I was tired of the shanty. The tower herder could see me, but I didn't care. The sounds of slack grew muffled and the peace of the desert settled in like fog, like time funneling away. I was remembering these denuded rocklike hills, thrown at crazy angles to the ground, protruding above orange groves and irrigation canals you could sit beside at night—the deep wet grass with fat green spears, the orchard-smelling earth. The stars descended at night and the moonlight rebounded from the jumbled rocks; and I would watch them with my friends, high on acid or cheap Red Mountain wine, talking about Bob Dylan's songs or the color Wallace Stevens meant when he said "the elephant coloring of tires." The loneliness of that time came through to me, too—the death of my father, our last handshake dismembered in my mind. He had left to go east to a scientific convention. We had shaken hands. A heart attack in a taxi and my mother returning home alone. And I was sent out to college here, missing him, and looking out at the desert. All those pictures he had taken of the Southwest. Where were the people? Why the endless blue ranges and vistas of the wandering mind alone?

I thought about Wrong Way, too. Not the gold itself, but looking for the gold. And when did I start to seek my father, start to look for him in those places he made maps for me of? Was it all some kind of circle I was feeling the .urn of now, here where I went into the world and found drinking and poetry and the desire to consume more and more life?

I awoke to find Rambo shaking my truck to let me know it was time to wake up and go home. Only today I was going to check out a room near the yard with some switchman's exwife. I needed a place to sleep after work. Somebody who knew railroad, who wouldn't wake me up during the day. Annie's place looked sleepy enough in the morning, weed-eaten and bushy, with a homemade fishpond and a hound dog behind the fence. Sitting on the fence was the biggest crow I had ever seen in my life. Glistening blue black with even blacker lifeless eyes. It cawed at me and hopped, but it didn't try to fly away. I rang the bell. A dark little woman came to the door, dressed in a chenille robe, with her long black hair pulled back and falling to her waist. There were circles under her eyes and she was blinking in the light.

"I'm Gypsy, the switchman. Called about the room."

"Oh yes, come in. I been up all night myself, waiting for a patient to die. This here's my daughter's room; she sleeps in the other room now, but I left her things just as they was. It'll be quiet for you here; I know what switchman's hours are like."

I looked around the room, a child's room with a canopy bed, stuffed animals, and pillow shams. Ruffled yellow gingham curtains and lace shades, yellow shag carpet on the floor. Yellow shag carpet on the walls. Every surface covered with toys.

"I won't need room for stuff. I just need to sleep here before I drive home. Maybe a few overnights. Not more than one a week."

"Well, I can make room—got plenty of room here now I kicked my son out. Now don't you let him in if he comes here drunk in the middle of the night. I told him the last time I wasn't going to have that in my house. Some woman he picked up in a bar—brought her right into the house, my daughter home and all. I told him I wasn't going to have it."

"Right; well, I think I'll go to sleep now, if that's all right."

"Sure, honey. Just eat what you find in the kitchen when you wake up. I just might sleep all day myself. Sure feel like I could."

I woke up in the afternoon to an oppressive feeling of closeness and stagnant air. Annie's living room was windowless and dark, a jukebox in one corner and a TV in the other, emitting blue light but no sound. There was shag carpet everywhere—interspersed, on the walls, with squares of gold-webbed mirror plate. There was a Nevada feeling about the place. It was as much like a mobile home as a house could be. The kitchen was strange in another way. There were institutional amounts of everything stacked on the pantry shelves. A forty-cup coffee urn was bubbling on brew. A huge bag of Oreo cookies lay on the formica table next to a loaded relish tray. Stacks of dishes were in the sink. Was Annie running a boarding house? Was she a camp cook? It didn't add up to a two-person household. I sat at the kitchen table, sweating and eating Oreos and drinking coffee, but nobody else woke up. At three I left for work, an afternoon shift pulling pins on the hump.

The Colton hump job was mindless brutal labor. You took a switch engine, coupled onto a track in the receiving yard, and started shoving it toward the hump. So that the engine could hold the cars without any airbrakes, the pinpuller had to tie ten hand-brakes on the end of the cut. You then rode the end of the cut as the engineer shoved slowly toward the crest of the hill. Before you could hump the cars, you then had to knock all the brakes off, so they could roll freely down the classification hill. After you did that, you started pulling the pins on the cars, guided by a readout board that lighted up the number of cars you had to let go each cut. The hump foreman sat in a small tower next to the track and watched the computer list and matched it up with the cars rolling by him. The yardmaster's tower loomed over the whole operation, and he made it a habit to oversee the pinpuller's efforts and offer helpful advice.

"Pinpuller, are you getting those brakes off those cars? That last car off the hill either had air or it had a brake on. I want all those brakes off those cars, pinpuller."

"I'm ordering you to walk each pin to the crest, pinpuller."

Walking each pin meant you had to run to get back to the next cut if it was more than two cars. The pins stayed up by themselves if you jiggled the cutlever, and any switchman knew which ones wouldn't.

"You hear me, pinpuller?"

It was, of course, the foreman's job to direct his crew, not the yardmaster's, but this was typical of the way things worked at Colton. The yardmaster thought he was all the foremen put together, and the tower herder thought he personally owned every switch in the yard, and there was no good feeling about being on a crew working anymore.

Just then a wildman with matted hair and a grease-covered dufflebag popped out from behind one of the reefers on our cut. He grabbed the pin I was about to pull and gave it a jerk to set it open.

"Do it like that. Don't be walking those pins. Walking pins'll take the stuff out of a strong man. You tell that sonofabitch in the tower if he wants 'em walked to come down here and walk 'em himself. All he is is a switchman, just like you."

He nodded sagely, glanced around checking his perimeter, and vanished down the tunnel under the hump. The field man stepped out of the foreman's tower and came over to relieve me.

"That was Cat Man. He's crazy."

"He looked crazy, but he didn't sound crazy."

"Well, he lives with hundreds of cats in a trailer in the L.A. yard. Always going on about something. He's been out here forever."

Well, that's what Wrong Way would have said, I thought. Wrong Way wouldn't take this crap for five minutes if he were the foreman.

I worked out the rest of the shift doing the same thing over and over. Up to the receiving yard, tie ten brakes, shove to the hump, climb up and knock them off, pull hundreds of pins, listen to the crap over the speaker. Finally it was time to go home.

To get off the hump, you went down through a tunnel under the running tracks of the yard. I met the engineer coming through. There was this spray-painted scrawl at the end that said "HUMP" with an arrow pointing up the stairs. Walking through the tunnel going to work, the daylight hit the sign. It looked like some obscene graffiti, and it looked like what this job was, too. The engineer had also spent the shift fighting with the yardmaster, but he looked none the worse for it now. He gave me a rare, cheerful smile.

"Say, girl, don't let these peckerwoods out here get to you. Just do your thing and pay them no mind at all."

"It's hard for me. I get so mad at them."

"It ain't worth it, girl. You got to learn how to shine people on, specially if you a chocolate child."

He patted me on the shoulder and left. As I walked toward my truck, some wild kittens ran out of a nearby bush. I had made friends with one of them by giving her some of my brakeman's tuna fish stash. I watched her wolf it down and then come over to be petted. Boomer cat, I thought; I ought to take her along.

Back at Annie's there was still no sign of life. I passed the crow and let myself in the front door. I peeled off my overalls and rolled my dirty boots up in them so I wouldn't stain the rug. Then I lay down on the child's bed and let the toy shapes grow more and more indistinct. It seemed like a few minutes later that the house was shaking from a pounding on the door.

"Goddammit Annie, let me in."

"Now you stop that, Ray. You'll wake up my boarder and the whole damn street."

"Well you shouldn'ta locked me out. You and your crazy notions."

I drifted back into sleep. I was pulling pins on the crest of the world, the globe of the earth with its maps of icecaps and blue rivers fanning out like veins. It was the world from far away, a view from outer space, where I stood waiting for the next boxcar to be shoved to the crest of the hill. Those aren't tracks, I thought. Those are rivers and oceans and clouds moving like freight trains running with the wind. The air was good up here, I thought. And the sun was warm on my skin. I had the feeling that I might just go anywhere, or I might just sit down here and let it all go on without me.

I found Annie in her kitchen in the morning. She wanted to tell me about her son. His drinking. His wild life. I told her what I knew about drinking and what I'd done about it. I could tell that something had caught her attention, stopped the ramble of complaint.

"You say you go to these meetings. Are they around here?"

"Yeah, they're everywhere. I was going to go to one today."

"Well you know, I guess I'm kind of what you call an alcoholic myself. I'm pretty sure I am. But I just would be afraid to stop, afraid of what might happen."

That was it, then, the feeling I had about the house. The hopelessness—the shutting up against the daylight, the overstock of food so she wouldn't have to go out, the drunken son who had to be worse than she was. This was going to be my life on the road, these scenes I would keep on finding myself in—now sober and feeling pity and compassion but also the desire to walk out the door and turn my back on this life.

The second ending was here. The final resonance of my drinking life, gasping in a waterless pool like the brakeman's craft itself, not at all what it had been like. And impossible to go back to, to do anything more than remember it as it had been. Working the cool Salinas Valley on one-day locals out of Watsonville. Parking the engine on a spur and finding the agent at Castroville with his feet propped up on his old oak desk. The crew would get coffee, read bulletins, gossip while the agent decided on the work.

"Well, D'Arrigo needs a pull, and put two empty reefers on the runaround. You can spot Bud at three."

And we would go out and do some work and watch the forklift drivers and the packers do theirs, and we would feel the day go slow in a human rhythm of sorting, stacking, and icing the boxes of produce inside the reefer cars. And we would gather them up like sheep and herd them back to Salinas to sort them out after beans, doing our skilled teamwork then, switching cars in a small switching yard, with hand signs and a crew that was going home that night. To their own beds. To their own lives.

Castroville is gone. Watsonville shut down. San Luis closed. Salinas a ghost yard from what it was. Brakemen blame the company for running off the business. The company blames the cost of labor, talks about the modern railroad, cost-efficient operations, cutbacks and givebacks in every contract. Harassment in between. At Colton, gossip about the drug tests, accusations of officials lying about test results to intimidate crews. Jobs up in the air, people who never did anything for thirty years but railroad seeing themselves on the street. Younger rails one check ahead of their mortgages. Anger, fear. I sit in the shanty after the ground herders lose their jobs. They ignore me today. They're worried about themselves.

"You're lucky," an old head tells me. "You can do something else. Most of these guys can't."

It's true. Many of them have spent twenty years in this craft and it's changing into a job, like everyone else's job. The work itself was leaving me, offering me payoffs and mechanical motions. Offering me nothing for what was gone.

Colton being a desert, the weather does one of its sudden turns. Marking the cusp of fall, the nights begin to freeze and blow. I catch a cold, working midnights, driving into Hollywood to sleep. I find I can't go back to Annie's. There's too much sadness there. The fever lasts for weeks, but I don't seem to mind it, lying in bed, giving in to weakness, feeling myself let go. I know I won't be back to work this year. I know I'm at the end of the booming road. I don't want it anymore. The road no longer beckons, no longer promises any more than it has already told.

Being out at Colton has brought other memories alive for me: my passionate awaking to the power of words; the nights I spent in college at Riverside in company with ideas, following them through novels and poems and out into the world; the citrus groves that grew green tangerines and pomegranates and mornings. The prison yard at Colton—the modern world of work with its searchlights and bleakness—seems like solitary confinement to money and RVs. The something more to be prized than much fine gold, the something sweeter than the honeycomb had been here once for me. I wanted to find it again.

I moved back up north and rented a beat-up house with a view of Monterey Bay. I found I was able to live in it. At night, sitting at my desk in the room I wrote in, I could see a string of lights where the land went out into the dark sea. The desert was there in that room, and I could hear the voices of people I cared for, if I listened and outwaited my fears. I decided to stay in Santa Cruz whether I could work in Watsonville or not, and I went back to teaching for a while. When railroad work was around, I worked it. But I didn't chase it, didn't race back to mark up whenever they needed a brakeman out of the blue. When the phone rang at midnight during a thunderstorm and I knew who it had to be, I didn't answer it even though I often wanted to. Even though the train and the storm called me.

I made many returns to the Southwest. On one of them, I was hiking a lateral canyon on the Colorado River in the Grand Canyon. It was late in the day. We were headed for a spring and I had fallen behind my friends; I had to go slower and slower as I saw more and more around me, noticed that the flower on the barrel cactus was magenta by a magenta rock and pink by a pink one. Magenta rocks? Magenta and grey rocks. And orange and sky blue. And black and red and white cliff walls. Ellen the boatman had been waiting at the spring for me.

"It's going to be dark by the time we get back to the boats. We have to leave now."

I followed her back down the trail, fighting the pull of the place to just look around, look deeper and wander some more. The path narrowed and skipped the stream several times; we leapt rock ledges and entered a thicket of Tamarisk leaves, roots woven into wet bands in the mud. Ahead of me, she stopped and stood still. The stream dove into a hole and disappeared. The sounds of the canyon grew louder as we listened.

"The first thing I learned about hiking," she said, "was that trails never end. When you come to the end of a trail, it means you've lost it somewhere."

We turned in the lessening light and went back up the stream to where a red flower grew by a red rock and the trail turned left along a narrow ledge and dropped boulder by boulder for a few hundred yards. I could see the sunlight still heating the Navaho sandstone of the top canyon walls thousands of feet above us. Below the river tossed with riffling foam. The river, made by the land, and the steel rivers of rails—boats on the river, boats of brakemen's lives. Where had I lost the trail? The red flower growing by the red rock, the purple lupin footprints on the brown California hills; the moon rising over Chinatown at shops yard in L.A.; braking partners I'd had on the road, people I'd loved, people who told me the truth; the sheets of fog cooling the Salinas Valley, the vines of Lucero's winery in the morning sun, the smell of the desert in a monsoon rain.

The passing of trains, rocking the tracks, marks one moment in a life. A milepost. Screen memory of a death. I see a Mexican cross beside the tracks. White sacred datura flowering between the rails.

A gentler river moves me now on its way to the sea. Under the grey stars, and wet from the earth, I light this signal fire.

GLOSSARY

Air The airbrake system that applies the brakeshoes to the wheels when it ruptures. It consists of a compressor on the engine, brake-pipes running underneath the cars, and flexible rubber hoses (called rubber), which are fastened together between the cars. When cars separate, the hoses uncouple, causing the brakes to set up.

Bad order Damaged, defective.

Beans Meal period.

Big hole An emergency application of the air brakes reducing the air pressure in the brakepipe and causing the brakes to apply. Makes a distinctive sound like a giant tire being popped.

Bleed a car To drain the air from a car's reservoir by pulling a rod on the side of the car. Bleeding removes airbrakes, but not hand-brakes. It allows the car to roll freely.

Boomer Brakeman who travels to places that are booming in order to work.

Bowl The fan-shaped tracks at the bottom of a hump, used to receive cars that are being classified. Tracks where trains are made up.

Bullringer See herder.

Bump A seniority displacement.

Callboy A clerk who locates crews that are called for duty. Trainmen have the right to be called in person by a callboy if they live within a two-miles radius of their on-duty point.

Check the list Compare the computer printout of the cars on a track against the cars actually on the track.

Conductor A mean-tempered individual who does absolutely nothing and has two men to help him.

Crossovers Switches that allow movement from one track to another.

Crummy Caboose.

CTC Centralized Traffic Control. Signal and switch system controlled by a dispatcher for authorizing mainline trains.

Cut lever Uncoupling lever that raises coupling pin, allowing cars to separate. Located on the side of the car.

Cut off To be laid off. Of cars: to separate.

Cut the crossing When a long train is delayed and blocks road crossing for more than ten minutes, the cars must be separated to allow traffic to cross.

Deadhead Travel to and from an on-duty point which is paid for by the company.

Derail A switch that, when thrown, opens a section of rail, causing a runaway car or engine to go on the ground.

Die on the law Work to the limit of the Federal Hours of Service Act (twelve hours).

Dog catching To relieve a crew on a train that has died under the Hours of Service Act.

Double To pick up a whole track and couple it to another whole track. Of working: to work two shifts in twenty-four hours.

Double runaround A complicated switching move used to switch the position of the engine on a cut of cars that won't fit into the available siding or runaround track.

Drag A slow train that isn't going anywhere fast. No priority with the dispatcher.

Drawbar The wrench-shaped piece of metal that the knuckle fits into. The heaviest component of a coupler and the part that remains rigid. If you break a drawbar in addition to the knuckle, you have really hit hard. Often take two people to adjust.

Drop A skilled move used in switching to reverse the position of a car in relation to the engine. Requires teamwork. One person tends the switch; one rides on the engine ready to uncouple it in motion; a third rides the car being dropped, ready to stop it in the clear with a handbrake. The engineer starts down the track, pulling the car behind the engine. At a signal, he reduces speed momentarily, allowing the slack to run in. The pinpuller pulls the pin uncoupling the car and gives the engineer a highball. The engine then outraces the car to the sidetrack switch, which is thrown when the engine goes over it. The car then sails up the sidetrack and is tied down by the brakeman riding it. The engine then reverses and picks the car up from the opposite end. End of drop.

Dynamic braking Using the power generated by the engine's electric motors to assist in braking it.

Dynamiter A car whose airbrake system reads any reduction in air pressure as an emergency application, sending the whole train into emergency.

Extra board List of available brakemen. As each brakeman is called for a job, the next in order moves up to first place (first out) to be called. The board rotates. As a brakeman reports back in from a job, he goes to the bottom of the list.

Field man Brakeman or switchman who works the position farthest from the engine. Like a centerfielder.

Gladhand Metal coupling piece on the end of an airhose. Heavy enough to break your jaw if suddenly filled with ninety pounds of pressure.

Hang Keep ahold of, as in "hang two," meaning hold onto two cars.

Heel Handbrakes placed on cars in a track. so that other cars may be kicked against them and the whole track will not roll out.

Herder Switchman who guides engines and trains in and out of a yard, lining switches and giving them a highball with a green flag or green light. The herder at the top end of the Watsonville yard was called a bullringer, from the slang term for an engine—a bull.

Highball Signal meaning "Get going," or "All's well with your train."

Hoghead Engineer. As in the Hog Law, for Hours of Service Act.

Hotshot A fast freight with priority on the mainline.

Hump Man-made hill in a classification yard used to separate cars from each other by gravity. A cut of cars is shoved to the crest of the hill; the pin on several cars is pulled, and those cars roll off down the hill into one of the bowl tracks at the bottom. The process is repeated until all the cars in the cut have been separated.

In the clear Of cars and engines: to be far enough back from the point where two tracks meet to avoid being crunched by a car on the other track. As in clearance point. Of people: to be far enough away from a track that a car rolling on that track won't hit you.

Joint a coupling between two cars. As in "make a joint; make a short joint," meaning the distance to the car to be coupled to is short.

Kick To shove cars with force ahead of the engine so that when the engine is stopped, the cars will roll into a track on their own.

Kicksign Lantern sign or handsign signaling the engineer to come ahead hard.

Knuckle The mobile component of a couple device, weighing eighty-five pounds. Two knuckles lock together to form a joint, or couple. Knuckles are the weakest link and often shatter when a train breaks in two.

Lead Yard track from which other tracks branch off. A lead track will typically have ten other tracks leading into it in a series.

Line behind Throw a switch back after you have passed through it.

Make the air Hook up the rubber airhoses and cut the air into them by turning the angle cock on the end of a car.

Midnight goat Switch engine on the midnight job.

Modules Railroad company dorms.

Old head Rail with a lot of seniority.

On the point To ride on the leading end of a car or engine to protect the movement.

On the spot Time out for coffee or rest. Also to designate exact location a freight car is to be delivered to. Spotting cars in industries provides good opportunities to go on spot.

Order board Post on which train orders are hung to be snatched up by crews on passing trains.

Piggyback railpack Long light flatcar used to transport containerized freight.

Pinpuller Switchman who works the position closest to the engine, lining switches ahead and operating the uncoupling (cut) lever on the side of cars during switching.

Pool freight Refers to the pool of crews available in a rotating order to work on through freight trains.

Pull the pin To uncouple something. To quit the railroad, to quit anything, to die.

Puzzle switch One huge switch with four levers which will throw four sets of switch points. Used as a crossover switch between adjacent tracks. Well named.

Rail Railroader. What the railroad runs on.

Road foreman Company official who supervises engineers.

Roll by Observation of a passing train for possible defects.

Roundhouse Facility where engines are worked on. Usually round brick building with lots of windows.

Runaround Siding track used to run around cars in switching.

Run through a switch To go through a switch without lining it for the movement, bending the switch points.

Shove Push ahead of engine.

Slack Amount of free motion in the coupling device between cars. Creates most of the problems in life.

Special agent Railroad police.

Spotter Company spy.

Stretch Order to the engineer to pull on a cut of cars to see if they are coupled up.

Switch list List of cars on a particular track and their destinations. Working instructions for a switch crew.

Tie 'em down Tie handbrakes on a cut of cars.

Train dispatcher Air traffic controller for trains. Operates power switches and signals in a specific territory. Issues train orders. Has Big Picture. Smokes too many cigarettes; drinks too much coffee.

Trainmaster Company official who is in charge of a terminal. Hides in bushes; asks questions on the Book of Rules.

Turn To reverse the direction of a car by either running around it or dropping it.

Unit Engine.

Walk the train Walk alongside the train from the rear to the head end, looking for defects.

Wye Tracks in the shape of a Y used for turning cars or engines.

Work train A train that serves the Maintenance-of-Way department in track repair. Unloads ties, ribbon rail, and ballast.

Yardmaster Person in charge of all moves within yard limits. A seniority position bid in by switchmen. Gives switchmen the dope (switch lists) in the can (can lowered on a string from yardmaster's tower).